MACROBII AVRELII THEODOSII VIRI CONSVLARIS ET ILLVSTRIS IN SOMNIVM SCIPIONIS EXPOSITI⸗ ONIS QVAMELEGANTISSIMAE LIBER PRIMVS.

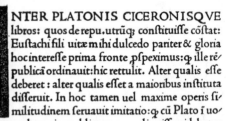

NTER PLATONIS CICERONISQVE libros: quos de repu.utrūqʒ constituisse cōstat: Eustachi fili uitæ mihi dulcedo pariter & gloria hoc interesse prima fronte ͵pspeximus:ꝙ ille rē publicā ordinauit:hic rettulit. Alter qualis esse deberet : alter qualis esset a maioribus instituta disseruit. In hoc tamen uel maxime operis si⸗ militudinem seruauit imitatio:ꝙ cū Plato ī uo⸗ luminis conclusione a quodam uitæ reddito quam reliquisse uidebatur īdicari faciat:qui sit exutarum corporibus status animarum: adiecta his quadam spærarum uel syderum nō ociosa descriptione rerum facies nō dissimilia significans a tulliano Scipione per quietem sibi ingesta nar⸗ ratur. Sed quod uel illi cōmento tali uel huic tali somnio in his potissi⸗ mum libris opus fuerit: ī quibus de rerumpu.statu loquebatur:quoue attinuerit inter gubernandarum urbium constituta circulos orbes glo⸗ bosꝗ describere: de stellarum modo de cæli conuersione tractare quæ situ dignum & mihi uisum est & aliis fortasse uideatur:ne uiros sapiētia præcellentes : nihilꝗ in inuestigatione ueri nisi diuinum sentire solitos aliquid castigato operi adiecisse supfluū suspicemur. De hoc prius ergo pauca dicenda sūt: ut liquido mens operis de quo loquimur inotescat. Rerum omnium Plato & actuum naturam penitus inspiciēs aduertit ī omni sermone suo de reipu.institutione ͵pposito īfundendum animis iustitiæ amorem: sine qua nō solū respu.sed ne exiguus hominū cœtus nec domus quidem parua constabit. Ad hūc porro iustitiæ affectū pec⸗ toribus inculcandum nihil æque patrocinaturum uidit: q̄ si fructus eius non uideretur cum uita hominis terminari. Hunc uero superstitem durare post'hominem:qui poterat ostendi: nisi prius de animæ immor⸗ talitate constaret? Fide autem facta perpetuitatis aīarum:cōsequens esse aīaduertit:ut certa illis loca nexibus corporis absolutis pro cōtēplatu ͵p bi improbiue meriti deputata sit. Sic ī Phedrone īexpugnabilium luce rōnum anima in ueram dignitatem propriæ īmortalitatis assertæ sequiē distinctio locoꝗ:quæ hanc uitam relinquentibus ea lege debent: quam sibi quisꝗ uiuendo sanxerit. Sic in Gorgia post pactam pro iustitia dis⸗ putationem de habitu post corpus aīarū morali grauitate socraticæ dul⸗ cedinis āmonemur. Igiē īdē obseruanter secutus est in illis præcipue uo⸗ luminibus:quibus statum reipublicæ formandum recepit. Nam postꝗ

First Page of the *Commentary* in the First Edition
Printed by Jenson in Venice, 1472

Macrobius

Commentary on the
Dream of Scipio

Records of Western Civilization

RECORDS OF WESTERN CIVILIZATION

A series of Columbia University Press

The Correspondence of Pope Gregory VII:
Selected Letters from the Registrum
Translated with an introduction by EPHRAIM EMERTON

Medieval Handbooks of Penance
Translated by JOHN T. McNEILL and HELENA M. GAMER

Medieval Trade in the Mediterranean World
Translated with introductions by ROBERT S. LOPEZ and
IRVING W. RAYMOND

The Cosmographia of Bernardus Silvestris
Translated with an introduction by WINTHROP WETHERBEE

Macrobius

Commentary on the Dream of Scipio

Translated with an Introduction
and Notes by
WILLIAM HARRIS STAHL

Columbia University Press
New York

Columbia University Press
New York   Oxford
Copyright © 1952, 1990 Columbia University Press
All rights reserved

Library of Congress Cataloging-in-Publication Data

Macrobius, Ambrosius Aurelius Theodosius.
[Commentarii in Somnium Scipionis. English]
Commentary on the dream of Scipio / Macrobius ;
translated with an introduction and notes by
William Harris Stahl.
p.   cm.—(Records of western civilization)
Translated from the Latin.
Includes bibliographical references and index.
ISBN 0-231-01737-5.—ISBN 0-231-09628-3 (pbk.)
1. Cicero, Marcus Tullius, Somnium Scipionis.
2. Neoplatonism.
I. Stahl, William Harris.
II. Title.
III. Series.
PA6498.E6A35 1990
129—dc20
90-2118
CIP

Casebound editions of Columbia University Press books are Smyth-sewn
and printed on permanent and durable acid-free paper

Printed in the United States of America

c 10 9 8 7 6 5 4 3 2 1
p 10 9 8 7 6 5 4 3 2

Records of Western Civilization is a new series published under the auspices of the Interdepartmental Committee on Medieval and Renaissance Studies of the Columbia University Graduate School. The Western Records are, in fact, a new incarnation of a venerable series, the Columbia Records of Civilization, which, for more than half a century, published sources and studies concerning great literary and historical landmarks. Many of the volumes of that series retain value, especially for their translations into English of primary sources, and the Medieval and Renaissance Studies Committee is pleased to cooperate with Columbia University Press in reissuing a selection of those works in paperback editions, especially suited for classroom use, and in limited cloth-bound editions.

M. W. S.

J. E. S.

S. J. S.

Caris quae tacita pectus dulcedine tangunt

Preface

THE PRESENT STUDY happens to be the second volume in the Records of Civilization series to deal with the Late Latin encyclopedists who were largely responsible for transmitting a knowledge of classical philosophy, liberal arts, and science to the medieval world. Professor Leslie W. Jones's study of Cassiodorus' *An Introduction to Divine and Human Readings* appeared in 1946. The small group of compilers to which Macrobius and Cassiodorus belonged, whose zeal it was, as the Roman Empire was expiring in the West, to preserve in digested form what they regarded as the most valuable contributions of classical civilization, are of major importance to medievalists because for centuries they served as the connecting link between the ancient and the medieval mind. And yet these authors have not received the attention they deserve from English-speaking scholars. Such neglect is perhaps understandable. Classical scholars cannot be blamed for overlooking fifth-hand epitomists and commentators when they often have access to the original works that these digesters pretend to be drawing upon. And medievalists are not readily attracted by compilations that appear to be wholly classical in content. Neither classical nor medieval, these late encyclopedists have not been widely studied in England and America, and their significance as an introduction to the medieval mind has not been generally appreciated.

Such has not been the case on the Continent. French interest in the Neoplatonic and patristic encyclopedists is well known; German interest in the late compilers has been focused mainly upon the investigation of sources—an undertaking that is fraught with difficulties. The rash *Quellenforschungen* of the nineteenth century were for the most part foolhardy guesses in the dark, and British and American scholars had reason to look askance at them; but in the present century the conjectures of French and German scholars have been gradually yielding results. Now we have a fairly clear picture of the intellectual background of the compilers of the fourth, fifth, and sixth centuries.

The present translation is the first in English, and the annotations are the first to cover the entire *Commentary* since Ludwig von Jan's edition a century ago. After completing the translation, I realized that the *Commentary* was not an original work, and my chief interest thereafter was in attempting to see how Macrobius' handling of his multifarious topics compared with the treatment given to the same subjects by the extant writers whose works resembled the *Commentary*. I devoted the leisure time of the next two years to the reading of the works of the Neoplatonists Proclus, Porphyry, Plotinus, and Iamblichus, and of the handbooks of Nicomachus, Geminus, Theo Smyrnaeus, Cleomedes, Chalcidius, and Martianus Capella. I am grateful to Professor Austin P. Evans, editor of the series, and to the authorities of the Columbia University Press for permitting me to refer to many analogous passages from these writers in the footnotes and for the opportunity to discuss Macrobius' sources at some length. It may be sufficient justification that any discussion of the sources of the *Commentary* has not previously appeared in English and that the likelihood of another detailed study of this aspect of the *Commentary* in the near future is very small. Moreover, the citing of analogues will help to place Macrobius in the stream of encyclopedic literature, a field in which the borrowing, early and late, was notoriously heavy. I feel that if this volume has any scholarly contribution to make, it is as a case history bearing out the recent contention of Professor Courcelle that Porphyry and not Plotinus was the guiding influence of Neoplatonism in the Latin West. My first draft of the section on sources in the Introduction, written before I knew about Courcelle's study, expressed essentially the same convictions as are presently stated.

I have been pleasantly in debt from the earliest stages of the preparation of this volume to Professor Austin P. Evans for his painstaking care and experienced guidance. To Professor Eva Matthews Sanford of Sweet Briar College I am deeply grateful for the numerous corrections and suggestions for improved wording which she introduced into the initial draft of the translation. I am also grateful to Mr. J. Christopher Herold, Assistant Editor of the Columbia University Press, for the special interest he has taken in the final stages of preparing the manuscript for publication. My expression of indebtedness to them does not hold them accountable in the least for any of the shortcomings of the book. To two others I have a particularly strong sense of obligation: to Mr. William A. Finn, Supervisor of Readers' Services at the University Heights Library of New York University, for his zealousness in assisting me with library problems; and to my wife, who, from earliest reactions to my phraseology and wording to final reading of proof, has been a constant source of help and encouragement.

WILLIAM HARRIS STAHL

New York University
October 1, 1951

Contents

Illustrations

Introduction

Note on Abbreviations

Abbreviations used in footnote references throughout this volume are listed in the Bibliography.

Introduction

THE AUTHOR

IN THE OLDEST MANUSCRIPTS of the *Commentary* the author is called *Macrobius Ambrosius Theodosius v[ir] c[larissimus] et in[lustris]*. In other manuscripts of his works the order of the names varies, and sometimes Ambrosius or Theodosius is omitted; but since the beginning of the Middle Ages, with perhaps the single exception of Boethius' citation of him as Macrobius Theodosius, he has been referred to simply as Macrobius.

Hardly anything is known for a certainty about his life. He is the author of three works that have been wholly or partially preserved: the *Commentary on Scipio's Dream* has come down to us intact; the *Saturnalia*, as it now stands more than twice as long as the *Commentary*, is incomplete, the missing portions being the end of Book II, the opening of Book III, the second half of Book IV, and the end of the closing Book VII; a treatise *On the Differences and Similarities of the Greek and Latin Verb* has been lost, but we have a medieval abridgement of it, doubtfully attributed to Johannes Scottus.[1]

The *Commentary* is interesting chiefly to medievalists. The *Saturnalia*, on the other hand, is valuable to classicists for the light it throws upon Roman society and letters at the end of the fourth century. It is a miscellany of pagan lore and antiquarianism, in many respects resembling Aulus Gellius' *Attic Nights*, and it is cast in the form of a series of dialogues in imitation of Plato. Books III–VI are devoted to comments on Virgil's works. As a contribution to Virgilian literary criticism Macrobius' remarks are practically worthless; they give no indication of an appreciation of Virgil's poetic merits. In the *Saturnalia* we have the culmination of a growing tendency to regard Virgil not as a great poet but as an authority of prodigious wisdom and

---

[1] For references regarding the authorship of this abridgement, see Johannes Scottus, p. ix.

learning, omniscient and infallible. His verses are oracular because they never prove false and because their meaning is often concealed and requires the acumen of a commentator to reveal it. This veneration of Virgil's erudition and infallibility was to continue for more than a thousand years and was essentially the attitude of Dante. The *Saturnalia* calls attention to many parallels between Homer and Virgil and to instances of Virgil's borrowing from earlier Latin writers. Trifling as Macrobius' comments are, we would regret the loss of this interesting insight into the mind of a critic of the fourth century. The *Saturnalia* has preserved, among other things, many of the extant fragments of the early Latin poet Ennius.

Little else is known about Macrobius. He flourished at the end of the fourth and at the beginning of the fifth century. He had a son, Eustachius, to whom he dedicated his major works and whom he professed to love dearly.[2] That he was not a native of Italy but probably of some fairly distant land is assumed from·his words "born under another sky."[3]

At this point we are reduced to speculation if we desire a fuller picture of the author. There have been many conjectures regarding his birthplace. Most scholars favor Africa, a few prefer Greece or some Greek-speaking part of the Empire. His name is Greek. Jan[4] thinks he may have been an African for the following reasons: Africa in this period produced many scholars versed in Latin and Greek; it would be less surprising for an African fluent in both languages to prefer to write in Latin at Rome than for a native Greek, whose mother tongue would be known to all readers whom he could hope to attract with his writings, to write in Latin; if Greek had been his native language, he would have used Greek authors more freely than Latin authors; lastly, Africa is far enough from Rome to fit his words "born

---

[2] See *Saturnalia* I.i.1; *Commentary on Scipio's Dream* I.i.1, II.i.1. In citations of Greek and Latin authors, small capital Roman numerals will refer to the book (large capitals are used for the volume); lower-case Roman numerals, to the chapter; and Arabic numerals, to the numbered section or paragraph (or, in poetical works, to the line). Where, in traditional practice, sections are numbered through from the beginning to the end of a book, the chapter reference will be omitted. In the few cases where there are no traditional divisions, citations will be made by Arabic numerals referring to the pages in the text edition listed in the Bibliography.

[3] *Saturnalia* Praefatio 11: *nos sub alio ortos caelo.*

[4] Jan, I, vii.

under another sky." Vogel,[5] Schanz,[6] Leonhard,[7] and Wessner[8] also favor Africa. Mras[9] argues that Latin was Macrobius' native language because of his frequent citations of Latin authors and his use of translations from the Greek. Wissowa[10] believes that Greek could not have been his vernacular because of his enthusiasm for Virgil and Cicero and because of his numerous mistranslations of Greek passages. English scholars, on the other hand, possibly following the lead of Glover, are inclined to regard Macrobius as a Greek or a native of some Greek-speaking land. Glover[11] finds no objections to the possibility of a Greek origin and feels that Macrobius' intimate knowledge of Greek literature suggests a birthplace in some Greek area of the East. Sandys[12] favors Greece over Africa as a possibility. I do not know to what Whittaker refers in his statement, "He seems, from what he says, to have been born in the Greek-speaking part of the Empire." [13] One gets the impression from reading the *Commentary*—and a perusal of the *Index auctorum* in Jan's edition bears out the impression —that Macrobius' familiarity with Latin literature is more extensive than is his familiarity with Greek literature.

Macrobius was probably born in the third quarter of the fourth century. Georgii[14] would set the date at approximately 360 and estimates that he was about ten years older than Servius. Georgii places the publication of the *Saturnalia* around 395 and believes that the *Commentary* appeared later, some time before 410. But Wissowa's contention[15] that the *Commentary* was the earlier work seems more reasonable. He argues that Macrobius' fuller treatment in the *Commentary* of topics that are common to both works indicates that he had the discussions of the *Commentary* in mind when he wrote the *Satur-*

[5] Review of K. Sittl, "Die localen Verschiedenheiten der lateinischen Sprache . . ." *Jahrbücher für classische Philologie*, CXXVII (1883), 180.
[6] Martin Schanz, *Geschichte der römischen Litteratur*, Vol. IV, Pt. 2, p. 191.
[7] In W. S. Teuffel, *Geschichte der römischen Literatur*, III, 383.
[8] Pauly, Vol. XIV, Pt. 1 (1928), col. 171.
[9] Mras, p. 285.
[10] G. Wissowa, *De Macrobii Saturnaliorum fontibus capita tria, dissertatio inauguralis philologica*, p. 15.
[11] T. R. Glover, *Life and Letters in the Fourth Century*, p. 172.
[12] J. E. Sandys, *A History of Classical Scholarship*, I, 238.
[13] Whittaker, *Macrobius*, p. 11.
[14] H. Georgii, "Zur Bestimmung der Zeit des Servius," *Philologus*, LXXI (1912), 518–26.
[15] Wissowa, *op. cit.*, p. 12.

nalia. It is quite possible that the Theodosius to whom Avianus dedicated his fables was our author.[16]

II

The most important question concerning Macrobius' life is whether he is to be identified with a contemporary Macrobius who held high governmental positions. The Codex Theodosianus mentions a pretorian prefect in Spain (399–400)[17] and a proconsul of Africa (410),[18] both by that name; it records that in 422 a grand chamberlain by the name Macrobius, in recognition of exceptional merit, was rewarded by having his office raised to equal rank with those of the pretorian and city prefects and of the masters of the soldiers.[19] In the last decree Macrobius is called a *vir inlustris,* one of the titles added to the name of the author of the *Commentary* in the manuscripts. The difficulty in attempting to identify the author with the official arises from the fact that it is unlikely that a pagan would have held the first two offices and the man holding the third office must certainly have been a Christian; but there is no evidence to indicate that the author Macrobius was a Christian. On the contrary, he presents as speakers in his *Saturnalia* the leading opponents of Christianity in that day, Praetextatus, Symmachus, and Flavianus, and he reveals his admiration for them; he also shows an intense interest in pagan deities. In his *Commentary* he is seen to be a devout follower of the Neoplatonists. Furthermore, there is not a single reference to Christianity in any of his works.

Ramsay,[20] Sundwall,[21] and Ensslin[22] deny the identification of the author with the official. Sandys[23] also shows disinclination to accept it, admitting the possibility of Macrobius' having been converted or of having become a nominal Christian after he had written the *Saturnalia.* Glover[24] feels that Macrobius' failure to mention Christianity

---

[16] See Schanz, *op. cit.,* pp. 32–33.

[17] XVI.x.15, VIII.v.61.

[18] XI.xxviii.6.

[19] VI.viii.1.

[20] In William Smith, ed., *Dictionary of Greek and Roman Biography and Mythology,* III, 888.

[21] Johannes Sundwall, *Weströmische Studien* (Berlin, 1915), p. 98.

[22] Pauly, Vol. XIV, Pt. 1 (1928), col. 169.

[23] Sandys, *op. cit.,* I, 238.   [24] Glover, *op. cit.,* p. 172.

is quite significant and suggests that, being a contemporary of Augustine, Jerome, Chrysostom, and Theodosius, he must have known about Christianity but chose to ignore it as his way of showing his displeasure at its victory. Inasmuch as the Macrobius who held the office of grand chamberlain would have had to become a Christian in later life, Glover sees "no probability, at least no certainty, in any of these identifications."

In any case, whether or not we identify the author Macrobius with the Macrobius of the Theodosian Code, the title *vir clarissimus et inlustris,* attached to his name in the manuscripts, is a designation reserved for the holders of only the highest offices, according to the orders of rank instituted by the Emperor Valentinian.[25] Since we can hardly dismiss the title as the result of a later confusion or as a meaningless designation, as Ramsay would have it, we are again confronted with the difficulty that the holder of such high rank during the later years of Honorius' reign would have had to be a Christian.

Whittaker[26] and Mras[27] speak of him as a high-ranking official without connecting him with the Macrobius of the Theodosian Code. Schanz[28] and Pallu de Lessert[29] accept the identification outright. Leonhard[30] considers it probable that the author was the holder of the aforementioned offices and assumes that he was converted to Christianity after he had written his major works and that the title of rank was added in the manuscripts after his tenure. Wessner[31] and Henry[32] think it likely that the writer was the officeholder and that he was converted after he had written the *Commentary* and *Saturnalia.*

It is strange that it has occurred to none of these scholars that Macrobius' failure to mention Christianity and the fondness for pagan antiquities revealed in his works do not necessarily indicate that he was not a Christian at the time he wrote. Paganism died very slowly

---

[25] See A. E. R. Boak and J. E. Dunlap, *Two Studies in Later Roman and Byzantine Administration,* p. 194.
[26] Whittaker, *Macrobius,* p. 11.
[27] Mras, p. 232.
[28] Schanz, *op. cit.,* p. 189.
[29] A. C. Pallu de Lessert, *Fastes des provinces africaines* (Paris, 1901), II, 121–22.
[30] In Teuffel, *loc. cit.*
[31] Pauly, Vol. XIV, Pt. 1 (1928), col. 170.
[32] Henry, pp. 146–47.

throughout the Empire. H. F. Stewart[33] attributes the persistence of paganism in the fourth and fifth centuries to the belief in the eternal destiny of Rome and to the cult of the city; to the attractions of the worship of Cybele, Isis, Mithra, and Orpheus, with their emphasis upon immortality; to the stern traditions of Stoicism inculcated by Marcus Aurelius; to the lofty idealism of the Neoplatonists; and, above all, to the heavy hand of the training in rhetoric, which was exclusively pagan, in the schools and colleges. Glover[34] also feels that the training in the rhetoric schools was chiefly responsible for continuing pagan traditions long after Christianity had won out.

The fourth century marks a revival of schools and education.[35] The schoolboy studied pagan mythology, history, and the maxims of pagan philosophers, and he learned to declaim by modeling his style on the classical writers. The conspicuous pagan tinge in the writings of the Church Fathers betrays their attendance upon the classes of heathen rhetoricians. Christian teachers used heathen textbooks in their courses. It is therefore not surprising that adult lay writers reflected the paganism of their childhood training. The more Christianity succeeded in spreading, the stronger seemed to be the yearning for the preservation of the antiquities and thoughts of the pagan past. A jealous rivalry and keen feeling of opposition grew up. There seems to have been a tacit agreement among writers on lay subjects to ignore Christianity completely. Stewart attributes this conspiracy of silence to "Roman etiquette."

So strong is the cleavage at times that even men of Christian sympathies wrote as if they had never heard of Christianity.[36] Boethius did not refer to it in his philosophical works. Nonnus, author of a hexameter version of the Gospel of St. John, did not mention Christianity in his lengthy *Dionysiaca*. Claudian, court poet of Christian emperors, spoke of Christianity only once, and then in a flippant lampoon. Synesius, both before and after becoming a Christian, used the language of Neoplatonism in his serious works. Of the two Albini who participate in the dialogues of Macrobius' *Saturnalia*, one had a Christian wife and the other was probably a Christian. Apollinaris

---

[33] *Cambr. Med. Hist.*, Vol. I, Chap. xx, especially pp. 569–72.
[34] Glover, *op. cit.*, pp. 108–9. See also the very full discussion of this subject in Samuel Dill, *Roman Society in the Last Century of the Western Empire*, Book v.
[35] Glover, *op. cit.*, p. 10.
[36] *Cambr. Med. Hist.*, I, 569.

Sidonius, who was a bishop of the Church, was often quite pagan in his writings. Among the pagans of this period who ignored Christianity one could find a host of writers, if he took the trouble to peruse their works. I do not recall coming upon any reference to it in my readings of the Neoplatonists, except possibly in Porphyry, whose bitter attack on the Christians has survived only in fragments. Eutropius, Symmachus, and Martianus Capella overlooked Christianity in their works. Rutilius Namatianus, like Dio Cassius in an earlier period, referred to it only as a Jewish superstition.

Rather than be surprised, we have no reason to expect Macrobius to mention Christianity in either the *Commentary*, an exposition on Neoplatonism, or in the *Saturnalia,* a work on pagan antiquities and literature. But he certainly could have been a Christian, by profession at least, when he wrote those works. Thus the objection on religious grounds, advanced by Glover and others, to the identification of the author with the official of the Theodosian Code does not appear to be valid.

THE COMMENTARY

MACROBIUS belongs to a small but important group of polymaths and encyclopedists who, in the fourth, fifth, and sixth centuries, attempted to epitomize and present in readily accessible form the classical liberal arts and the more attractive teachings of classical philosophy. Although the compilations of these scholars[1] were quite inadequate to convey the more precise and advanced achievements of the classical mind to the medieval world, they were largely responsible for keeping alive a knowledge of the liberal arts and classical philosophy and science in the early Middle Ages. Apart from the disinclination or inability of both writers and readers to comprehend the more recondite matters of Greek philosophy and the more specialized developments of Greek science, the main reason that these works are poor representatives of classical thought is that the authors follow the traditional practice of a long line of compilers and commentators who had long since lost contact with the classical originals. In many cases

[1] The list would also include Boethius, Martianus Capella, Chalcidius, Cassiodorus, and Isidore of Seville. The handbooks and translations prepared by these authors, together with the *Natural History* of Pliny the Elder (and the *Collectanea* of his epitomator, Solinus), were the basic works in the preservation of the classical arts and science in the early Middle Ages.

the late encyclopedists were removed from classical Latin authors by
five or six, and from Greek authors such as Plato and Aristotle, by ten
intermediate sources, and in many cases the separation was probably
greater. Yet they give the impression that they are handling the
original works. As a consequence these compilations hold little interest for classical scholars, who are annoyed at the frequent garbling
and misrepresentation of material and falsification of sources, at the
lack of regard for chronology in the classical period, and at the seeming inability to distinguish between classical events and events of their
own age. Notwithstanding their shortcomings, these rudimentary
compendia were to hold a central position in the intellectual development of the West for nearly a millennium.

To the medievalist, Macrobius' *Commentary* is an intensely interesting document because it was, as we shall see, one of the basic source
books of the scholastic movement and of medieval science. Next to
Chalcidius' *Commentary,* it was the most important source of Platonism in the Latin West in the Middle Ages. As an exposition of
Neoplatonism it has been praised for its succinctness and lucidity.
The frequent references throughout the Middle Ages to Macrobius
as an authority on Neoplatonism testify to his ability to make the
system intelligible to his readers. And yet the modern scholar who
wishes to study Neoplatonism would of course do well to ignore
Macrobius and go directly to the masters of the school, to Plotinus,
Porphyry, Iamblichus, and Proclus.

Classical scholars can hardly be blamed for feeling that the *Commentary* has served only one useful purpose—the preservation of the
excerpt on which it is the commentary. This excerpt, known as
Scipio's Dream, constituted originally the closing portion of Cicero's
De re publica. Forming a complete episode, it is one of the most pre-
cious compositions in Cicero's entire collection and was, with the
exception of a few brief fragments, all that had been preserved from
the *De re publica* through the greater part of the Middle Ages and up
until the last century. The text of *Scipio's Dream* was appended to
various manuscripts of Macrobius' *Commentary* and was thus preserved. In 1820 the distinguished Angelo Mai discovered in the Vati-
can Library a very early palimpsest (probably fourth or fifth century), containing beneath a commentary on the *Psalms* by Augustine

about one third of the missing portions of the *De re publica*. Mai published his editio princeps in Rome in 1822.

Although Cicero used Plato's *Republic* as a model for his *De re publica* and imitated it in many respects, he approached his subject from an entirely different point of view. Plato's work treats of an ideal commonwealth, a utopia; Cicero, with typically Roman instincts, preferred to trace the development of the Roman Republic and to discuss an ideal state with the example of Rome always prominently in mind.[2] Perhaps the most striking resemblance to Plato's work is found in *Scipio's Dream*. It is an obvious imitation of the Vision of Er, which is also a closing episode, in Plato's *Republic*. The grandeur and poetic beauty of Plato's account evidently impressed Cicero, for he appears to have made a conscious effort to rival his master. The splendor of his theme also must have inspired him. It would be hard to find in all of Latin prose literature so much poetry in so little compass. One of the most discerning of modern critics, Mackail, compares passages in it to organ music and sums up his appraisal: "Hardly from the lips of Virgil himself does the noble Latin speech issue with a purer or a more majestic flow."[3]

The unusual qualities of style and content of *Scipio's Dream* and the fact that it formed a complete episode resulted in its being published separately. One other commentary on it has come down to us, a comparatively insignificant one by Favonius Eulogius, a pupil of Augustine. It is about one tenth as long as Macrobius' and is concerned chiefly with the numbers of the Pythagorean decad and the numerical ratios of the chords in the harmony of the spheres.

II

The method adopted by Macrobius in preparing his *Commentary* resembles that used by other Neoplatonic commentators, Iamblichus, Chalcidius,[4] Syrianus, and Proclus, for example. His customary prac-

---

[2] See Cicero *De re publica* II.3. For a discussion of Cicero's own ideas on handling the subject and for an appreciation of this work, see Torsten Petersson, *Cicero: a Biography*, Chap. XIII.

[3] J. W. Mackail, *Latin Literature* (New York, 1923), p. 71.

[4] In the case of Chalcidius, the excerpts quoted are from his own Latin translation of Plato's *Timaeus*.

tice is to place a passage excerpted from *Scipio's Dream* at or near the beginning of a chapter and to devote the remainder of the chapter to a discussion of the passage. He omits treatment of about one quarter of Cicero's text, mostly introductory material. Nevertheless the text of the *Commentary* is sixteen or seventeen times as long as that of the *Dream.* The excerpted passages are nearly always kept in their original order. Macrobius' discussions of them are at times to the point, at times diffuse, and occasionally almost irrelevant. He has a zeal, characteristic of Late Latin commentators, for displaying his erudition at the slightest provocation. Cicero would have been highly amused at Macrobius' ingenuity in twisting his plain and simple meaning to fit some precise Neoplatonic doctrine. It is true that the realization has been growing that Neoplatonism represents an accretion from the leading schools of philosophy, as far back as Pythagoreanism and perhaps even beyond, with emphasis upon Platonism, and that Platonism has much that is compatible and familiar to Neoplatonists. But in Macrobius' eyes the Platonizing Cicero is a full-fledged Neoplatonist, and nowhere is there the slightest indication of the anachronism involved in this conception. Macrobius' best opportunity to impress his readers with his learning is presented in his long excursuses on Pythagorean arithmetic, the harmony of the spheres, astronomy, geography, and the immortality of the soul. These five subjects occupy about two thirds of the *Commentary.*

The excursuses give to the *Commentary* an appearance of disproportionateness, and frequent abrupt changes of subject matter seem to indicate faulty organization. To be sure, a commentary is not expected to have a well-proportioned structure—particularly if the commentary is based upon a work as discursive and pregnant as *Scipio's Dream,* ranging, as it does, from heaven to earth and introducing numerous topics any one of which might readily provide material for a book. The rambling character of the *Commentary* is to be accounted for by Macrobius' practice of commenting upon passages of Cicero's work in the order in which he found them.

III

Macrobius' introduction to the *Commentary* extends over the first four chapters. After pointing out the difference between the approaches of Plato and Cicero to the study of an ideal commonwealth, Macrobius deems it necessary, as did Porphyry and Proclus, to defend the use of fiction in serious treatises on government. He argues that an orderly society is based upon a general acceptance of the principles of right and that the most effective way of instilling in a man a desire to lead an upright, law-abiding life is by revealing to him the habitations and rewards of departed souls. This is the function of the Vision of Er in Plato and of *Scipio's Dream*. In reply to the clamorous objections of the Epicureans that imaginary events do not belong in serious treatises, Macrobius offers a classification of the types of fiction and points out that there is nothing incompatible between philosophical discourses and the type of fiction to which the vision and dream belong. The third chapter, presenting in clear and concise Latin Artemidorus' authoritative classification of dreams with some later revisions, was sufficient to establish the *Commentary* as one of the leading dream books of the Middle Ages, even though the remainder of the work has very little to do with this subject. The last of the introductory chapters furnishes the reader with the setting of *Scipio's Dream;* for what little is known of the setting we are indebted to Macrobius.

In the fifth chapter the author is ready to discuss the text of the dream and announces his intention of taking up only those passages that "seem worth investigating." Immediately it begins to be apparent that his work is not so much a commentary as it is an encyclopedia of general information and an exposition of the basic doctrines of Neoplatonism, and that he uses passages from *Scipio's Dream* as pretexts for entering upon lengthy excursuses which, in some cases, might be called digressions. A meager statement about Scipio's life span, couched in prophetic language, starts the author off on one of his most protracted investigations, a study of number lore. It was customary for the encyclopedists to include a discussion of Pythagorean arithmetic in their works, and Macrobius' treatment bears close resemblances to the arithmologies of Theo Smyrnaeus, Nicomachus, Philo Judaeus, Aulus Gellius, Chalcidius, pseudo-Iamblichus, Martianus Capella, and numerous others. A comparison of their texts would serve to introduce the reader to the general practice among encyclopedists and commentators of extensive and frequent borrowing and incorporation, usually with no acknowledgement and often with misrepresentation of their sources. The textual resemblances are closer in the sections dealing with mathematics than in other fields. Large portions of Macrobius' text would serve as an adequate translation of the Greek of pseudo-Iamblichus' *Theologoumena arithmeticae*. The fifth chapter deals with figurate numbers and the numerical origin of material objects and the sixth (by far the longest chapter) is devoted almost exclusively to the virtues of the numbers of the sacred decad of the Pythagoreans. These doctrines are probably as old as the master himself. Only the first eight numbers of the decad are taken up, and, as is true of the other arithmologies, the number seven receives the fullest treatment.

A brief chapter accounting for the ambiguity in the prophecy about Scipio's death follows. Here, as elsewhere, the reader is given an opportunity to choose among the explanations offered.

The eighth chapter, containing his classification of the virtues, was one of the most popular portions of Macrobius' work. Cicero implies in *Scipio's Dream* that the efforts of statesmen and military leaders are most gratifying to the Ruler of the universe. Macrobius cites Plotinus' treatise *On the Virtues*—although he is probably more dependent upon Porphyry—and points out that Plotinus admitted political virtues into his scheme. Political virtues have their rightful place, although they are not on as high a plane as the contemplative virtues. Hereupon it is revealed that this truth was apparent to the profoundly wise Cicero, for in his statement that "nothing that occurs on earth is more gratifying to that supreme God than the establishment of commonwealths" the words *on earth* allude to the practical virtues and at the same time intimate that there are other types of virtues. To Macrobius, Cicero is incapable of error; his wisdom, often concealed in subtle language, will be discovered upon careful examination of his words (or through the assistance of the commentator). Cicero's subtlety is of course usually imagined by Macrobius, whose diligent search for hidden meanings to serve as substantiation for particular Neoplatonic doctrines or as excuses for displaying his erudition is an indication of how far removed he was from a true appreciation of the work upon which he was commenting.

The next six chapters (1.ix–xiv), on the origin and descent of souls, might be said to comprise the core of the *Commentary*. The underlying purpose of Macrobius' work is to reinforce the belief of Plato and Cicero that there is a life beyond the grave. All of these chapters, to be sure, were cherished in the Middle Ages and widely quoted. From their habitations in the celestial or "fixed" sphere souls descend into mortal bodies. Those souls that never lose sight of their divine origin and do not become defiled by the impurities of the corporeal realm are taken back to their rightful abode. Guilty souls, on the other hand, shun the sky and hover about the bodies they recently inhabited or seek lodging in new ones, of beasts as well as of men, choosing the body best suited to their depraved conduct. As long as souls reflect on the "singleness of their divine state," they reside in the sky; but when they are overtaken by a longing for a body, they gradually slip down, taking on corporeal accretions as they pass through each of the spheres. These accretions are explained in the twelfth and fourteenth chapters. The creature's death is the soul's life, since the soul is released and restored to the imperishable realm. Sojourn in a mortal body is death for the soul. The traditional stories of punishment in Hades are merely allegories and figures representing the distress of the souls of wretched mortals on earth. Macrobius finds that there are three divisions of opinion among the followers of Plato as to what constitute the boundaries of the "infernal regions of the soul." He does not specify who the groups were but they are clearly identifiable as Aristotelians, late Pythagoreans, and Neoplatonists. Macrobius of course favors the Neoplatonic view and devotes most of the twelfth chapter to a detailed discussion of it. Souls descend from the sky at the place where the Milky Way intersects the zodiac. In each of the planetary spheres they acquire an attribute which they are to exercise on earth.

The thirteenth chapter, condemning suicide, was particularly attractive to readers in the Middle Ages. Macrobius cites Plato to show that we have no jurisdiction over the souls that tarry in our bodies and calls Plotinus to witness that the act of destroying oneself is a grievous sin. Anyone who contemplates suicide because he feels that he has attained perfection and is only delaying his soul's enjoyment of its rewards by prolonging his life is mistaken, for his very impatience is a passion sufficient to contaminate his soul. It is highly unlikely that Macrobius had read Plato. The latter's views Macrobius probably derived indirectly through Porphyry, who could also very well have been the transmitter of Plotinus' doctrines.

Again, in the fourteenth chapter, Cicero's Platonism proves to be congenial to the Neoplatonic commentator. The occurrence of the word *animus* offers Macrobius the opportunity to expound on *deus, mens, animus,* the Neoplatonic trinity of God, Mind, and Soul which is the foundation of the system. An authority on medieval philosophy and theology considers this passage about as capable a summary of the Neoplatonic hypostases as it is possible to find in Latin.[5] Macrobius then cites the opinions of twenty-one philosophers in support of the immortality of the soul.

The long cosmographical section which follows, from I.xiv.21 to the end of II.ix, comprising nearly half of the *Commentary,* was frequently bound separately and given the title of a work on astronomy. Numerous manuscripts have been preserved which consist only of this section. Other manuscripts of the complete *Commentary* have marginal glosses or markings indicating where the astronomy section begins and ends and marginal notations which serve as headings for the more important topics discussed. No other subject received such attention in the manuscripts. Such evidence testifies to the great interest which this subject held for readers in the Middle Ages and is corroborated by the recent studies of historians of science who, on the basis of Macrobius' known influence, consider him one of the leading authorities on astronomy and geography, particularly in the twelfth century.

His description of the universe and earth bears many resemblances to material found in the works of Vitruvius, Geminus, Cleomedes, Theo Smyrnaeus, Chalcidius, Martianus Capella, and Isidore of Seville. Theirs are for the most part general introductions, concise handbooks, or sections of encyclopedias which avoid the more difficult refinements of Alexandrian science. Such resemblances as are found here do not necessarily throw any light upon Macrobius' sources. If it were possible to draw up a stemma of Macrobius' cosmographical sources, none of the earlier authors just mentioned might appear in the lineage. The similarities here are rather one more instance of the widespread borrowing that characterizes the compilations of ancient encyclopedists.

We find in Macrobius the familiar statements about a spherical earth situated in the exact center of the universe, encircled by the

[5] H. F. Stewart in *Cambr. Med. Hist.,* I, 573.

seven planetary spheres, which rotate from west to east, and by the celestial sphere, which rotates from east to west. The courses of the planets are confined within the zodiac, which is one of eleven great circles girding the celestial sphere. The others are the Milky Way, the celestial arctic and antarctic circles, the celestial tropics and equator, the two colures, the meridian, and the horizon. When he comes to the horizon he makes the mistake of discussing the visible instead of the celestial horizon. The handbooks usually distinguish between the two or omit the visible horizon.

The only difficult point about Macrobius' astronomy is found in the nineteenth chapter, in which he takes up the order of the planets. The arrangement of the superior planets, Mars, Jupiter, and Saturn, is easily determined by the duration of their orbits, but the order of the sun, Venus, and Mercury puzzled those ancient astronomers who did not accept the Heraclidean explanation or Aristarchus' heliocentric theory. According to Heraclides Ponticus, Mercury and Venus revolve about the sun, and the sun and the superior planets revolve about the earth. In Heraclides' system there is no fixed order: Mercury and Venus are sometimes above and sometimes below the sun, Mercury being the nearer to it. Macrobius finds himself in the awkward predicament of having to choose between Plato's order and Cicero's order, for both authors are infallible in his estimation. Cicero, he says, belongs to the Chaldean school, whereas Plato follows the Egyptians. The Egyptians maintain the correct order and they also understand what has misled those who adhere to the Chaldean order. Venus and Mercury course now through the upper portions of their tracts and now through the lower portions, and during the latter periods they appear to be below the sun though they never really are. He goes on to explain why they are never found beneath the sun. It is clear that Macrobius adopted a fixed order for the planets, the one approved by Plato and his faithful adherents.

It is also obvious that when Macrobius mentions upper and lower courses for Venus and Mercury he is alluding to Heraclides' theory, perhaps without understanding it himself. Three ancient writers, Vitruvius, Chalcidius, and Martianus Capella, clearly described the Heraclidean system, Chalcidius being the only one who attributed it to its discoverer by name. But up until the present it has always been assumed that Macrobius was the fourth Heraclidean. During the

Middle Ages Heraclides' theory was referred to as the "Egyptian" system on the authority of Macrobius. Duhem, author of a monumental history of ancient astronomy in five volumes, includes Macrobius with Chalcidius and Capella as the transmitters of the Heraclidean view, and points out various medieval astronomers who interpreted Macrobius' passage as an exposition of it. Dreyer and Heath, the other modern authorities who have dealt with the problem in detail, also agree that Macrobius is a Heraclidean.

In my opinion there is no question that Macrobius has been misinterpreted through the ages and that he is defending the fixed order of Plato.[6] About this very point he is explicit here and elsewhere. With regard to the Heraclidean system he is extremely vague, and the fixed order is incompatible with Heraclides' beliefs. The modern scholars ignore what Macrobius says immediately after the passage in question. He explains that the moon is the only planet that has to borrow its light, lying, as it does, beneath the sun. All the other planets shine forth with their own light because they are situated above the sun in the region of natural light. It would have been impossible for Macrobius' discussion to serve as an exposition of Heraclides' views. Any medieval astronomer who offers a clear statement of that system on the authority of Macrobius must have been familiar with the details from the writings of Chalcidius or Capella or some intermediary.

The lengthy accounts of two astronomical discoveries, occupying the twentieth and twenty-first chapters, aroused much wonder and admiration in the Middle Ages. It would be interesting to know what the source of his first account was because it involves a painstaking and tedious procedure which could have been obviated by a simple geometrical proposition and achieves a result that is woefully inaccurate—an apparent diameter for the sun that is 1⅔ degrees of celestial arc, compared with the correct estimate of approximately ½ degree, and an actual diameter that is twice as great as the earth's. Nevertheless the latter result was widely adopted in the Middle Ages. Macrobius describes the instrument used in determining the sun's size, arbitrarily gives a figure for the sun's distance without telling how it was obtained, and proceeds to ascertain what part of its orbit the sun's apparent diameter occupies. He baldly states that the cone

[6] For a discussion of the arguments involved, see Stahl, pp. 236–42.

of the earth's shadow extends just as far as the sun's orbit. Elementary geometry would have demonstrated to him that in that case the sun's diameter would be twice the earth's. After drawn out calculations that yield a figure of 140,000 stades for the sun's diameter as compared with 80,000 stades for the earth's diameter, he concludes that the sun's diameter is approximately twice as great and its volume eight times as great as the earth's!

The twenty-first chapter contains an interesting account of how the Egyptians divided the zodiac into twelve signs by means of containers of water that measured the rotation of the celestial sphere, and the twenty-second sets forth his proofs, satisfactory to medieval geographers, that the earth is in the center of the universe.

IV

Book Two opens with a discussion of the numerical ratios of the fundamental musical concords, a subject which is treated in most of the ancient encyclopedic compendia. As might be expected, we also find here marked similarities and correspondences in the treatments of the subject. Particularly in the account of Pythagoras' discovery of the numerical ratios does Macrobius' report bear close resemblances to those of Nicomachus, Iamblichus, and Boethius. He goes on in the second chapter to explain how the divine Creator used these ratios in weaving the fabric of the World-Soul. The third chapter reveals two matters that are not related to each other: that the harmony present in human souls is derived from the World-Soul, and that the previously discussed numerical ratios also govern the distances of the planets. The last chapter of the section on music deals with the causes of the harmony of the spheres and the reasons why our ears cannot catch the heavenly sounds.

The next five chapters (ii.v–ix) comprise the geographical section. Macrobius' basic conception of the earth conforms with the view that has been traced back to Crates of Mallus (second century B.C.). The so-called Cratesian theory represents the earth as spherical and divided into four great continents separated by an equatorial and meridional ocean. Macrobius, more than any other author, is responsible for transmitting this conception to the Middle Ages. His geographical excursus also repeats much of the data that are familiar to readers of the ancient handbooks dealing with the subject, particularly those of Geminus, Cleomedes, Theo Smyrnaeus, Chalcidius, and Martianus Capella. Once again the similarities here do not necessarily indicate anything about Macrobius' sources. He accounts for the temperate, frigid, and torrid climates and for the reversal of seasons in the northern and southern hemispheres, gives the dimensions of the five zones, and assures his readers that the antipodeans enjoy climatic conditions that correspond exactly with those in Europe. Inhabitants of the known quarter of the globe will never be able to establish contact with those who dwell in the other quarters because of the barriers of ocean and torrid zone.

As an authority on geography, Macrobius was extremely influential in the Middle Ages. Historians of geography give him and Martianus Capella credit for keeping alive the belief in the earth's sphericity and in the antipodeans and for the retention of Eratosthenes' figure of 252,000 stades for the measurement of the earth's circumference. Macrobius' explanation that the tides are caused by the impact of the oceans colliding at the poles became one of the three leading tidal theories. Here his influence was not favorable, for it served to cast doubt upon the more reasonable lunar explanation. His insistence that the inhabitants of the other quarters of the globe were forever cut off from the known world also probably had a detrimental effect. The maps of the eastern hemisphere that accompanied the manuscripts of the *Commentary* became the basis for one of the leading types of *mappaemundi* cartography, the so-called zone maps.[7] Macrobius' hemisphere map, such as it appears in the earliest extant manuscripts, is primitive in comparison with the map of the known world in Ptolemy's *Geography*. As a cartographer Macrobius certainly does not lack courage. He indicates where the Caspian Sea connects with the eastern ocean and assures his readers that there is a sea in the southern hemisphere corresponding to the Mediterranean, although its precise location will always be unknown.

The whole of the eighth chapter is devoted to a curious investigation of the meaning of one puzzling preposition in a passage in Virgil's *Georgics*. This learned disquisition is characteristic of the blind zeal of the commentator. Is Virgil's *per* an example of the

---

[7] For a fuller account of the influence of Macrobius' geography and for some reproductions of medieval zone maps, see Stahl, pp. 249–58.

grand epic style, or of poetic license, or does he use it to mean *inter?* We may be sure that Virgil never troubled his head about the matter. Another amusing discussion of this sort occurs near the beginning of the astronomical section. Cicero has described the speed of the planets as *mirabilis.* Macrobius explains (i.xiv.27) that he is referring to the fact that although the planets all travel at the same speed, their periods of revolution differ.

Macrobius closes the geographical discussion with a reminder that the earth, when viewed from the sky and compared with its dimensions, is but a small point, and that the known portion of the earth is only a small part of that. This revelation brings him to the subject of the next two chapters (ii.x–xi), that it is senseless for men to strive for glory as a reward for their efforts, since a man's reputation cannot extend over much territory and its endurance would have to be cut short by one of the alternate floods or conflagrations that sweep over the earth periodically. Civilization is young, for recorded history goes back only two thousand years, and such nations as the Gauls have been introduced only recently to some of the most useful boons known to man. Cicero's statement in the *Dream* that a man's reputation cannot endure a single year refers, Macrobius explains, to the "great year" or world-year mentioned in Plato's *Timaeus.* Macrobius estimates a world-year to be 15,000 solar years. This Platonic year has no connection with Hipparchus' precessional period of 36,000 years.

After a brief recapitulation of the contents of *Scipio's Dream* near the opening of the twelfth chapter, Macrobius declares that the *Commentary* will be consummated by the revelation that the soul is not only immortal but is a god. Two inspiring passages from *Scipio's Dream,* quoted at the beginning of this and the following chapter, lead Macrobius back to the main theme of his work. Again he speaks with a homiletic fervor, as in the earlier discussion of the soul's origin and reward, but this time he has a vigor and assurance that rise in a tremendous crescendo, climaxed by a lyrical comparison of the source of the soul's motion to a spring which is the beginning of a great river (ii.xvi.22–24).

The first Ciceronian quotation states that the body is mortal and that the mind of the individual represents his true self, that he is in reality a god. Macrobius fortifies this conviction by citing opinions of Plotinus from the opening chapters of his *Enneads*. The second quotation, at the beginning of the thirteenth chapter, is Cicero's translation of an immortal passage from Plato's *Phaedrus*. Cicero was so fond of this passage that he used it again in his *Tusculan Disputations*. In fact it was always cherished by Platonists as the crux of their aspirations. Chalcidius included his translation of it in his *Commentary on Plato's Timaeus*. Macrobius uses it now as the basis of a defense of Plato against the attacks of Aristotelians. The thirteenth chapter consists mainly of syllogisms which Platonists set up to demonstrate that the soul is self-moved and immortal.

In the next chapter Macrobius pretends to be quoting directly from Aristotle's arguments that the soul not only is not self-moved but that it does not even move. There is no reason to suppose that Macrobius read either Plato or Aristotle. The evidence in the *Commentary* makes it quite clear that he did not, and recent studies have shown that the late commentators preferred to derive their knowledge of Plato and Aristotle from their immediate predecessors. The arguments presented here are the clichés of Platonists and Aristotelians worn threadbare through centuries of wrangling. The quotations supposedly taken directly from Aristotle in this chapter prove to be oversimplified statements of doctrines of his found mainly in the *Physica* and *De anima,* removed from their context and sequence, and set up in such a way as to be vulnerable to Macrobius' attacks which follow in the fifteenth and sixteenth chapters.

As he begins his refutation of Aristotle, Macrobius admits that his own powers are too feeble and that he must draw upon the arguments which the Platonists have prepared. Obviously his version of Aristotle's doctrines comes from the same source. However, after his opening acknowledgement of indebtedness to the Platonists, he proceeds to flail at Aristotle as if he were answering him directly. As he progresses, his confidence rises and his abuse increases. He accuses his adversary of quibbling and raillery and returns full measure. He graciously gives in on a point because he does not wish "to seem eager to refute every assertion," but the point quickly turns into a pitfall for the poor master (II.xvi.10, 13). In the end Aristotle is completely devastated. Enough of him who turns his back on what is obvious. His doctrines with regard to the soul do not become him, admittedly great as he is in other respects.

The seventeenth chapter brings the *Commentary* to a hasty close. Once again Macrobius speaks on behalf of virtues exercised in public life. Some men combine both political and contemplative virtues, as did Scipio the Younger. In conclusion, *Scipio's Dream* embraces the three divisions of philosophy, moral, physical, and rational; consequently nothing could be more complete, in Macrobius' opinion, than this work.

SOURCES

MOST of the studies of Macrobius' *Commentary* in the past century have dealt mainly with his sources. It is not surprising that this subject has received the greatest attention, for it has long been recognized—and it is evident to anyone who is familiar with Platonist and Neoplatonist literature—that the *Commentary* is a compilation containing few, if any, original doctrines. It is true, as Mras, Henry, and Courcelle have asserted, that Macrobius is not a mechanical compiler who has merely excerpted from earlier works. He has organized his material and incorporated his borrowings with such skill that the reader is unaware of his heavy debt to his predecessors. One has only to read the *Commentary* in translation to appreciate that the author has blended his material into a coherent and lucid exposition. But it is now feasible to offer analogues or possible sources for practically every doctrinal statement made by Macrobius in the *Commentary,* and an examination of those passages from earlier works in their contexts will aid immeasurably in understanding the *Commentary.*

Before we look into what is known about Macrobius' sources and the extent of his indebtedness to them, it would be well to point out some of the difficulties that have confronted the scholars who have attempted to trace his sources. Macrobius belongs to a group of Late Latin compilers who, as it has long been suspected and is now known, made it a practice to borrow from, or plunder, recent works and cite classical authors as their sources. In the greater number of cases in which the compilers drew their material from Greek sources, the Greek works have not survived. This has necessitated a comparison of the texts of the Latin borrowers (frequently a number of them have been found using the same sources), or a careful study of later

Greek writers who drew upon the lost works used by the Latin compilers. Such investigations are admittedly highly conjectural. In the case of Macrobius it has been generally agreed that he borrowed extensively from many works of Porphyry. Since the greater number of these have been lost, a search has had to be conducted through the bulky commentaries of Proclus and the works of other authors, Latin and Greek, who borrowed from Porphyry. Some scholars have seen fit to add another complication by assuming that Macrobius was not using the Greek works directly but Latin translations, now lost. To defend or disprove such an assumption is of course extremely difficult.

II

Let us take a cursory glance at the contributions made by Macrobian scholars during the past century. Although Ludwig von Jan in his elaborate 1848 edition cited many analogous passages from earlier authors, he ignored the problem of sources and had no inkling of Macrobius' heavy indebtedness to Porphyry. Only a few Porphyrian parallels are to be found listed in his notes to the *Commentary* and *Saturnalia,* although Macrobius' debt to Porphyry was extensive in both works. In 1866 Petit made the important discovery that Macrobius' citations were not reliable, and that occasionally Plotinus was given credit for material drawn from Porphyry.[1] Ever since this discovery it has been the practice of most investigators of the sources to scan the extant works of Porphyry and of writers who borrowed from Porphyry for additional parallels to Macrobian material. Their efforts have always been successful; each investigator has added to the existing store of references. In 1888 Linke propounded a theory, long influential but now discarded, that the ultimate source of Macrobius' *Commentary* was Porphyry's lost *Commentary on Plato's Timaeus,* and that Macrobius' direct source was a Latin commentary on *Scipio's Dream,* perhaps by Marius Victorinus, which in turn was based upon Porphyry's *Commentary* and a commentary on Virgil.[2] In 1905 Borghorst, apparently unaware that Zeller had already

[1] See Petit, pp. 67, 75, 79.
[2] Hugo Linke, "Ueber Macrobius' Kommentar zu Ciceros Somnium Scipionis," in *Philologische Abhandlungen, Martin Hertz zum siebzigsten Geburtstage,* pp. 240–56.

pointed out that Macrobius' *Commentary* had none of the "phan-tastische Scholastik" which characterizes Iamblichus' writings, of-fered the abortive suggestion that Iamblichus' lost *Commentary on the Timaeus* was Macrobius' source.[3] Bitsch's theory bore strong resemblances to that of Linke. He assigned as Macrobius' source a Latin commentary on *Scipio's Dream*, drawn mainly from Porphyry's *Commentary on the Timaeus* and an assumed *Quaestiones Vergil-ianae*, a Virgil commentary probably compiled by Marius Victorinus and itself largely dependent upon Porphyry.[4] In 1916 Schedler pro-duced the longest and most documented study of Macrobius since Jan's edition, but it contained no substantial contribution to the in-vestigation of the sources. He adopted Linke's conjectures and felt that he had strengthened Linke's theory by discovering many new Porphyrian parallels to Macrobian material. Schedler went so far as to say that wherever Plotinus was cited the true source was Porphyry.[5]

Up to this time Macrobian investigators had shown the typical weaknesses that have long been associated with the more enthusiastic Continental *Quellenforschung* specialists. Instead of exercising the caution and restraint that would seem to be called for in a field of research that is necessarily so uncertain in its findings, they plunged in and assigned sources with utmost assurance on the basis of most tenuous evidence. Any sort of resemblances of doctrine were regarded as certain proof of direct borrowing. At times they were so intent upon gleaning further references to substantiate a preconceived theory that they lost any perspicacity that they might have had. The single-source theory adhered to by some of the scholars men-tioned above has been successfully disposed of by Mras, Henry, and Courcelle, for reasons which we shall take up in a moment. Lastly, it is hard to understand why some scholars felt the need of a Latin intermediary, for Macrobius' two longer works and the abstract of his comparative study of Greek and Latin verbs demonstrate that he was almost as familiar with the Greek language and literature as he was with Latin. It has been seen that one eminent scholar thought Macrobius' knowledge of the Greek language indicated that he might have been born in Greece or some Greek-speaking land.[6]

---

[3] A dissertation by Gerhard Borghorst, *De Anatolii fontibus* (Berlin, 1905).
[4] Friedrich Bitsch, *De Platonicorum quaestionibus quisbusdam Vergilianis*, pp. 71–73.
[5] Schedler, p. 4.
[6] T. R. Glover, *Life and Letters in the Fourth Century*, p. 172.

Crude as these early attempts to trace Macrobius' sources were, they were pointing in the right direction. By this time it had become clear that the *Commentary on Scipio's Dream* was a misleading title and that Macrobius had used Cicero's text merely as a framework upon which to hang Neoplatonic doctrines gathered from his readings. It had also become clear that Macrobius' citations could not be relied upon and that Porphyry was the main inspiration for his *Commentary*.

In 1919 Cumont wrote an ingenious article on Macrobius' chapter on suicide (1.xiii) in which he suggested that Macrobius did not consult the two works that he cites as his authorities—Plotinus' *Enneads* and Plato's *Phaedo*—but that instead he drew his ideas from the *De regressu animae* of Porphyry. Cumont noted that it was characteristic of the erudition of Late Latin compilers merely to allude to the work from which they had appropriated their material and to give as their own authorities the authorities that had been cited by the author of the book they were consulting.[7]

Whittaker, well known for his studies on Neoplatonism, wrote a slender volume on Macrobius in 1923, containing numerous discursive philosophical reflections stemming from a digest of the contents of Macrobius' works. He paid very little attention to sources and remarked that "there is no prospect of an end to the search for sources."[8] In a review of this work Professor Shorey commended Whittaker for "wasting little space on the dissertations that guess at Macrobius' sources."[9] On behalf of Whittaker and Shorey it must be admitted that the attempts to trace Macrobius' sources had not been very successful up to that time. On the other hand, it is a deplorable attitude to express disinterest about a matter that is basic in the understanding and evaluation of an author whose doctrines are wholly unoriginal.

III

Three recent studies by Mras, Henry, and Courcelle have thrown considerable light on Macrobius' sources and it would be well to summarize their arguments and conclusions here.

[7] Cumont, pp. 113–20.
[8] Whittaker, *Macrobius*, p. 18.
[9] *Classical Philology*, XVIII (1923), 190.

Mras believes that Macrobius' two main sources were Porphyry and Plotinus,[10] and he offers the following evidence, which he feels is convincing, to show that Macrobius consulted Plotinus' works at first hand: Macrobius translates the titles of chapters of Plotinus' *Enneads* (i.xix.27, ii.xii.7); his remark that "Plotinus is more concise than anyone" could have been made only by one who had studied his works; on a few occasions when Macrobius finds Plotinus and Porphyry differing in their views, he distinguishes between them, and on one occasion,[11] on the question whether human souls pass into the bodies of beasts, he adopts the Plotinian attitude that they do.

In refutation of the single-source theory of Linke, Schedler, and others, Mras offers the following arguments: the scope of the source material of the Linke-Schedler theory is not far-reaching enough to take into account such subjects as Macrobius' chapters on geography and his chapter on the virtues; the proof presented in his own study that Macrobius used numerous works of Porphyry; Macrobius' remark that the literature on music is limitless (ii.iv.12); his contemporary references (ii.iii.4, 5; *Saturnalia* vii.vii.5);[12] his individualistic style, which has many characteristic traits, and his occasional independent additions (ii.xv.13–19, ii.xvi.16); his emphasis upon the political virtues, which may be partly explained by his almost certain identification with the Macrobius who held high state offices; and his practices in the *Saturnalia*, which indicate that he was not a mechanical copyist, that he borrowed from different sources, and that he made use of the material in an original manner.[13]

[10] See Mras, *passim*, and especially pp. 281–82.

[11] *Commentary* i.ix.5.

[12] The contemporary reference in *Commentary* ii.iv.13 might be added.

[13] There is no denying the correctness of the attitude expressed by Mras in the last statement; Henry and Courcelle fully agree with him, and any reader of the *Commentary* would readily admit that Macrobius has assimilated his borrowings and woven them into his text with great skill. Nevertheless it is necessary at this time to call the reader's attention to a practice of Macrobius which can be traced more clearly in his *Saturnalia* than in the *Commentary*.

Fortunately two of the most influential sources (ultimate or direct) of the *Saturnalia* are extant, Aulus Gellius' *Attic Nights* and Plutarch's *Symposiacs*. At the opening of the *Saturnalia* (Praefatio 4) Macrobius admits that he has borrowed freely from earlier writers, frequently verbatim or with minor changes; the evidence of this is seen in an examination of the passages he excerpts from Gellius. He copies with slight modifications, sometimes omitting, sometimes altering the order, and rarely adding. There are one passage of ten pages in the Teubner edition, one of more than three, two of two, three of one, and numerous smaller passages in which the correspondence is very close. He weaves them into

IV

A year after Mras's study appeared, Paul Henry published a volume on Plotinus' influence in the West containing a chapter on
Macrobius[14] in which he confirmed many of Mras's findings, although he had reached his conclusions without the knowledge of
Mras's work. Henry's book is a manifest attempt to vindicate the
supreme importance of Plotinus' influence upon Western Neoplatonism in the face of views held by previous scholars who had depre-
ciated or minimized Plotinus' contribution. As a result Henry's position with regard to Plotinus' influence upon Macrobius becomes
almost as extreme as the attitude of Schedler, reported above,
maintaining the all-importance of Porphyry. Nevertheless Henry's
arguments are worthy of examination.

Henry stresses the importance of conclusions based upon a careful study of parallel texts. He begins by comparing the texts of *Commentary* II.xii and Plotinus' *Enneads* I.i and I.ii. He notes that Macrobius accurately translates the title of Plotinus' treatise and that one
short passage could almost be considered a translation of Plotinus'
words. He points out that Macrobius' expert abstracting of Plotinus'
doctrines, his easy and familiar transitions from one chapter of Plotinus to another, and his penetrating remarks about Plotinus' style
indicate without a doubt that he studied the *Enneads* carefully.

Henry next turns his attention to Macrobius' chapter on the virtues
(I.viii), the chapter which, since the time of Petit, has furnished sup-
porters of Porphyry as the chief source of Macrobius with their

---

the pattern of the whole, putting the words of Gellius and his authorities into the mouths
of the savants of his dialogue. His ultimate indebtedness to Plutarch in Book VII is also
great, although the similarity is not so marked. There is a theory that the text of the *Symposiacs* which he used was substantially different from the one that has come down to us.

Similar close correspondence between Macrobius' text and passages in earlier writings can
also be found in the *Commentary*. In his chapter on the virtues of the number seven we find
many passages that are free but adequate translations of a Greek treatise, falsely ascribed to
Iamblichus, on the virtues of the numbers in the sacred Pythagorean decad (see notes to
I.vi). In one passage of five Teubner pages Macrobius' text follows the Greek text rather
closely, with some omissions and additions and very few changes in order. Despite these
and other extended borrowings there is little of the unevenness and irregularity about
Macrobius' writings that would ·betray a mechanical compiler. For a full discussion of the
sources of Macrobius' *Saturnalia*, see G. Wissowa, *De Macrobii Saturnaliorum fontibus
capita tria;* G. Lögdberg, *In Macrobii Saturnalia adnotationes;* Courcelle, pp. 9–20.

[14] Henry, pp. 146–92.

strongest evidence. An examination of the texts of Macrobius, Plotinus, and Porphyry, placed side by side, forces him to admit that there
are numerous points common to Porphyry and Macrobius but not
found in Plotinus. Nevertheless he concludes that Macrobius used
Porphyry to supplement the doctrines of Plotinus, as he used Virgil
elsewhere.[15]

At this point Henry attempts to refute Cumont's arguments regarding Macrobius' chapter on suicide. Cumont, as we have seen, believes
that Macrobius did not consult the two works which he lists as his
authorities, Plotinus' *Enneads* and Plato's *Phaedo,* but instead used
Porphyry's *De regressu animae.* Henry's arguments are too detailed
to be taken up in full here, and since Courcelle has pointed out flaws
in some of them, it would be well to postpone consideration of them.
Suffice it to say that Henry denies Cumont's contentions and feels
that Macrobius' chief sources were Plotinus and Plato. At the same
time he admits the possibility of Macrobius' having read Porphyry's
De regressu animae.

V

The latest investigation of Macrobius' sources, forming a part of an
elaborate study by Pierre Courcelle[16] of the influence of Greek writers
upon the Latin writers of the West in the fifth and sixth centuries,
is in my opinion the most successful attempt yet made at reconstruct-
ing Macrobius' scholarly background, and it serves to show how
great has been the progress since Jan's edition of a century ago. The
success of this work lies in the author's recognition of the fact that
the compilations of the Late Latin encyclopedists exhibit so many
common phenomena as to represent a distinct genre. He has accordingly made a careful study of what is known of the backgrounds and
practices of all the important compilers. His volume is a synthesis of
the arguments and conclusions of recent scholars concerning the
erudition, borrowing habits, and extent of indebtedness of these compilers, and it contains many original contributions and interpretations.

[15] Henry, p. 191.
[16] Courcelle devotes the first chapter, pp. 3–36, of his study to Macrobius and refers to
him constantly thereafter.

Courcelle finds that, Neoplatonist and Christian alike, the compilers preferred to ransack recent commentaries and to give their
readers the impression that they were drawing upon classical sources.
In compounding commentary upon commentary they lost all regard
for chronology and were seemingly unable to distinguish between
contemporary events and the events of the classical period referred
to in their commentaries. Courcelle remarks that in these practices
we see a clear sign of the approaching Dark Ages.[17] Because he has
demonstrated (perhaps anew, but probably more forcefully than any
of his predecessors) that the compilers had similar habits and similar
literary backgrounds, Courcelle's statements regarding any one of
them carry more conviction than those of a scholar dealing with a
single author. His final conclusion, which he regards as the most
important result of his study and which he claims to be the first
to have pointed out, is that Porphyry, and not Plotinus, was the
guiding light of Neoplatonism in the West:

Only one [pagan Greek] philosophy survives—Neoplatonism. Its master
spirit is Porphyry, the archenemy of the Christians. This all-important
fact has never before been elucidated, for the history of Latin Neoplatonism
has not yet been written. The only one who has made an attempt at it,
Father Paul Henry, was of the opinion that a study on Plotinus could
"serve as basis to the central chapter of the history of Neoplatonism in the
West." In my judgment, this opinion reflects an error of perspective. . . .
It was neither the lofty metaphysics of Plotinus—although he was still read
and appreciated—nor the mystical lucubrations of Iamblichus and Julian,
whose works seem to have remained almost unknown in the West, that
conquered Roman intellects. Roman readers were much more receptive to
the doctrines of Porphyry, which are both a philosophy and a religion.[18]

---

[17] Courcelle, p. 393: "Les Latins les plus férus de Platon ou d'Aristote, un Macrobe, un
Augustin, un Boèce, ne connaissent le texte ancien qu'à travers le commentaire le plus
récent et ne peuvent détacher l'un de l'autre. Cette absence d'un contact direct avec les
chefs-d'œuvre classiques, ce défaut de perspective, ce manque de sens historique est l'un
des signes les plus graves de la décadence; les meilleurs esprits ne s'y peuvent soustraire; ils
réfléchissent, non sur les textes, mais sur les commentaires qu'ils commentent à leur tour;
de commentaire en commentaire, la pensée s'affadit et dégénère." See also pp. 111–12.
Throughout the volume Courcelle gives numerous instances of the commentators' misrepresentation of their sources. It is interesting to note that Macrobius cites Plotinus'
Enneads six times in the *Commentary* but refers only twice to Porphyry, a more important
source.
[18] Courcelle, pp. 394–95.

In my opinion Courcelle has given a convincing demonstration of the truth of his position. Unlike Henry, an ardent admirer of Plotinus who was determined to maintain Plotinus' key position in Latin Neoplatonism before he undertook his work, Courcelle begins in the spirit of true research, weighing all the evidence with an open mind and championing no theory. The evidence supporting his statement quoted above is abundant, as any reader of his volume will admit.

Let us turn now to Courcelle's discussion of the sources of Macrobius' *Commentary*. Here, too, we find him better prepared to handle the subject than his predecessors because he has already carefully investigated the sources of Macrobius' *Saturnalia* and believes that Porphyry's influence predominates in the Neoplatonic passages of that work as well.[19]

After agreeing with Henry and Mras that the evidence indicates that Macrobius probably read Plotinus' *Enneads* carefully, Courcelle then proceeds to undermine some of their strongest arguments on behalf of Plotinian influence. Mras, as we have seen, notes that Macrobius preferred Plotinus' view to Porphyry's regarding the possibility of the transmigration of human souls into the bodies of animals. Courcelle points out that Porphyry's attitude on the subject is not fixed, and that in his *Peri Stugos* he accepts Plotinus' view. Courcelle therefore feels that Macrobius may have been following Porphyry here too.[20]

When he comes to the Cumont-Henry controversy over whether Macrobius was following Plotinus or Porphyry in his chapter on suicide, Courcelle in the main sides with Cumont. He cites a passage from Augustine's *De civitate Dei* which refers to the *De regressu animae,* the work which Cumont claims was the source of Macrobius' chapter, and by an extraordinary coincidence, as Courcelle points out, the passages of Macrobius and Augustine reveal a similarity. Courcelle agrees with Cumont in concluding that Macrobius followed the *De regressu animae* and interpreted Plotinus' chapter in the light of Porphyrian doctrines. He moreover is by no means convinced that Macrobius had read directly from Plato's *Phaedo* the

[19] Courcelle, pp. 16–20, 34.
[20] Courcelle, p. 22.

pages, cited by Henry, having to do with suicide. Courcelle believes that Macrobius was using Porphyry's *Commentary on the Phaedo* or, more likely, the *De regressu animae,* and offers cogent reasons for his belief. He uncovers evidence to show that Porphyry quoted verbatim long extracts from the *Phaedo* in the *De regressu* and suggests that the literal echoes of Plato and Plotinus which Henry finds in Macrobius can be explained by accepting what Courcelle feels was undoubtedly true—that long passages of Plato and Plotinus were available to Macrobius in Porphyry's work.[21]

Courcelle does not accept Cumont's assumption that the *De regressu* was also the source of Macrobius' chapters on the descent of the soul into the lower regions (i.x–xii). Striking resemblances between a passage from Porphyry's *Peri Stugos,* preserved by Stobaeus, and *Commentary* i.x.9–11, and between two passages, cited by Olympiodorus, from Porphyry and *Commentary* i.xii.7–8, 12, lead Courcelle to believe that the *Peri Stugos* was the main source of Macrobius' doctrines on the soul's descent. It would seem that Macrobius did use the *De regressu,* however, as the source for his catalogue of the philosophers' definitions of the soul (i.xiv.19–20). Courcelle points out that Claudianus Mamertus drew a similar catalogue from that work.

In concluding his discussion of the sources, Courcelle agrees with Mras that the doctrines on the immobility of the soul, ascribed by Macrobius to Aristotle, were in reality derived from Porphyry's *Peri psyches,* and he accepts the traditional view that Porphyry's *Commentary on the Timaeus* was the principal source for Macrobius' chapters on astronomy.

VI

The accompanying table summarizes the results of the most recent investigations of the sources of the *Commentary* and will give the reader a glimpse of the extent of the evidence at present available in attempting to ascertain Macrobius' indebtedness. All of the conclusions tabulated are based upon textual and not mere doctrinal resemblances, except in the few cases embracing larger sections of the *Commentary,* where the investigator is of the opinion that Macrobius

[21] Courcelle, pp. 27–28.

was drawing his material largely from some one source. These have been indicated by the word *mainly* in parentheses after the source. The great amount of uncertainty and difference of opinion in the results arises from the fact that the large majority of the works by Porphyry listed in the table have not survived, and in their absence the scholars have been forced to base their conclusions upon quotations or citations of those works preserved by later Greek and Latin authors. Some of the difference of opinion may be explained perhaps by assuming that Porphyry expressed the same doctrines in two or more works. We would then never know which source Macrobius used.

The columns are arranged from left to right in chronological order of the authorities. When an entry in a right-hand column is found to agree with that of a column to the left, it indicates that the later scholar has either accepted the earlier view or has confirmed it in some way. On the other hand a blank in a right-hand column does not necessarily imply that the later scholar is unwilling to commit himself, but probably indicates that he saw no reason to give the passage attention. The three scholars are of course heavily indebted to earlier investigators of the sources, but their indebtedness could not be conveniently indicated in the table.

A perusal of the table will show that Macrobius seems to have drawn most of his doctrines from Porphyry's works, and that he read many of them. The most important question that arises is: What was the extent of Macrobius' debt to Plotinus? Henry's position that Macrobius' citations are reliable and that Plotinus was the main source wherever he is the acknowledged source is an extreme one, and it does not take into account Porphyry's great influence elsewhere in the *Commentary*. Moreover, Courcelle has shown quite convincingly that Henry's attempts to refute Cumont's arguments are for the most part unsuccessful. Mras, as we see from the table, acknowledges that Macrobius' debt to Porphyry was by far the more extensive, but he is convinced that Macrobius read Plotinus carefully and referred directly to his *Enneads* in the *Commentary*. Courcelle does not deny the contention of Mras and Henry that Macrobius used the *Enneads* at first hand, but he feels that Plotinus' influence was very small and that Porphyry's doctrines dominated Macrobius' thinking throughout the *Commentary*. When Courcelle proceeds to

Source, According to

Passage in Macrobius' Commentary	Mras	Henry	Courcelle
i.i.6-7			Porphyry Commentary on Plato's Republic
i.ii	Porphyry Commentary on Plato's Republic		Porphyry Commentary on Plato's Republic
i.iii	Porphyry Quaestiones Homericae		Porphyry Commentary on Plato's Republic
i.v-vi	Porphyry Commentary on Plato's Timaeus; Nicomachus Theologoumena arithmeticae (?)		Some Latin commentator, whose work ultimately was derived from Posidonius through Varro
i.vi.41			Porphyry Vita Pythagorae
i.vii.4-6	Porphyry Quaestiones Homericae		Porphyry Commentary on Plato's Republic
i.viii.3-12	Plotinus Enneads; Porphyry	Plotinus Enneads; Porphyry Sententiae	Porphyry Sententiae
i.ix.5	Plotinus Enneads		Plotinus Enneads or Porphyry Peri Stugos
i.x-xii			Porphyry Peri Stugos (mainly)
i.xi.3-11	Porphyry Commentary on Plato's Timaeus		
i.xii.1-2	Porphyry De antro nympharum		Porphyry De antro nympharum
i.xii.3			Porphyry Commentary on Plato's Republic
i.xii.7			Porphyry Commentary on Plato's Phaedo
i.xii.12	Porphyry Commentary on Plato's Timaeus		
i.xii.14	Porphyry Commentary on Plato's Timaeus		Porphyry Commentary on Plato's Timaeus
i.xiii	Plotinus Enneads; Porphyry	Plotinus Enneads; Plato Phaedo	Porphyry De regressu animae
i.xiv.5-7		Plotinus Enneads	Plotinus Enneads
i.xiv.19-20			Porphyry De regressu animae
i.xv-xxii			Porphyry Commentary on Plato's Timaeus (mainly)

I.xvii.8-11	Plotinus *Enneads*	Plotinus *Enneads*	Plotinus *Enneads*
I.xvii.14	Porphyry *Commentary on Plato's Timaeus*		
I.xvii.15	Porphyry *Peri agalmaton*		
I.xix.1-13	Porphyry *Commentary on Plato's Timaeus*		
I.xix.20-26	Ptolemy *Harmonica*		Ptolemy *Harmonica* or Porphyry *Commentary on Ptolemy's Harmonica*
I.xix.27	Porphyry *Commentary on Plato's Timaeus*	Plotinus *Enneads*	Plotinus *Enneads*
I.xxi.23	Porphyry *De antro nympharum*		
I.xxi.24-26	Porphyry *Commentary on Plato's Timaeus*		
I.xxi.27	Porphyry *Vita Pythagorae*		
II.i.4-12	Porphyry *Commentary on Plato's Timaeus*		
II.i.13-25	Porphyry *Commentary on Plato's Timaeus*		
II.iii.17-19	Porphyry *Commentary on Plato's Timaeus*		
II.iii.i-xi	Porphyry *Commentary on Plato's Timaeus*		Porphyry *Commentary on Plato's Timaeus* (mainly)
II.iii.1	Porphyry *Commentary on Plato's Timaeus* (?)		
II.iii.14-15	Porphyry *Commentary on Plato's Timaeus*		
II.iv.11	Porphyry *Commentary on Plato's Timaeus*		
II.iv.14	Porphyry *Vita Pythagorae*		
II.x	Porphyry *Commentary on Plato's Timaeus*		
II.xii.7-10, 14-15	Plotinus *Enneads*	Plotinus *Enneads*	Plotinus *Enneads*
II.xiii.7	Plotinus *Enneads*	Plotinus *Enneads*	Plotinus *Enneads*
II.xiii.9-16, 26	Plotinus *Enneads*; Porphyry *Peri psyches*		Porphyry *Peri psyches*
II.xv.6-10			Porphyry *Peri psyches*

demonstrate that Porphyry held the same key position in the works of many other compilers of the fifth and sixth centuries, his position with regard to Macrobius becomes, it would seem, unassailable.

VII

In my opinion it would be justifiable to reduce the importance of Plotinus still further. I think that stress should be placed upon Macrobius' known falsifications of his sources and his withholding of acknowledgement of any debt to Porphyry, as in ı.viii and ı.xiii. Although it appears clear now that Porphyry was his most important source, Macrobius—following the accepted practice of late encyclopedists—refers to him only twice in the *Commentary*.[22]

Other instances of misrepresentation of sources and, in the first case, of complete disregard for chronology may be pointed out. In ı.xx.9-10 Macrobius has the audacity to pretend that he has detected a fallacy in the mathematical demonstrations of one of the leading Greek astronomers and mathematicians, Eratosthenes, who in his *Libri dimensionum* attempted to determine the relative sizes of the sun and the earth. (Obviously this observation was not original with Macrobius but was drawn from some commentator.) Macrobius offers instead (ı.xx.11-32) what he asserts to be the correct method of ascertaining their relative sizes, and attributes the method and operations to the ancient Egyptians, although he must have known that they had been performed by the ancient Greeks. His calculations are based upon an estimate of 252,000 stades for the earth's circumference, a figure which is known to have originated with Eratosthenes; but Macrobius does not mention Eratosthenes' name although he has just pretended to be drawing upon his *Libri dimensionum*. In ı.xxi.27 Macrobius gives Plato's order of the planets as moon, sun, Mercury, and Venus, whereas the true Platonic order (*Timaeus* 38D; *Republic* x.616E) is moon, sun, Venus, and Mercury. In ıı.xiv he gives the impression that he is quoting directly from Aristotle's works, but his version is so different that he could hardly have consulted the original. His alleged quotations have no regard for context or sequence and give the appearance of having been selected merely because they could be most effectively undermined.

[22] ı.iii.17, ıı.iii.15.

He admits that his refutation of Aristotle was taken from the clichés of Platonists and Neoplatonists who contradicted Aristotle before him (II.xv.2), and it is probable that these were also the source of his version of the Aristotelian arguments.

Moreover, the arguments of Mras and Henry on behalf of Macrobius' first-hand familiarity with the *Enneads* leave some room for doubt, it seems to me. Of the three main points of Mras, cited above, the third might be invalidated by a question raised by Courcelle,[23] and the first two are flimsy indeed. Mras draws attention to the fact that Macrobius correctly translates the titles of two of Plotinus' chapters (Henry also uses this as an argument), but we know that occasionally Porphyry repeated the titles of Plotinus' chapters, as he does in *Sententiae* XXXII, when commenting upon the same subject. Mras and Henry both feel that Macrobius' remark that "Plotinus is more concise than anyone" [24] indicates that Macrobius must have been thoroughly familiar with his style. Is it not possible that he drew this comment from Porphyry as well? Henry admits that the closest correspondence between Plotinus' text and the *Commentary* is found in II.xii.8–9,[25] but even if Macrobius had been drawing directly from the *Enneads* here, it would have little significance, for these are the opening passages of that work, sacred to all Neoplatonists. And is it not likely that the opening passages of the *Enneads* were quoted by Porphyry somewhere in his works? Courcelle has given his reasons for believing that substantial portions of the *Enneads* and Plato's *Phaedo* were quoted by Porphyry in his *De regressu animae*.[26] Finally, we have the extant evidence of Porphyry's copying from the *Enneads* in his *Sententiae*.[27]

Since there was such a considerable reproduction of Plotinus' doctrines and words in Porphyry's works, it would seem quite possible that even in the passages listed in the table in which Mras, Henry, and Courcelle (or two of the three) agree that Macrobius was drawing directly from Plotinus, he may have been using Porphyry instead. Plotinus, as many modern scholars have acknowledged, is an extremely difficult author to understand, and Porphyry by comparison

---

[23] See above, p. 31.
[24] II.xii.7.
[25] Henry, pp. 151–52.
[26] Courcelle, pp. 27–28.
[27] The parallel texts may be found in Henry, pp. 155–57.

is quite simple and lucid. It is not likely that Plotinus' "haute méta-physique," as Courcelle expresses it, had very much attraction for Macrobius.

No one has called attention to the similarity between Proclus' chapter on the purpose of myths in his *Commentary on Plato's Republic*[28] and Macrobius' discussion of the same subject in the opening chapter of the *Commentary*. Proclus, who names Porphyry as his chief authority, reaffirms the view of Socrates that the main purpose of the myth is to offer an incentive for virtuous conduct. This is further indication of Macrobius' possible indebtedness to Porphyry's lost commentary on Plato's *Republic*.

The chapters on the properties and virtues of the numbers of the sacred Pythagorean decad (i.v–vi) have received considerable attention outside the field of Macrobian studies because they belong to a numerous group of Greek and Latin arithmological writings in which the correspondence among Greek texts is very close and in which the Latin texts are frequently faithful translations of the Greek. Most scholars have followed the theory of Schmekel, who believes that all these ancient arithmological passages and works could ultimately be traced to Posidonius. Courcelle adopts the views of Fries and Praechter, according to which Macrobius was following a tradition of Latin handbooks going back to Posidonius by way of Varro. But in 1921 Professor Robbins, after attacking the textual problem much more critically than the European scholars, disposed of Schmekel's theory of Posidonian authorship and set up a table of family relationships based upon a very careful comparison of texts.[29] According to Robbins the close agreement between Macrobius and the pseudo-Iamblichus *Theologoumena arithmeticae* indicates that Macrobius was following, directly or indirectly, the *Theologoumena* of Nicomachus, which was also the source of pseudo-Iamblichus. Or, if Macrobius was following a Neoplatonic source here, that source was in turn drawing from Nicomachus. Robbins's view with regard to Macrobius agrees with the conjecture of Mras, who apparently did not know of Robbins's studies.

Still another important question remains. Did Macrobius consult

[28] Proclus (Kroll), II, 96–101.
[29] F. E. Robbins, "The Tradition of Greek Arithmology," *Classical Philology*, XVI (1921), 97–123.

earlier Latin commentaries on *Scipio's Dream* in addition to his Neoplatonic sources or did he depend upon his own ingenuity in adapting
Neoplatonic doctrines to Cicero's work? There is one statement in
the *Commentary* that would lead us to believe that he did look into
such works: he speaks of the doubt of certain scholars regarding the
correct interpretation of a passage in *Scipio's Dream*.[30] The only other
surviving commentary on *Scipio's Dream* is a very scanty one by
Favonius Eulogius. Only twenty-two Teubner pages in length and
devoted almost wholly to two topics, the Pythagorean decad and
musical concords, it offers little opportunity, by comparison with
Macrobius' work, to form an opinion about a tradition of commentators on Cicero's work. It is interesting to note that Favonius, like
Macrobius, opens his commentary with a comparison between the
Vision of Er and *Scipio's Dream* and explains why Cicero chose the
setting of a dream. Although there is no reason to suppose that Macrobius had read Favonius' work, my conjecture is that he did consult
some Latin commentary on *Scipio's Dream*.

INFLUENCE

IT IS NOT DIFFICULT to account for the great popularity of
Macrobius' *Commentary* in the Middle Ages. Perhaps no other book
of comparably small size contained so many subjects of interest and
doctrines that are repeatedly found in medieval literature. All chapters with the exception of four (i.iv, vii, xvi; ii.viii), which are devoted
to clarifying minute points of *Scipio's Dream* and which are written
in the characteristically dull style of commentators of that period,
have been referred to or used by writers in the Middle Ages, and most
of the chapters were used extensively. The following list of the more
popular topics discussed in the *Commentary* will make clear to anyone who has browsed in medieval literature why this work had such
a wide appeal: a classification of dreams; the attributes and abilities
of the numbers of the sacred Pythagorean decad; a classification of
the virtues; philosophers' views on the boundary of the infernal realm
of change and decay and on the nature of the soul; the steps by which
the soul descends from its celestial origin to human bodies; the Neoplatonic hypostases and man's endowment therefrom with intellect,

[30] I.vii.I.

sense-perception, and growth; how man differs from animals and the vegetable kingdom; the motions of the celestial sphere and planets; the order of the planetary spheres; the method of determining the relative sizes of the sun and the earth; the method first used in marking off the signs of the zodiac; the proof that the earth is in the center of the universe; the account of Pythagoras' discovery of the numerical ratios of the musical concords and their physical explanation; the numerical ratios of planetary distances; the explanation of the origin of the harmony of the spheres; the location of the four inhabited quarters of the globe and the impossibility of intercommunication; the equatorial and meridional oceans and the causes of the tides; the duration of the world-year; the doctrines of Plato on the immortality of the soul; and the refutation of Aristotelian views.

At the same time, a work that contains so many popular doctrines presents a problem for the medievalist who would attempt to trace its influences or to distinguish between direct and indirect influences. How can one say with confidence that an author of the late Middle Ages drew his classification of dreams directly from Macrobius, when John of Salisbury and pseudo-Augustine reproduced Macrobius' material? Or how can one say that a later writer derived from Macrobius the doctrine that a man is a small universe (microcosm), when at least a score of the more popular authors of the Middle Ages repeat the doctrine? Any attempt to separate the direct from the indirect sources of a medieval or Renaissance author—in the absence of *reliable* acknowledgement or significant textual discrepancies—presumes that we know precisely what books that author had read. In the absence of such precise knowledge the direct sources of many authors will remain a matter of conjecture. Many of the doctrines found in the *Commentary* later became commonplaces in the Middle Ages, but of course that does not mean that Macrobius was responsible for the transmission of all, or even a large proportion, of them. Rather these doctrines are to be traced in many cases to other encyclopedic compilations, pagan and Christian, of the fourth, fifth, and sixth centuries; these were in turn derived from the same ultimate sources as the *Commentary*—from the writings of Neoplatonists, Latin encyclopedists, Platonists, Aristotelians, Neopythagoreans, and beyond that even from the Pythagoreans and Orphics. In the closing centuries of the Roman Empire in the West commentators pillaged from each other these doctrines, which thus became commonplaces before they were transmitted to the Middle Ages. The attempt to trace direct influences therefore becomes an extremely difficult problem, where it is at all possible. The present writer is not a medievalist and he does not feel qualified to express an opinion as to how familiar some later writer, Chaucer or Dante for instance, was with the contents of the *Commentary*. For that reason the bulk of this section will be based upon the findings and views of competent medievalists.

II

If we had to depend upon manuscript evidence alone, and did not have the positive proof of Macrobius' popularity recorded in the extensive use of his *Commentary* by medieval authors, we should still conclude that he was widely read and that he was esteemed as an authority in certain fields. The very number of surviving manuscripts points to the wide circulation of the work. Professor Lynn Thorndike, an authority who is unusually well qualified to speak on the subject, notes that the *Commentary* "is one of the treatises most frequently encountered in early medieval manuscripts." [1]

Ludwig von Jan describes forty-eight manuscripts of the *Commentary* in the Prolegomena of his 1848 edition, some elaborately and some briefly. It would appear from the marginal and interlinear glosses, added titles, incipits, diagrams, and illustrations in these manuscripts that Macrobius was cherished as an authority in two fields in particular—cosmography and dreams. In fact, no subject receives as much attention from the scholiasts as does the long section on astronomy and geography (i.xiv–ii.ix). Four manuscripts (C, E2, H1, and H3) are fragments containing only this section. E1 is a fragment ending with ii.ix. Complete manuscripts and longer fragments indicate in the margin at i.xiv.21 that the section on astronomy is beginning, and at the end of ii.ix that it is closing. Marginal notation at the beginning and end of this section is so common that Jan has noted (p. lxxv) that three manuscripts do not have notations here. R1, a thirteenth-century manuscript of the complete *Commentary*, has on the first page, written in a fifteenth- or sixteenth-century hand: *Macrobius in astronomia,* and the initial letter at i.xiv.21 is larger than usual.

Many manuscripts, in addition to notations marking the beginning

[1] Thorndike, I, 544.

and end of the astronomical section, have marginal glosses which serve as headings for the more important divisions of the section, such as those found in C at 1.xiv.21: *Ex libris Macrobii de differentia stellarum et siderum;* at 1.xiv.24: *De circis et spera;* at 1.xv.8: *De decem circulis;* and at 1.xx.9: *De solis magnitudine.* On the verso of folio 17 of Harleian MS. 647 (not listed by Jan), immediately under the last line of a fragment of Cicero's translation of Aratus, begins an excerpt from the *Commentary* (1.xx.14), with the following heading in uncials: "Ambrosii Macrobii Theodosii de mensura et magnitudine terrae et circuli per quem solis iter est."

That Macrobius was looked upon in the Middle Ages as an authority on the interpretation of dreams is shown by the titles of many manuscripts. A typical one reads: *Macrobii Theodosii Oriniocensis in Somnium Scipionis commentarium incipit.* There are many variants of the puzzling epithet *Oriniocensis* in other manuscripts: *Ornicensis, Ornicsis, Onocrisius, Orinecresis, Orincrisis, Oricresis, olimcretes, ho.....tes;* usually they are accompanied by explanatory phrases such as *quasi somniorum iudex; id est somniorum interpres.* Caspar von Barth (1587–1658) rightly concluded that *Oriniocensis* was a bad attempt to transliterate into Latin the Greek word *oneirocrites,* "an interpreter of dreams."

III

An excellent appreciation of the extent of Macrobius' influence upon writers of the Middle Ages is afforded by the detailed and comprehensive studies of Schedler and Duhem.[2] Fortunately, their interests and treatment of the subject complement each other. Schedler is mainly interested in the intellectual (*rationalis*) and moral (*moralis*) aspects of Macrobius' work, and he pays little attention to the physical (*naturalis*) side. Duhem, on the other hand, deals almost exclusively with Macrobius' cosmological doctrines. Usually they do not handle

[2] Any consideration of the influence of a Latin author upon the writers of the Middle Ages would of course be incomplete without mention of the great general work on the subject, *Geschichte der lateinischen Literatur des Mittelalters,* by Max Manitius. Manitius refers to many authors not found in Schedler and Duhem, but for the most part they are lesser-known writers.

In the summary of Schedler's and Duhem's studies given here, no page references will be cited because the authors dealt with are easily found from their indexes.

the same authors or the same works. In the few cases in which they both discuss the same work, they have selected different passages as instances of Macrobian influence. Thus we see that their studies, revealing as they are, must not be considered exhaustive treatments of Macrobian influence upon the authors and upon the works that they discuss.

A brief summary of the results of these two studies will serve as a guide to Macrobius' influence throughout the Middle Ages. For fuller details and citations of borrowings the reader is referred to the original works.

Judging from Schedler's study, it would seem that Macrobius' influence in the early Middle Ages, from the sixth to the eleventh century, was not nearly so great as it became later.[3] Boethius, in his *Commenta in Isagogen Porphyrii,* calls Macrobius a *vir doctissimus* and refers to his discussion of the incorporeality of the termini of geometric figures (i.v). The greater part of what Isidore of Seville has to say on the months (*Origines* v.xxxiii) comes from *Commentary* ii.xi.6 and from passages in the *Saturnalia.* There are other possible traces of the influence of the *Commentary* upon Isidore, but there is no evidence of direct borrowing; he did, however, use the *Saturnalia* directly. Bede drew extensively from the *Saturnalia* in his *De temporibus* and *De temporum ratione.*[4] Macrobius' *Commentary* was the main source of pseudo-Bede's *De mundi constitutione.* Johannes Scottus Erigena names Macrobius as a source in his *Martiani expositio,* but Schedler was unable to find in him any use of the *Commentary* and found only slight use of the *Saturnalia.* It is Duhem's opinion, as we shall see later, that Erigena did not come under the influence of the *Commentary.*[5] Dungal, an Irish monk at Saint Denis, in a letter replying to Charlemagne's queries about solar eclipses, cites the *Commentary* as his authority.[6] The *Commentum Martiani* of

[3] Schedler's main deficiency is his failure to realize the importance of Macrobius' influence in the tenth and eleventh centuries. Duhem has shown, as we shall see, that Macrobius began to be widely read and quoted early in the tenth century.

[4] For the extent of Bede's indebtedness to Macrobius, see the index to *Bedae opera de temporibus,* ed. by Charles W. Jones.

[5] Both Schedler and Duhem are mistaken here. Macrobius' *Commentary* is cited at least twice by Johannes (xiii.1, ccclxv.21). According to Cora Lutz, Johannes derived his ideas on the soul and World-Soul from Chalcidius and Macrobius, and his astronomical doctrines from the same authors and from Pliny the Elder. See Johannes Scottus, p. xx.

[6] Manitius, I, 371.

Dunchad lists Macrobius as one of four Latin sources.[7] Helpericus of Auxerre refers to a passage in the *Commentary* in his *Liber de computo.*

From the twelfth century on, Schedler finds, the *Commentary* exerted much greater influence. Abelard calls Macrobius "a remarkable philosopher and interpreter of the great Cicero" and places him in first rank among Platonists. Schedler considers Macrobius a most important source and cites numerous cases of borrowing from the *Commentary* in Abelard's *Introductio ad theologiam* and *Theologia Christiana*. Resemblances to Macrobian material are frequently found in Peter Lombard. Honorius of Autun used the *Commentary* extensively in his *De imagine mundi* and *De solis affectibus,* as did Hugh of Saint Victor in his *Eruditio didascalica*.[8] Godfrey of Saint Victor, in the poem *Fons philosophiae,* expresses doctrines taken from many chapters of the *Commentary*.

The classification of dreams found in pseudo-Augustine's *De spiritu et anima* xxv is mainly a reproduction of Macrobius' classification. Schedler believes that John of Rupella, Vincent of Beauvais, and Albertus Magnus, on the other hand, derived their classification from pseudo-Augustine and not from Macrobius.

Adelard of Bath borrowed heavily from the *Commentary* in his *De eodem et diverso*. It was also the main source of the Neoplatonic doctrines of the *De mundi universitate* of Bernard Silvester of Tours, although Macrobius' name is never mentioned. Another writer to make extensive use of the *Commentary* was William of Conches in his *Dragmaticon*. William used the *Saturnalia* freely, too.

John of Salisbury made greater use of the *Saturnalia* than of the *Commentary* in his *Policraticus*. He excerpted whole passages, often without changing a word, and evidently possessed a fuller edition of the *Saturnalia* than we. His classification of dreams also came from Macrobius. Traces of Macrobian influence are to be found in almost all the writings of Alanus de Insulis, especially in his encyclopedic *Anticlaudianus*. The *Commentary* is also an important source of the *Summa universae theologiae,* by Alexander of Hales.

[7] *Ibid.,* p. 526.
[8] In another work, *Practica geometriae,* Hugh of Saint Victor refers to the measurements given by Macrobius of the earth's diameter and of the sun's distance and orbit. See Manitius, III, 116.

Schedler points out many instances of Bartholomaeus Anglicus' use of Macrobius' cosmographical doctrines in his *De rerum proprietatibus* and remarks that Macrobius' thoughts are reported in an inexact manner, as if Bartholomaeus had been depending upon his memory. In his *Summa philosophiae* Robert Grosseteste reckons Macrobius among the leading Latin philosophers and is frequently found drawing upon the *Commentary*. John of Fidanza, better known as St. Bonaventura, refers to Macrobius' discussion of the virtues (i.viii) in his *Collationes in Hexaemeron* and in his *Commentarii in quatuor libros Sententiarum Petri Lombardi*. In the latter work he also points out (as did many others) Macrobius' error in making the Milky Way intersect the zodiac at Capricorn and Cancer (i.xii.1).

Vincent of Beauvais made free use of the *Commentary* in all three of his great works, *Speculum naturale, Speculum doctrinale,* and *Speculum historiale*. In each instance he acknowledged Macrobius as his source, with one exception, according to Schedler. A passage on Pythagoras' discovery of the musical concords (*Speculum doctrinale* xvi.xxiv) betrays Macrobian origin. Vincent's failure to acknowledge his source here is understandable, for the account of Pythagoras' discovery was recorded by so many authors, Greek and Latin, in substantially the same wording, as to have become common property.

Macrobius was an important source of Platonic dogma for Albertus Magnus. In the *Summa de homine* Macrobius is ranked with Plato as an authority on the immortality of the soul. Schedler cites the influence of the *Commentary* upon seven of Albertus Magnus' works. He also lists numerous passages dealt with or used by Thomas Aquinas in his *Summa theologica*. Maximus Planudes' translation of the *Commentary* and of *Scipio's Dream* into Greek was widely used as a textbook, as were his other translations from Latin into Greek.[9] Macrobius is one of the most frequently cited of classical authors in Petrarch's works,[10] and he is included among approximately twenty classical writers that Rabelais read.

Schedler concludes with the opinion that there can be no doubt that

---

[9] See Karl Krumbacher, *Geschichte der byzantinischen Litteratur von Justinian bis zum Ende des oströmischen Reiches* (Munich, 1897), pp. 544–46.

[10] Pierre de Nolhac (*Pétrarque et l'humanisme* [Paris, 1892], pp. 132–33), in his list of classical citations uses *passim* for Virgil and Macrobius instead of giving specific references.

Dante was familiar with the *Commentary* and offers as his authorities Schlosser[11] and Kraus.[12]

We see from Schedler's study that the influence of Macrobius upon medieval philosophy and the Scholastics was quite considerable. The author of the article "Scholasticism" in the eleventh edition of the *Encyclopaedia Britannica* lists the following as the sum of the works available to the schoolmen in the early Middle Ages: the translations and commentaries of Boethius, Chalcidius, and Macrobius, the *De dogmate Platonis* of Apuleius, the works of Augustine, the *Satyricon* of Martianus Capella, the *De artibus* of Cassiodorus, and the *Origines* of Isidore of Seville. W. H. V. Reade, in a chapter "Philosophy in the Middle Ages," in *The Cambridge Medieval History*,[13] says of Macrobius:

> The debt of the Middle Ages to him was immense. To him was due what little was known of Plotinus, the fourfold classification of the virtues,[14] the threefold gradation of *Deus, mens,* and *anima,* the illumination of all creatures as in an orderly series of mirrors by the *unus fulgor,* the descent of the soul to its material habitation, and its yearning for restoration to its eternal home.

In the opinion of Charles H. Haskins[15] and George Sarton,[16] Macrobius is to be ranked second to Chalcidius as a source of Platonism in the West in the Middle Ages.

IV

Macrobius was no less important as a source of medieval astronomical and geographical conceptions. Duhem, in a lengthy chapter on the influence of the three Heraclideans—Chalcidius, Macrobius, and Martianus Capella—upon the Middle Ages, provides us with a cursory glance at the effects, good and bad, which Macrobius' doctrines had upon medieval astronomers and geographers.[17]

[11] Friedrich C. Schlosser, *Universalhistorische Uebersicht der Geschichte der alten Welt und ihrer Cultur* (Frankfurt, 1834), Pt. 3, § 4, p. 9.

[12] F. X. Kraus, *Dante* (Berlin, 1897), pp. 363, 426.

[13] V, 790.

[14] Henry (pp. 248–50) traces Macrobius' fourfold classification in the Middle Ages.

[15] C. H. Haskins, *Studies in Medieval Science,* p. 88.

[16] G. Sarton, *Introduction to the History of Science,* I, 385.

[17] Duhem, III, 44–162. I have stated my reasons in the footnotes to I.xix for disagreeing with Duhem (and Dreyer and Heath) in regarding Macrobius as one of the Heraclideans.

Duhem would set the time when the *Commentary* first came into vogue at the beginning of the tenth century. Johannes Scottus Erigena, coming just before this period, is to Duhem a significant figure. He feels certain that Erigena knew about the *Commentary,* but finds no trace of its influence upon his doctrines. Rather Erigena's Neoplatonism seems to him to have been derived wholly from Chalcidius. For this reason Duhem would assign the *De mundi constitutione* of pseudo-Bede, a work which is heavily indebted to the *Commentary,* to a date after Erigena.[18]

The first avowed disciple of Macrobius among astronomers is, according to Duhem, Helpericus of Auxerre. In a little known treatise, *In calculatoria arte,* which Duhem has examined in manuscript, Helpericus draws from the *Commentary* the method of determining in which sign of the zodiac a planet is said to be and the arguments establishing the true motions of the planets in relation to the celestial sphere.

A clergyman Adalbold, later to become bishop of Utrecht, wrote to Gerbert, when the latter was pope, about problems in geometry and suggested that he read Macrobius. Gerbert's *Geometria* acknowledges his indebtedness to the *Commentary* for certain passages.

There is evidence to show that belief in the earth's sphericity and in the existence of antipodeans was regarded by some members of the clergy and hierarchy as heretical. The attacks of Lactantius and Augustine upon these doctrines of pagan philosophers are probably the best-known statements of the Church's position.[19] There is an-

---

I feel that Macrobius is explicit in defending the Platonic order—a fixed order of the planets will not admit of the Heraclidean system—and that Macrobius' short and vague statement about the upper and lower courses of Mercury and Venus (i.xix.6) could be interpreted as a reference to the Heraclidean system only by a reader who was familiar with the system from the account of some other author, from Vitruvius, Chalcidius, or Martianus Capella. It is true that in the Middle Ages, as Duhem has shown, Macrobius was thought to be expounding the Heraclidean system; but that was not his intention, and anyone who is so interpreting him is reading between the lines and is drawing upon a previous knowledge of Heraclides. This point does not detract in the least from the value of Duhem's chapter on the influence of Macrobius' cosmological doctrines, however. Again, in this summary of Duhem's study, page references will be omitted because they are easily found in the index.

[18] Duhem's argument is invalid. See note 5 above.

[19] Lactantius *Divinae institutiones* iii.xxiv; Augustine *De civitate Dei* xvi.ix. For instances of accusations of heresy, see M. L. W. Laistner, *Thought and Letters in Western Europe: A.D. 500–900* (London, 1931), pp. 145–46; Wright, pp. 56–57; J. Oliver Thomson, *History of Ancient Geography,* p. 386; Duhem, III, 64–65; Thorndike, I, 480–81, feels that too much attention has been drawn to the opposition of early churchmen to natural science.

other exceedingly interesting attitude on this matter expressed by Manegold of Lautenbach, abbot of Marbach. In a tract directed against a certain Wolfelm of Cologne, Manegold relates a long conversation with Wolfelm, the principal subject of which was Macrobius' *Commentary*. Manegold then proposes to chide Wolfelm for entertaining the heretical notions found in that work. He points out that the acceptance of Macrobius' doctrine that there are four inhabited quarters of the globe, three of which are permanently cut off from the European-Asiatic quarter by vast oceans and an impassable belt of scorching heat about the earth's equator necessitates a denial of Christ's prophecy that he is coming to save the entire human race. How could all the ends of the earth bow down before God if it were impossible for the gospel to reach the inhabitants of three quarters of the earth's surface? [20]

Hugues Métel (died c. 1157) writes to another Hugues, probably Hugues de Saint Jean, that he has been reading over the *Commentary*, and says that he is not concerned about Manegold's allegations of heresy. The tendency abroad in the twelfth century to forsake previous teachings regarding the nature of the earth and the universe and to revert to classical doctrines preserved by Neoplatonist authors is most clearly discerned among the scholars of the school of Chartres. Bernard Silvester of Tours sought his inspiration in Chalcidius, Macrobius, and Martianus Capella. He acknowledged his indebtedness to Macrobius in the opening lines of his *Commentary on the Aeneid*. The influence of Macrobius and Chalcidius also dominates the *Peri didaxeon*, which, Duhem argues, should be attributed to William of Conches, another member of the school.[21]

There is little that is original about twelfth-century attempts to explain the phenomena of the tides. According to Duhem, the theories may be classified as physical, based upon the views of Macrobius and Paulus Diaconus, as astrological, stemming in the main from Pliny the Elder and Bede, or as a cautious combination of the two schools. Macrobius believed that a great equatorial ocean separates in the east and west into smaller oceans, running north and south, and that the tides are caused by the impact of the ocean currents colliding

---

[20] *Opusculum contra Wolfelmum Coloniensem* iv (Migne, *Pat. Lat.*, CLV, 154).
[21] On the influence of Macrobius upon the school of Chartres, see also Wright, pp. 134–35.

at the north and south poles;[22] Paulus Diaconus assumed that the tides are caused by the action of great whirlpools. The astrological school attributed tidal phenomena to the influence of the moon. In Duhem's opinion, Macrobius' doctrine served only to confuse and obscure twelfth-century thought on the subject.

If the "Adelandus" referred to by Pico della Mirandola in his *Disputationes adversus astrologos* is really Adelard of Bath, as Duhem supposes, then Adelard was clearly opposed to the theory of lunar influence. In his *Quaestiones naturales* (which Duhem did not examine) Adelard adopted the greater part of Macrobius' tidal theory but felt that the impact at the poles would not be sufficient and that there would have to be a mountain or land mass interposed. Whether or not Adelard denies a lunar influence in this passage depends upon the reading of a certain word in the manuscripts.[23] If Adelard was opposed to the lunar theory, other natural scientists of the school of Chartres did not share his attitude. Bernard Silvester saw the moon as the sole cause of the tides while William of Conches cautiously embraced something of each of the prevailing theories, attributing the tides in part to the moon's drying powers and in part to the ocean streams meeting at the poles and striking against submerged mountain masses.

Still other views about the tides are found in this period. Lambert of Saint Omer accepted the Macrobian explanation in his *Liber floridus*. The author of the *De imagine mundi* offered a theory that is reminiscent of Bede's cycle of lunar influence and of the description of the great whirlpool of Paul the Deacon. The *Topographia hibernica* of Giraldus Cambrensis presents a combination of the astrological theory of Abu Mashar, of the whirlpool theory of Paulus Diaconus, and of Macrobius' belief in a collision of ocean streams at the poles.

The manuscript maps of the eastern hemisphere accompanying Macrobius' discussion of the four inhabited quarters of the earth were

[22] Macrobius' conception of a great equatorial and a great meridional ocean girding the globe and dividing it into four large land masses originated with Crates of Mallus, of the second century B.C. Wright (p. 158) refers to the theory as the "Crates-Macrobian system" and points out that Macrobius and Capella introduced it to the western world. On the currency of the theory in the Middle Ages and on Macrobius' importance in its transmission, see Wright, pp. 18–19, 56, 158–59; J. Oliver Thomson *History of Ancient Geography*, p. 203.

[23] See Wright, p. 440.

the basis of one of the commonest types of medieval *mappaemundi* cartography, the so-called zone maps. The influence of the Macrobian maps is clearly seen in the maps appearing in the *Liber floridus* of Lambert of Saint Omer, in the *Dragmaticon* and *De philosophia mundi* of William of Conches, and in the *De imagine mundi*.[24]

In his *De proprietatibus rerum*, Bartholomaeus Anglicus continued the practice of twelfth-century scholars of borrowing his astronomical information from Macrobius and Martianus Capella. A chapter devoted to the planet Venus shows that he interpreted Macrobius' statements about the upper and lower courses of Venus and Mercury as an exposition of the Heraclidean system.[25]

L'Introductoire d'astronomie, written in the prose of the Île-de-France by the court astrologer of Baudoin de Courtenay and examined in manuscript by Duhem, derives its doctrines on planetary motions from the works of Pliny, Martianus Capella, Macrobius, and the natural scientists of Chartres, particularly William of Conches. The author cites Macrobius on the distinction between the Chaldean and Egyptian orders of the planets.

Another writer who interpreted Macrobius as referring to the Heraclidean system in his discussion of the courses of Venus and Mercury was Peter of Abano. His *Lucidator astrologiae,* written in 1310, points to the *Commentary* as representative of the views of astronomers who believe that these planets describe epicycles about the sun.

V

We have seen that the notations made on the manuscripts of the *Commentary* indicate that the portion dealing with astronomy and geography held the greatest interest for readers in the Middle Ages, and the specific instances of borrowing uncovered by Duhem have given us an insight into the extent of the influence of the *Commentary* in these fields. It seems to be the consensus of recent historians of science that Macrobius ranked with Chalcidius and Martianus Capella among the three most influential writers on astronomy, and

---

[24] See Wright, pp. 121–22; M. C. Andrews, "The Study and Classification of Medieval Mappae Mundi," *Archaeologia,* LXXV (1925), 71.
[25] *Liber de proprietatibus rerum* VIII.xxvi.

that he and Capella were the most potent influences on medieval geographic lore, at least for the period from the tenth to the twelfth century.

Duhem regards Macrobius as third in importance after Chalcidius and Capella as a transmitter of cosmological doctrines.[26] Dreyer, in his masterly *History of the Planetary Systems from Thales to Kepler*, credits Macrobius and Capella with keeping alive classical traditions in the West, as did Simplicius in the East.[27] Elsewhere the same author includes Pliny's *Natural History* with the works of Chalcidius, Macrobius, and Capella as the sources from which such knowledge of Greek science as they had was derived by medieval students in the West.[28]

In geography it would appear that Macrobius ranks second to Martianus Capella. This is the opinion of the eminent authority, C. R. Beazley.[29] Kimble asserts that in the twelfth century the works of Capella and Macrobius became the leading textbooks in the schools; he sees in their popularity a "barrier to the resurrection of scientific geography" but does admit that "these two works did serve to keep alive belief in the sphericity of the earth."[30] John K. Wright, whose *Geographical Lore of the Time of the Crusades* is a mine of information on the persistence of classical doctrines in the writings of medieval geographers, also attributes to Macrobius responsibility for the survival of the belief in a spherical earth and in the antipodes[31] and estimates Macrobius' popularity among geographers of the Middle Ages, particularly in the twelfth century, as next to that of Capella.[32] Wright[33] and Kimble[34] agree that Macrobius and Capella were the authorities responsible for the wide adoption of Eratosthenes' figure of 252,000 stades for the earth's circumference in the Middle Ages.

[26] Duhem, II, 411.
[27] Dreyer, p. 207.
[28] J. L. E. Dreyer, "Medieval Astronomy," in *Studies in the History and Method of Science*, ed. by Charles Singer (Oxford, 1921), II, 103.
[29] Beazley, *The Dawn of Modern Geography*, I, 343.
[30] G. H. T. Kimble, *Geography in the Middle Ages*, p. 11. That the currency of this belief was a factor in the discovery of America is the opinion of M. Cary and E. H. Warmington (*The Ancient Explorers*, p. 192) and of Whittaker (*Macrobius*, p. 83).
[31] Wright, pp. 160, 386.
[32] Wright, pp. 11, 366–67.
[33] Wright, pp. 55, 155.
[34] Kimble, *Geography in the Middle Ages*, pp. 8–9, 24.

VI

Macrobius' *Commentary* is best known to English readers through the numerous references to it in Chaucer's works, and particularly as the book, called by Chaucer his "olde bok totorn," which he read "the longe day ful faste . . . and yerne" and which started him on the dream that forms the *Parliament of Fowls*. I am not so rash as to propose to answer the question, which has puzzled accomplished Chaucerians, as to just how familiar the poet was with the contents of the *Commentary,* but I feel that the problem is so vital that it is fitting here to indicate some of the difficulties and to point out some of the more significant studies that have been made.

Usually Chaucer does not seem to be aware of the fact that Macrobius was the author of only the *Commentary* and that *Scipio's Dream* was the work of Cicero. In the opening lines of the *Romaunt of the Rose* Macrobius is supposed to be the author of the *Dream* and Scipio the Younger is referred to as "king Cipioun." Again in the *Book of the Duchess* (284–87) it is

> Macrobeus
> (He that wrot al th' avysyoun
> That he mette, kyng Scipioun

In the *House of Fame* (916) Scipio is "kyng, Daun Scipio," and in the *Nun's Priest Tale* (VII, 3123–25) *Scipio's Dream* is attributed to Macrobius. In the *Parliament of Fowls,* however, Chaucer understands that Cicero is the author of the *Dream*

> Tullyus of the Dream of Scipioun (31)

and that Macrobius wrote the *Commentary*

> Of which Macrobye roughte nat a lyte (111).

Martha Shackford suggests that the solution of this difficulty may lie in the chronology of the poems.[35] Chaucer's blunder of referring

---

[35] Martha Shackford, "The Date of Chaucer's *Hous of Fame*," *Modern Language Notes*, XXXI (1916), 507–8. Recently her suggestions were adopted by Robert A. Pratt in "Chaucer Borrowing from Himself," *Modern Language Quarterly*, VII (1946), 264, in support of his assumption that the *Parliament* Invocation is based partly on that of the *House of Fame*, which accordingly must antedate it. It is widely agreed that the *Book of the Duchess* is one

to Scipio as "kyng" arose, she feels, in the translation of "roi Cipion" from the opening lines of the *Roman de la Rose,* and she might have added that Chaucer's mistaken notion that Macrobius wrote *Scipio's Dream* may also have originated in the same passage. She concludes that Chaucer had not read the *Dream* when he wrote Book II of the *House of Fame* but that he had read it carefully by the time he wrote the *Parliament,* and she offers this as another bit of evidence in support of the prevailing view that the *House of Fame* is earlier than the *Parliament.*

There can be no doubt that Chaucer knew the *Dream* at the time that he wrote the *Parliament.* At the beginning of the poem he speaks of having read the *Dream* eagerly all the day long, and in lines 29–84 he presents a lucid summary of its contents. But how familiar was he with the contents of Macrobius' *Commentary?* This is a question which may never be answered satisfactorily.

Professor Anderson makes out a likely case for Chaucer's familiarity with the *Commentary* but his arguments are not conclusive.[36] He points out that Chaucer, facile Latinist that he was, would not have required "the longe day ful faste" (*Parliament* 21) and "al the day" (28) to read the 228 lines of easy Ciceronian Latin that constitute the entire *Dream,* and that he must have been reading the *Commentary* as well; for Chaucer refers (111) to Macrobius' high praise of the *Dream* found at the end of the *Commentary,* and Chaucer's stanza on the cause of his dreaming (99–105) is reminiscent of Macrobius' discussion in his chapter on the classification of dreams. Lastly, there were no known manuscripts of the *Dream* in Chaucer's day that were not attached to manuscripts of the *Commentary.*

It does appear probable that Chaucer at least read from the *Commentary,* but the evidence in favor of his having read the whole of it is not convincing. On the other side it may be pointed out that Chaucer specifically identifies the book he was reading all day as the *Dream,* that it is the *Dream* alone that is summarized, and that he makes no mention of reading the *Commentary.* Line 111 does not necessarily refer to Macrobius' commendation of the *Dream;* even if

---

of Chaucer's early works. On the dating of the *House of Fame* and of the *Parliament* and on the chronological order of Chaucer's works, see *The Complete Works of Geoffrey Chaucer,* edited by F. N. Robinson, pp. xxiv–xxv, 887, 900–901.

[36] E. P. Anderson, "Some Notes on Chaucer's Treatment of the *Somnium Scipionis,*" *Proceed. of the Amer. Philol. Assoc.,* XXXIII (1902), xcviii–xcix.

it did, it would matter little. A reference to the closing words of a work is not proof that the work has been read in entirety. Only one line (105) of Chaucer's stanza on the cause of his dreaming bears resemblance to the Macrobian treatment, and any conclusions based upon Macrobius' chapter on dreams are dangerous because this discussion became common property in the Middle Ages. What is more, the material on dreams appears near the beginning of the *Commentary*. The titles of a large proportion of the manuscripts call Macrobius "dream-interpreter," and the *Commentary* was commonly regarded as one of the leading dream books of the Middle Ages. This would indicate that many readers got no further than the third chapter of Book I and wrongly supposed that the whole *Commentary* dealt with dreams. The most persuasive of Anderson's arguments, it seems to me, is his first one, and it is here that someone possessing an intimate knowledge of Chaucer's personality and reading habits might express an enlightening opinion.

John Livingston Lowes has done that very thing in a chapter, "The World of Books," in his *Geoffrey Chaucer and the Development of his Genius*. There is no doubt in his mind that Chaucer read the *Commentary;* in fact, he names Boethius' *Consolation* as "the Latin treatise which most profoundly influenced his thought," and says that "with Boethius must be named another treatise . . . the commentary of Macrobius upon Cicero's *Somnium Scipionis*." [37] The almost insurmountable difficulties that Professor Lowes would encounter if he attempted to defend this opinion are revealed in an article of his on the sources of the *Second Nun's Prologue*.[38] He draws attention to striking parallels between the wording of lines 71–74 and some passages in the *Commentary* and then admits that resemblances might also be traced to Servius. There is still another possible source, Albericus, who, according to Raschke, drew from Macrobius and Servius as well as others and who, according to Rand, drew from Donatus. Now the question arises: Did Chaucer draw upon Macrobius or Servius (or both) directly, or upon Albericus, Donatus, Remigius, or Johannes Scottus? Professor Lowes concludes that perhaps it is impossible to answer the question. The doctrines of Macro-

---

[37] J. L. Lowes, *Geoffrey Chaucer and the Development of his Genius,* pp. 112–13.
[38] J. L. Lowes, "The Second Nun's Prologue, Alanus and Macrobius," *Modern Philology,* XV (1917), 193–202.

bius that would appeal to Chaucer would be likely to be the very ones that are found here, there, and everywhere in the Middle Ages.

A number of scholars have noted the similarity between Chaucer's remarks about dreams in the Proem of the *House of Fame* and the Macrobian classification in *Commentary* i.iii, and have accordingly regarded Macrobius as the main source of Chaucer's knowledge of dreams. It should be remembered, however, that Macrobius' classification was also available to Chaucer in John of Salisbury, pseudo-Augustine, Vincent of Beauvais, Albertus Magnus, and numerous other writers, and that Chaucer, at the time that he wrote the *House of Fame,* apparently did not know that Cicero wrote the *Dream* and that Scipio was not a king. Professor Curry has made an intensive study of medieval dreamlore in order to obtain a clearer picture of the sources of Chaucer's information.[39] His painstaking research makes it perfectly obvious that Chaucer could not have obtained all the details of his dreamlore from Macrobius, and that he was drawing upon many other popular authorities on dreams of the time.

In summary it may be said that it seems probable that Chaucer read all or most of the *Commentary,* but to prove it would be extremely difficult, if it is at all possible.

STYLE

ALTHOUGH the *Commentary* cannot be said to be an easy work to translate, the author's chief literary characteristic is his earnest desire to be clear and to keep his reader in mind at all times. It must be admitted that his efforts are eminently successful and that herein lies one of the main reasons for his great popularity in later ages. Encyclopedic in scope as the *Commentary* is, it never gets beyond the comprehension of a layman. Most of the extant classical and post-classical encyclopedias or handbooks, such as those of Theo Smyrnaeus, Geminus, Cleomedes, Chalcidius, Capella, and Boethius, will usually become quite complex in their discussions of technical matters; but Macrobius will call a halt, avowedly in the interests of brevity and of his readers, whom he is trying to instruct and not to overawe with a "worthless display of erudition." A more likely reason for his reluctance to proceed to the complicated details of mathematics,

[39] Walter Clyde Curry, *Chaucer and the Mediaeval Sciences,* pp. 195–218.

music, astronomy, and geography is his own apparent inability to comprehend the more difficult points. In no field of interest does he reveal more than a dilettante's grasp.

But dilettantism may often be a helpful trait when found in a pedagogue in the lower forms or in an expositor writing for the general public. In fact, Macrobius' style suggests that of a devoted schoolmaster trying to impart to his pupils the day's lessons. If we had no information about his life and, on the basis of his literary style, were called upon to venture a guess as to what his occupation was, we might reasonably suppose him to have been a schoolteacher. Mras,[1] calling to mind Macrobius' study *On the Differences and Similarities of the Greek and Latin Verb,* speaks of him as a "Grammatiker."

Specific examples from the *Commentary* will serve to indicate Macrobius' pedagogic instincts and his devotion to clarity. In i.xii.18 and i.xiii.20 he expresses confidence that his discussion has cleared up any obscurity in Cicero's text. In i.xviii.19 he points out that he has used simple cases to enable the reader to comprehend less obvious ones. In i.x.8, i.xx.17, and ii.ii.2 he avows his intention of being brief and explicit and of avoiding involved explanations; to take up minor details would befit one "showing off his knowledge rather than one teaching" (ii.iv.11). Occasionally he states in advance what aspects of a subject he intends to treat, as at i.ii.2, i.xvii.7, ii.vii.1, ii.xi.4, or he includes a summary of topics which have been previously discussed, as at i.v.1, i.xix.14, i.xxi.28–32, ii.ii.23–24, and ii.xii.2–6. Sometimes he inserts a transitional statement, as at i.iv.1, which calls attention both to what has been discussed and what is going to be discussed. There are occasional cross-references to matters previously treated, as at i.xiii.5 and ii.xvii.4, or to be treated later, as at ii.xiv.14. He fulfills every promise made to discuss a point at a later time. He uses Greek words sparingly, rarely without making their meaning clear, translates excerpts from Plato, and on one occasion (i.ix.7) refrains from quoting Hesiod in the original "for fear of annoying some readers."

Macrobius' faculty for making himself readily understood is best demonstrated in his clear and simple handling of technical or abstruse topics which, when treated by the other encyclopedists, require of the reader considerable background. Macrobius' explanation of the

---

[1] Mras, p. 278.

Pythagorean doctrine that numbers are the basis of the entire creation
(i.v.4–13) is much easier to grasp than is Nicomachus' treatment. The
simplicity and advantages of the method used to reveal how the sun
goes counter to the celestial sphere in its apparent backward course
through the zodiac (i.xviii.12–18) will be appreciated by any enthusiastic watcher of the sky who has tried to explain this phenomenon
to a beginner by any other method. Macrobius' description of the
instrument used in determining the sun's apparent diameter (i.xx.-
26–27) is easier to follow than is the description given by Archimedes
in his *Arenarius*[2] of an instrument used for the same purpose, and
Macrobius' whole discussion of the measurement of the sun's orbit
(i.xx.28–32) is more readily comprehended than Cleomedes' treatment of the same subject.[3] The painstaking care with which Macrobius reports the method and describes the water-clocks used by the
Egyptians in marking off the signs of the zodiac (i.xxi.12–21) may be
compared with the extreme compression of Cleomedes' account[4] of
the use by the Egyptians of a water-clock in measuring the sun's apparent diameter or with the obscurity of the concise account of the
measurement by a water-clock of the moon's apparent diameter
found in Martianus Capella.[5]

In fact, the last two accounts of Macrobius, instead of being hard to
understand as might be expected, are too drawn out and oversimplified. Again, in ii.ii.3–13, he tediously repeats much of the material
which he has presented earlier and expands his discussion unduly.
At times (e.g., i.xx.16, ii.i.15–20) his illustrations are extremely simple
and hardly necessary at all. In a similar manner he is fond of introducing diagrams to assist the reader (i.xxii.11–12, ii.v.13–17, ii.vii.4,
ii.ix.7), and on at least two occasions (i.xxi.3–4, ii.vi) his discussion is
so clear and elementary that a diagram is really not needed. It should
be pointed out here that there is a possibility of accounting for Macrobius' elementary approach to technical subjects by assuming that his
address to his son at the opening of Books i and ii was not a token
dedication, but that Macrobius was directing his treatise first to his
son and second to the general reader.

[2] i.12–15.   [3] Cleomedes ii.82.
[4] Cleomedes ii.75. Of course it will be acknowledged that the readers of the treatises of
Nicomachus, Archimedes, and Cleomedes were more highly trained than Macrobius' readers
and the discussion throughout is accordingly on a higher level.
[5] Martianus Capella viii.860.

II

Further evidence of Macrobius' love of clarity may be found in the close-knit coherence of his sentences. Indeed, his abundant use of transitional expressions and words of reference is the most striking feature of his Latinity. I know of no Latin author, unless it be Martianus Capella, who uses this device as liberally as Macrobius. For this reason it may be worth while to consider for a moment some tabulations based upon an analysis of the first half of the *Commentary* (i.i–xix).

Seventy-three percent of his sentences contain a transitional word or expression (adverbial or conjunctive), fifteen percent contain introductory words of reference (demonstrative or relative), and only twelve percent lack such connecting expressions. When these tabulations were being prepared, no count was kept of repetition of words—an important device in securing coherence—or of equivalent words or expressions, such as *ut diximus, similis,* and *par.* If these had been included, the figure of twelve percent would have been substantially reduced. There are comparatively few sentences in the *Commentary* that are completely divorced from immediate context. In twenty-two percent of his sentences he combines two or more transitional devices, such as two adverbs, a conjunction and a demonstrative, a conjunction and a relative, or some other combination.

Among pronouns referring to the preceding sentence, Macrobius shows a decided preference for *hic* (147 times). *Ille* (12), *idem* (3), and *ipse* (2) are by comparison rarely used. The transitional relative *qui* is found 18 times. His favorite transitional adverbs are *enim* (69), *ergo* (51), *autem* (45), *nam* (39), and *vero* (39). *Ideo* (21), *quoque* (18), *tamen* (16), *hinc* (15), *sic* (11), *igitur* (9), *ita* (8), *denique* (7), *nunc* (6), *hic* (6), *unde* (5), *item* (5), *tunc* (4), *quidem* (4), *etiam, inde, immo,* and *illic* (3), *adeo, iam, tum, idem, verum,* and *rursus* (2), and *rursum, praeterea, similiter, interim, ceterum, deinde,* and *porro* (1) are the others. Among transitional conjunctions, *et* (61), *sed* (26), and *nec* (21) are the more popular. *Ac* (3), *neque* (2), and *atque* (1) complete the list.

To Macrobius, Cicero and Virgil are the "founders of Roman eloquence," [6] and their influence upon his style is evident everywhere.

---

[6] *Commentary* ii.v.7.

Macrobius demonstrates his complete familiarity with Virgil's works in his *Saturnalia*, particularly in Books IV–VI. The influence of Cicero upon Macrobius is apparent in almost every sentence of the latter's writings. Macrobius' vocabulary is predominantly Ciceronian throughout, and he appropriates numerous neologisms which Cicero coined to express Greek philosophical concepts and which were not used again in Latin until the postclassical period. Macrobius' syntax shows comparatively few deviations from the syntax of classical writers.[7]

Mingled with the Ciceronian vocabulary of the *Commentary* is a considerable number of words found almost exclusively in the works of Late Latin authors. Among the nouns, the rarest and most interesting are *circumflexio, competentia, concinentia, contrarietas, digeries, discussor, globositas, incorporalitas, influxio, interstitium, nimietas, obvolutio, omnipotentia, principalitas,* and *profunditas.* Both masculine and neuter forms of *stadium* are found in the plural and *cingulum* is declined as a masculine in the plural. Among the nouns used in a rare and postclassical sense are *actus* (to translate Artemidorus' ἀναθήματα), *adsertio, ambitio, fermentum, integritas, post animal* and *post corpus* (i.e., *post vitam*), and *spiramentum.*

The least frequently found of the postclassical adjectives are *actualis, incorporeus, Iovialis, iugabilis, materialis, mundanus, silvestris* (i.e., ὑλικός), *sphaeralis,* and *testeus.* A few of the more interesting adverbial forms are *iusum, rationabiliter, regulariter,* and *susum.*

Among Macrobius' Late Latin verbs, *deviare, obviare,* and *sequestrare* are noteworthy; among verbs used in a special sense may be mentioned *adserere* (i.e., *contendere*) and *astruere* (i.e., *affirmare*). Macrobius is fond of the Greek accusative with the passive voice of *induere*[8] and *exuere.*[9]

MANUSCRIPTS, EDITIONS, AND TRANSLATIONS

INASMUCH as the present translation has been prepared from printed editions and not from a new collation of the manuscripts, it would be inappropriate to include here a list of the manuscripts.

---

[7] For a comprehensive discussion of Macrobius' syntax, forms, vocabulary, and orthography, see Jan, I, xxxviii-xlvi.

[8] *Commentary* I.ix.3, xi.12, xiv.7. Cf. Virgil *Aeneid* II.392–93; VII.639–40.

[9] *Commentary* I.xiii.6; II.x.15, xii.5. Cf. *Aeneid* IV.518.

Such a list would quickly run into the hundreds for, as Thorndike has noted, manuscripts of the *Commentary* are among the commonest from the early Middle Ages. The reader will find a list of some of the more important manuscripts, together with references to the catalogues containing descriptions of them, in Max Manitius, *Handschriften antiker Autoren in mittelalterlichen Bibliothekskatalogen* (Leipzig, 1935), pp. 227–32. Manitius' list includes thirty-eight manuscripts from libraries in Germany, twenty-eight from France, eleven from Great Britain, twelve from Italy, and four from Spain. Descriptions of some of the more important manuscripts are to be found in Jan, I, lxii-lxxix. These number forty-eight and are classified as follows: (1) manuscripts used by others in emendations of certain passages; (2) manuscripts examined by Jan or by others as a favor to him; (3) manuscripts examined by others but not yet used in emending the text; (4) manuscripts examined by others for emending certain passages as a favor to Jan.

II

Jan's list of printed editions to 1848 is almost complete and offers an adequate description of thirty-five editions. His list has been checked by the standard catalogues, for editions before 1501 by those of the British Museum,[2] Hain,[3] Copinger,[4] Reichling,[5] Polain,[6] and Stillwell,[7] and for editions after 1500 by those of the British Museum,[8] Bibliothèque Nationale,[9] Maittaire,[10] Panzer,[11] and Graesse.[12] A new

[1] Jan, I, lxxxviii-xcviii.

[2] British Museum, *Catalogue of Books Printed in the XV Century Now in the British Museum*, Pts. I–VII (London, 1908–35). (BMC)

[3] Ludwig Hain, *Reportorium bibliographicum . . . usque ad annum MD*, 2 vols. (Stuttgart, Paris, 1826–38). (H)

[4] W. A. Copinger, *Supplement to Hain's Reportorium bibliographicum*, Pt. I (London, 1895). (HC)

[5] Dietrich Reichling, *Appendices ad Hainii-Copingeri Reportorium bibliographicum* (Munich, 1905–11). (HCR); *Appendices ad Hainii-Copingeri Reportorium bibliographicum: Additiones et emendationes* (Münster, 1914). (R. Suppl.)

[6] M.-Louis Polain, *Catalogue des livres imprimés au quinzième siècle des bibliothèques de Belgique*, 4 vols. (Brussels, 1932). (Pol.)

[7] Margaret Bingham Stillwell, *Incunabula in American Libraries* (New York, 1940). (St.)

[8] British Museum, *Catalogue of Printed Books* (London, 1881—). (BM)

[9] Bibliothèque Nationale, *Catalogue général des livres imprimés* (Paris, 1910—). (BN)

[10] Michael Maittaire, *Annales typographici* (Amsterdam, 1733–41). (Maittaire)

[11] Georg Wolfgang Panzer, *Annales typographici* (Nuremberg, 1793). (Panzer)

[12] Johann Georg Theodor Graesse, *Trésor de livres rares et précieux* (Dresden, 1859–69). (Graesse)

list with additions to and corrections of Jan's list, together with references to catalogues authenticating or describing the editions, follows:

Editions before 1501

(Abbreviations in this list are explained in notes 1–12 above)

1472   Venice: Nicolaus Jenson: BMC V.172 (IB 19655); HCR 10426; St. M4; Jan, I, lxxxviii. Editio princeps.

1483   June 6, Brescia: Boninus de Boninis: BMC VII.968 (IB 31072); HC 10427*; St. M5; Jan, I, lxxxviii, gives incorrect year (1484). First edition to contain printed geometric diagrams and map.

1485   May 15, Brescia: Boninus de Boninis: BMC VII.969 (IB 31084); HC 10428*; Pol. 2551; St. M6; Jan, I, lxxxviii, gives incorrect year (1480).

1485   May 31, Brescia: Boninus de Boninis (variant of H 10428*): BMC VII.969 (IB 31085); R. Suppl. 112; St. M7.

1492   June 29, Venice: [Joannes Rubeus Vercellensis]: BMC V.417 (IB 23151); HC 10429*; Pol. 2552; St. M8; Jan, I, lxxxix.

1500   Oct. 29, Venice: Philippus Pincius: BMC V.499 (IB 23690); HC 10430*; Pol. 2553; St. M9; Jan, I, lxxxix.

Editions after 1500

(Abbreviations in this list are explained in notes 1–12 above)

1501   Jan. 18, Brescia: Angelus Britannicus: BM; Maittaire II.153; Panzer VI.338.1: Graesse IV.330; Jan, I, lxxxix.

1513   June 15, Venice: Augustinus de Zannis de Portesio: BN; Maittaire Index II.43; Panzer VIII.411.616; Graesse IV.330; Jan, I, xc.

1515   Feb. 1, Paris: ed. Ascensiana: BM; BN; Maittaire II.272; Panzer VIII.21.778; Jan, I, xc.

1515   July, Florence: Philippus Junta: BM; BN; Panzer VII.21.98; Graesse IV.330; Jan, I, xc.

1517   April, Venice: Aldus (with Censorinus *De die natali*): Panzer VIII.439.842.

1519   Nov. 5, Paris: ed. Ascensiana (with Censorinus *De die natali*): BM; BN; Panzer VIII.53.1067; Graesse IV.330; Jan, I, xc.

1521 July 18, Venice: Joannes Tacuinus de Tridino: BM; BN; Panzer VIII.465.1057.

1521 August, Cologne: Eucharius Cervicornus: Maittaire II.616; Panzer VI.384.339; Graesse IV.330; Jan, I, xci.

1524 Nov. 5, Paris: ed. Ascensiana (with Censorinus *De die natali*): BM; BN; Maittaire II.654; Panzer VIII.86.1404.

1526 Jan. 4, Cologne: Eucharius Cervicornus: Maittaire II.676; Panzer VI.397.451; Jan, I, xci.

1527 August, Cologne: Opera et impensa Joannis Soteris: Panzer VI.401.489; Jan, I, xci.

1528 April, Venice: Aldus (with Censorinus *De die natali*): BM; BN; Maittaire II.709; Panzer VIII.508.1445; Graesse IV.330; Jan, I, xci.

1532 Lyons: Sebastianus Gryphius: Panzer VII.353.661.

1535 Basle: Joannes Hervagius: BM; BN; Maittaire II.830; Panzer VI.306.1017; Graesse IV.330; Jan, I, xcii.

1538 Lyons: Sebastianus Gryphius: Jan, I, xcii.

1542 Lyons: Sebastianus Gryphius: Jan, I, xciii.

1548 Lyons: Sebastianus Gryphius: BN; Jan, I, xciii.

1550 Lyons: Sebastianus Gryphius: BN; Jan, I, xciii.

1556 Lyons: Sebastianus Gryphius: BM; Jan, I, xciii.

1560 Lyons: Apud haered. Gryphii: BM; BN; Jan, I, xciii.

1560 Lyons: T. Paganus: BN.

1565 Venice: Joannes Gryphius: BM; Jan, I, xciii.

1574 Venice: Joannes Gryphius: Jan, I, xciii.

1585 Paris: Henricus Stephanus: BM; BN; Maittaire III.794; Graesse IV.330; Jan, I, xciii.

1585 Lyons: A. Gryphius: BM; BN; Jan, I, xciii.

1597 Leiden: Franciscus Raphelengius: BM; BN; Graesse IV.330; Jan, I, xciv.

1597 Geneva: Jacobus Stoer: Graesse IV.330; Jan, I, xciii.

1607 Geneva: Jacobus Stoer: BM; BN; Graesse IV.330; Jan, I, xciii.

1628 Leiden: Joannes Maire: BM; BN; Graesse IV.330; Jan, I, xcv.

1670 Leiden: Arnoldus Doude, Cornelius Driehuysen: BM; BN; Graesse IV.330; Jan, I, xcvi.

1694 London: T. Dring and C. Harper: BM; BN; Jan, I, xcvi.

1736 Padua: Jos. Cominus: BM; BN; Graesse IV.330; Jan, I, xcvii, gives incorrect year (1737).

1774 Leipzig: G. Theophilus Georgius: BM; BN; Graesse IV.330; Jan, I, xcvii.

1788 Zweibrücken: ed. Bipontina: 2 vols.: BM; BN; Graesse IV.330; Jan, I, xcvii.

1848–
1852 Quedlinburg and Leipzig: Godofredus Bassius: 2 vols.

This edition, by Ludwig von Jan, represents the fullest collation of the manuscripts, including B (Bambergensis 875) and P (Parisinus Regius 6371), and also compares the readings of eleven printed editions. It remains the most serviceable of the editions of the *Commentary*.

1868 Leipzig: B. G. Teubner.

Eyssenhardt's edition is a hurried piece of work, based upon a comparison of only two manuscripts (B and P) and prepared during a six-year period when Eyssenhardt also edited Phaedrus, Apuleius, Ammianus Marcellinus, Martianus Capella, and the *Historia Miscella*.

1893 Leipzig: B. G. Teubner.

Eyssenhardt's second edition is virtually a reprinting of the first edition. A few emendations suggested by scholars in the intervening years have been incorporated, but unfortunately this edition is marred by a greater number of typographical errors than the first contained, and the first was poor in this respect. The eminent Wissowa's scathing criticism[13] of this work is probably justified.

Doubtful Editions

1485 Leipzig: Panzer I.473; Catal. Bibl. Ernesti 174.
1513 Leipzig: Panzer VII.182.446; Bauer VII.154.

III

An anonymous Latin commentary on Macrobius' *Commentary* is to be found in manuscript, in a twelfth- or thirteenth-century hand, in the Bibliothèque d'Avranches.[14]

Cicero's *Dream of Scipio* and Macrobius' *Commentary* on it were

---

[13] G. Wissowa, in *Wochenschrift für klassische Philologie*, XII (1895), 689: "Mein Urteil, dass wir es mit einer von Anfang bis zu Ende nachlässigen und unbrauchbaren Arbeit zu tun haben, glaube ich im vorstehenden ausreichend begründet zu haben."

[14] *Catalogue général des manuscrits des bibliothèques publiques de France*, X (1889), 104.

among the numerous Latin works which the well-known Byzantine scholar and theologian Maximus Planudes (c.1260–1320) translated into Greek.

An anonymous French translation, based upon the Pontanus edition (1628), is to be found in manuscript, in an eighteenth-century hand, in the Bibliothèque de Châlons-sur-Marne.[15]

The interest of French scholars in Neoplatonism during the nineteenth century is reflected in the numerous editions of French translations of Macrobius' works:

Œuvres de Macrobe, traduites par Ch. de Rosoy. 2 vols. Paris, 1827.

Macrobe, Œuvres complètes, avec la traduction en français, publiées sous la direction de M. Nisard. Paris, 1845. In the preface A. J. Mahul is indicated as the translator of this work. The series in which this translation appeared, "Collection des auteurs latins," was republished at various times.

Œuvres de Macrobe, traduction nouvelle, par MM. Henri Descamps, N. A. Dubois, Laas d'Aguen, A. Ubicini Martelli. Paris, 1847. "Bibliothèque latine-française," seconde série, tome 33.

In 1937 a new translation, by Henri Bornecque, of the *Saturnalia* appeared: *Les Saturnales, traduction nouvelle, avec introduction et notes* (2 vols., Paris, 1937).

The present translation is based upon a comparison of Jan's edition and the 1868 and 1893 editions of Eyssenhardt. I had once intended to make a new collation but this became impossible during the war years. After completing the translation I realized that there were very few textual difficulties. Nearly all the discrepancies that are found in the three texts employed are the result of obvious typographical errors, negligent omissions of words or phrases, and variant spellings. In the main I have found Jan's text the most reliable and have used it as the basis of the translation. Lacking the opportunity to consult the manuscripts, I had to adopt the unscholarly practice of choosing the reading that made the better sense. On about a half-dozen occasions, indicated in the notes, Eyssenhardt's reading (usually the emendation of some other scholar since Jan) seemed more sensible. The Chaucer Section of the Modern Language Association is planning a

[15] *Ibid.*, III (1885), 57.

series of critical editions of texts that were used by Chaucer, and a new edition of the *Commentary* is being prepared by Professor Claude W. Barlow, of Clark University.

The task of translating the *Commentary* has not been easy. The encyclopedic range of the author's interest draws upon many disciplines. But it has been a more difficult problem to adapt Macrobius' pedantry, flowery phraseology, and forced rhetoric to modern tastes and at the same time to retain the flavor and charm of the original. In general it seemed best to translate quite literally. Long sentences have been broken down and the author's overfondness for transitional particles has had to be reconciled with English usage.

Marcus Tullius Cicero

Scipio's Dream

Scipio's Dream[1]

CHAPTER I

[1] WHEN I ARRIVED in Africa in the consulship of Manius Manilius[2] (I was military tribune in the fourth legion, as you know), the intention that was uppermost in my mind was to meet King Masinissa,[3] who for very good reasons was most friendly to my family. [2] When I came before him, the old man embraced me with tears in his eyes and, after a pause, gazing heavenward, said: "To you, O Sun on high, and to you other celestial beings, my thanks are due for the privilege, before I pass from this life, of seeing in my kingdom and beneath this very roof Publius Cornelius Scipio, at the mere mention of whose name I am refreshed; for the memory of that excellent and invincible leader never leaves my mind.[4]

Then we questioned each other, I about his kingdom and he about our commonwealth, and in the ensuing conversation we spent the whole day. [3] Moreover, enjoying the regal splendor of our surroundings, we prolonged our conversation far into the night; the aged king could talk of nothing but Scipio Africanus, recollecting all his words as well as his deeds.

After we parted for the night, I fell into a deep slumber, sounder

---

[1] *Scipio's Dream* was originally the closing portion of the sixth book of Cicero's *De re publica*. This translation is based upon the interpretation that Macrobius gave to Cicero's words. It will consequently deviate on a few occasions from Cicero's intended meaning. A careful rendition of the Ciceronian meaning may be found in C. W. Keyes's translation of the *De re publica* and *De legibus* in The Loeb Classical Library (London and New York, 1928), pp. 261–83. See Boyancé for a detailed study of *Scipio's Dream*.

[2] 149 B.C.

[3] An ally of Rome in the Second Punic War, he materially assisted Scipio the Elder in defeating Hannibal in 202 B.C. By the terms of the peace treaty he was made king of Numidia. He remained an ally throughout his long reign. In 151 B.C. report of hostilities between Carthage and Masinissa was used as a pretext by the Romans for engaging in a third war against Carthage.

[4] The elder Publius Cornelius Scipio Africanus, conqueror of Hannibal in 202 B.C. and adoptive grandfather of the narrator of this dream, Publius Cornelius Scipio Africanus the Younger.

than usual because of my long journey and the late hour of retirement. [4] I dreamt that Africanus was standing before me—I believe our discussion was responsible for this, for it frequently happens that our thoughts and conversations react upon us in dreams somewhat in the manner of Ennius' reported experiences about Homer,[5] of whom he used to think and speak very often in his waking hours. My grandfather's appearance was better known to me from his portrait-mask than from my memories of him.[6] Upon recognizing him I shuddered, but he reproved my fears and bade me pay close attention to his words.

CHAPTER II

[1] "DO YOU SEE that city which I compelled to be obedient to the Roman people but which is now renewing earlier strife and is unable to remain at peace?" (From our lofty perch, dazzling and glorious, set among the radiant stars, he pointed out Carthage.) "To storm it you have now come, ranking not much higher than a private soldier. Two years hence as consul [7] you will conquer it, thus winning for yourself the cognomen which until now you have had as an inheritance from me.[8] After destroying Carthage and celebrating your triumph, you will hold the office of censor;[9] you will go as legate to Egypt, Syria, Asia, and Greece;[10] you will be chosen consul a second time in your absence, and you will bring to a close a great war, destroying Numantia.[11] [2] Arriving at the Capitol in a chariot, you will find the commonwealth gravely disturbed because of the policies of my grandson.[12] Then, Scipio, it will behoove you to display to your people the brilliance of your intellect, talents, and experience.

[5] Cf. Lucretius *De rerum natura* 1.123–25; Cicero *Academica* 11.51; Persius *Satirae* VI.10–11.

[6] The descendants of a Roman who held one of the higher magistracies were accorded the privilege of displaying a wax mask of him in their atrium. Cicero (*De senectute* xix) places the death of the elder Scipio and the birth of the younger Scipio in 185 B.C.; Polybius (Livy *Ab urbe condita* XXXIX.52) gives the date of the elder Scipio's death as 183.

[7] Elected consul in 147 B.C., Scipio was proconsul when he destroyed Carthage in 146.

[8] The cognomen Africanus.

[9] In 142 B.C.

[10] Cicero (*Academica* 11.5) places the date of the embassy before that of the censorship.

[11] Again chosen consul in 134 B.C., he destroyed Numantia in 133 after a siege of fifteen months.

[12] Tiberius Gracchus.

"But at that point I see the course of your life wavering between two destinies, as it were. When your age has completed seven times eight recurring circuits of the sun, and the product of these two numbers, each of which is considered full for a different reason, has rounded out your destiny, the whole state will take refuge in you and your name; the Senate, all good citizens, the Allies, and the Latins will look to you; upon you alone will the safety of the state depend; and, to be brief, as dictator you must needs set the state in order, if only you escape death at the hands of your wicked kinsmen."

[3] Hereupon Laelius[13] let out a cry, and the others groaned deeply; but Scipio said with a smiling expression: Hush! please; don't awaken me from my sleep; hear the rest of the dream.

CHAPTER III

[1] "BUT THAT YOU may be more zealous in safeguarding the commonwealth, Scipio, be persuaded of this: all those who have saved, aided, or enlarged the commonwealth have a definite place marked off in the heavens where they may enjoy a blessed existence forever. Nothing that occurs on earth, indeed, is more gratifying to that supreme God who rules the whole universe than the establishment of associations and federations of men bound together by principles of justice, which are called commonwealths. The governors and protectors of these proceed from here and return hither after death."

[2] At this point, though I was greatly dismayed, not at the fear of dying but rather at the thought of being betrayed by relatives, I nevertheless asked whether he and my father Aemilius Paulus[14] and the others whom we think of as dead were really still living.

"Of course these men are alive," he said, "who have flown from the bonds of their bodies as from a prison; indeed, that life of yours, as it is called, is really death. Just look up and see your father Paulus approaching you."

[3] When I saw him, I wept profusely, but he embraced and kissed

---

[13] A very dear friend of the younger Scipio and one of the speakers in Cicero's dialogue *De amicitia*. Here Cicero interrupts Scipio's narrative, which is resumed in the following chapter.

[14] Became one of Rome's greatest heroes by his defeat of Perseus, king of Macedonia, in 168 B.C. He had his son (the dreaming Scipio) adopted by the son of the elder Scipio Africanus.

me and forbade me to weep. As soon as I could check my tears and
speak out, I said: "I pray you, most revered and best of fathers, since
this is truly life, as I hear Africanus tell, why do I linger on earth?
Why do I not hasten hither to you?"

[4] "You are mistaken," he replied, "for until that God who rules
all the region of the sky at which you are now looking has freed you
from the fetters of your body, you cannot gain admission here. Men
were created with the understanding that they were to look after
that sphere called Earth, which you see in the middle of the temple.
Minds have been given to them out of the eternal fires you call fixed
stars and planets, those spherical solids which, quickened with divine
minds, journey through their circuits and orbits with amazing speed.
[5] Wherefore, Scipio, you and all other dutiful men must keep your
souls in the custody of your bodies and must not leave this life of
men except at the command of that One who gave it to you, that
you may not appear to have deserted the office assigned you. But,
Scipio, cherish justice and your obligations to duty, as your grandfather here, and I, your father, have done; this is important where
parents and relatives are concerned, but is of utmost importance in
matters concerning the commonwealth. [6] This sort of life is your
passport into the sky, to a union with those who have finished their
lives on earth and who, upon being released from their bodies, inhabit
that place at which you are now looking" (it was a circle of surpassing
brilliance gleaming out amidst the blazing stars), "which takes its
name, the Milky Way, from the Greek word."

[7] As I looked out from this spot, everything appeared splendid
and wonderful. Some stars were visible which we never see from this
region, and all were of a magnitude far greater than we had imagined. Of these the smallest was the one farthest from the sky and
nearest the earth, which shone forth with borrowed light. And, indeed, the starry spheres easily surpassed the earth in size. From here
the earth appeared so small that I was ashamed of our empire which
is, so to speak, but a point on its surface.

CHAPTER IV

[1] AS I GAZED rather intently at the earth my grandfather said:
"How long will your thoughts continue to dwell upon the earth? Do

you not behold the regions to which you have come? The whole universe is comprised of nine circles, or rather spheres. The outermost of these is the celestial sphere, embracing all the rest, itself the supreme god, confining and containing all the other spheres. In it are fixed the eternally revolving movements of the stars. [2] Beneath it are the seven underlying spheres, which revolve in an opposite direction to that of the celestial sphere. One of these spheres belongs to that planet which on earth is called Saturn. Below it is that brilliant orb, propitious and helpful to the human race, called Jupiter. Next comes the ruddy one, which you call Mars, dreaded on earth. Next, and occupying almost the middle region, comes the sun, leader, chief, and regulator of the other lights, mind and moderator of the universe, of such magnitude that it fills all with its radiance. The sun's companions, so to speak, each in its own sphere, follow—the one Venus, the other Mercury—and in the lowest sphere the moon, kindled by the rays of the sun, revolves. [3] Below the moon all is mortal and transitory, with the exception of the souls bestowed upon the human race by the benevolence of the gods. Above the moon all things are eternal. Now in the center, the ninth of the spheres, is the earth, never moving and at the bottom. Towards it all bodies gravitate by their own inclination."

CHAPTER V

[1] I STOOD DUMBFOUNDED at these sights, and when I recovered my senses I inquired: "What is this great and pleasing sound that fills my ears?"

"That," replied my grandfather, "is a concord of tones separated by unequal but nevertheless carefully proportioned intervals, caused by the rapid motion of the spheres themselves. The high and low tones blended together produce different harmonies. Of course such swift motions could not be accomplished in silence and, as nature requires, the spheres at one extreme produce the low tones and at the other extreme the high tones. [2] Consequently the outermost sphere, the star-bearer, with its swifter motion gives forth a higher-pitched tone, whereas the lunar sphere, the lowest, has the deepest tone. Of course the earth, the ninth and stationary sphere, always clings to the same position in the middle of the universe. The other eight spheres, two of which move at the same speed, produce seven different tones, this number being, one might almost say, the key to the universe. Gifted men, imitating this harmony on stringed instruments and in singing, have gained for themselves a return to this region, as have those who have devoted their exceptional abilities to a search for divine truths. [3] The ears of mortals are filled with this sound, but they are unable to hear it. Indeed, hearing is the dullest of the senses: consider the people who dwell in the region about the Great Cataract, where the Nile comes rushing down from lofty mountains; they have lost their sense of hearing because of the loud roar. But the sound coming from the heavenly spheres revolving at very swift speeds is of course so great that human ears cannot catch it; you might as well try to stare directly at the sun, whose rays are much too strong for your eyes."

I was amazed at these wonders, but nevertheless I kept turning my eyes back to earth.

CHAPTER VI

[1] MY GRANDFATHER then continued: "Again I see you gazing at the region and abode of mortals. If it seems as small to you as it really is, why not fix your attention upon the heavens and contemn what is mortal? Can you expect any fame from these men, or glory that is worth seeking? You see, Scipio, that the inhabited portions on earth are widely separated and narrow, and that vast wastes lie between these inhabited spots, as we might call them; the earth's inhabitants are so cut off that there can be no communication among different groups; moreover, some nations stand obliquely, some transversely to you, and some even stand directly opposite you; from these, of course, you can expect no fame. [2] You can also discern certain belts that appear to encircle the earth; you observe that the two which are farthest apart and lie under the poles of the heavens are stiff with cold, whereas the belt in the middle, the greatest one, is scorched with the heat of the sun. [3] The two remaining belts are habitable; one, the southern, is inhabited by men who plant their feet in the opposite direction to yours and have nothing to do with your people; the other, the northern, is inhabited by the Romans. But look closely, see how small is the portion allotted to you! The whole

of the portion that you inhabit is narrow at the top and broad at the sides and is in truth a small island encircled by that sea which you call the Atlantic, the Great Sea, or Ocean. But you can see how small it is despite its name! [4] Has your name or that of any Roman been able to pass beyond the Caucasus, which you see over here, or to cross the Ganges over yonder? And these are civilized lands in the known quarter of the globe. But who will ever hear of your name in the remaining portions of the globe? With these excluded, you surely see what narrow confines bound your ambitions. And how long will those who praise us now continue to do so?"

CHAPTER VII

[1] "NOT EVEN if the children of future generations should wish to hand down to their posterity the exploits of each one of us as they heard them from their fathers, would it be possible for us to achieve fame for a long time, not to mention permanent fame, owing to the floods and conflagrations that inevitably overwhelm the earth at definite intervals. [2] What difference does it make whether you will be remembered by those who came after you when there was no mention made of you by men before your time? They were just as numerous and were certainly better men. Indeed, among those who can possibly hear of the name of Rome, there is not one who is able to gain a reputation that will endure a single year. [3] Men commonly reckon a year solely by the return of the sun, which is just one star; but in truth when all the stars have returned to the same places from which they started out and have restored the same configurations over the great distances of the whole sky, then alone can the returning cycle truly be called a year; how many generations of men are contained in a great year I scarcely dare say. [4] As, long ago, the sun seemed to be failing and going out when Romulus' soul reached these very regions, so at the time when it will be eclipsed again in the very same quarter, and at the same season, and when all constellations and planets have been returned to their former positions, then you may consider the year complete; indeed, you may be sure that not a twentieth part of that year has yet elapsed.

[5] "Therefore, if you despair of ever returning to this region in which great and eminent men have their complete reward, how in-

significant will be that human glory which can scarcely endure for a fraction of a year? But if you will look upwards and contemplate this eternal goal and abode, you will no longer give heed to the gossip of the common herd, nor look for your reward in human things. Let Virtue, as is fitting, draw you with her own attractions to the true glory; and let others say what they please about you, for they will talk in any event. All their gossip is confined to the narrow bounds of the small area at which you are gazing, and is never enduring; it is overwhelmed with the passing of men and is lost in the oblivion of posterity."

CHAPTER VIII

[1] AFTER HE SAID these words, I interrupted: "If, as you say, Africanus, a man who has served his country steadfastly finds a passage to the sky, so to speak, then, though I have walked in your steps and those of my father from boyhood and have never forsaken your brilliant example, I shall now strive much more zealously, with the promise of such a reward before me."

[2] "Do you then make that effort," he said, "and regard not yourself but only this body as mortal; the outward form does not reveal the man but rather the mind of each individual is his true self, not the figure that one designates by pointing a finger. Know, therefore, that you are a god if, indeed, a god is that which quickens, feels, remembers, foresees, and in the same manner rules, restrains, and impels the body of which it has charge as the supreme God rules the universe; and as the eternal God moves a universe that is mortal in part, so an everlasting mind moves your frail body.

[3] "For that which is always self-moved is eternal, but when that which conveys motion to another body and which is itself moved from the outside no longer continues in motion, it must of course cease to be alive. Therefore, only that which is self-moved never ceases to be moved, since it never abandons itself; rather, it is the source and beginning of motion for all other things that move. [4] Now a beginning has no origin: all things originate in a beginning, but a beginning itself cannot be born from something else, since it would not be a beginning if it originated elsewhere. But if it has no beginning, then indeed, it has no ending: for if a beginning were

destroyed it could not be reborn from anything else; nor could it create anything else from itself if, indeed, everything has to come from a beginning. [5] Thus it happens that the beginning of motion, that which is self-moved, originates in itself; moreover, it cannot experience birth or death; otherwise the whole heavens and all nature would have to collapse and come to a standstill and would find no force to stir them to motion again."

CHAPTER IX

[1] "THEREFORE, since it is clear that that which is self-moved is eternal, is there anyone who would deny that this is the essence possessed by souls? Everything that is set in motion by an outside force is inanimate, but that which has soul is moved by its own inward motion, for this is the peculiar function and property of soul. If the soul is unique in being self-moved, surely it is without birth and without death.

[2] "Exercise it in the best achievements. The noblest efforts are in behalf of your native country; a soul thus stimulated and engaged will speed hither to its destination and abode without delay; and this flight will be even swifter if the soul, while it is still shut up in the body, will rise above it, and in contemplation of what is beyond, detach itself as much as possible from the body. [3] Indeed, the souls of those who have surrendered themselves to bodily pleasures, becoming their slaves, and who in response to sensual passions have flouted the laws of gods and of men, slip out of their bodies at death and hover close to the earth, and return to this region only after long ages of torment."

He departed, and I awoke from sleep.

Macrobius Ambrosius Theodosius

Commentary on Scipio's Dream

Book One

CHAPTER I

[1] IN OUR READING of Plato's *Republic* and Cicero's *Republic,*
my son Eustachius, my joy and boast in life, we noted this difference
at a glance: the former drafted plans for the organization of a state,
the latter described one already in existence; the one discussed an
ideal state, the other the government established by his forefathers.[1]
[2] In one respect, however, imitation has produced a striking similarity, namely, that whereas Plato, at the conclusion of his work, has
a man who apparently had died and was restored to life reveal the
conditions of souls liberated from their bodies, introducing as well
an interesting description of the spheres and constellations, the
Scipio of Cicero's work treats of the same subjects, but as revelations
which came to him in a dream. [3] The reason for including such a
fiction and dream in books dealing with governmental problems,
and the justification for introducing a description of celestial circles,
orbits, and spheres, the movements[2] of planets, and the revolutions
of the heavens into a discussion of the regulations governing commonwealths seemed to me to be worth investigating; and the reader,
too, will perhaps be curious. Otherwise we may be led to believe that
men of surpassing wisdom, whose habit it was to regard the search
for truth as nothing if not divine, have padded their treatises, nowhere else prolix, with something superfluous. A brief explanation
of this point must be made, therefore, so that the reader may clearly
comprehend what follows.

[4] With a deep understanding of all human affairs Plato advises
throughout his discussion of the establishment of a republic that a
love of justice must be instilled in men's minds, without which it is
impossible to maintain not only a state, but human fellowship and

[1] Cf. Cicero *De re publica* II.3.
[2] Following Eyssenhardt (for this and other editions, see Introduction, pp. 60–63), who
adopts Zeunius' emendation *motu* instead of the reading *modo* in the MSS.

family life as well. [5] He realized that in order to implant this fondness for justice in an individual nothing was quite so effective as the assurance that one's enjoyments did not terminate with death. But how could Plato show that these continued after death except by demonstrating the immortality of souls? After he had created a belief in the immortality of souls he drew the obvious conclusion that the souls, upon being released from their bodies, had definite places allotted them according to their deserts. [6] For example, in the *Phaedo*,[3] when he has proved by brilliant and incontrovertible arguments that the soul is immortal, there follows a comparison of the abodes that are destined for those departing from this life, as each one has merited by his mode of living. Likewise in the *Georgias*,[4] after a defense of justice, the reader is admonished in that characteristically grave but charming Socratic manner about the condition of souls after death. [7] This subject is also painstakingly treated in those books that deal with the establishment of a republic. After Plato has given the chief place to justice and has taught that the soul does not perish at death, he points out by means of that closing fable[5] —for that is what many call it—whither the soul goes on leaving the body and whence it comes to the body. This he does in order to show that rewards for the pursuit of justice and penalties for its neglect await the souls of men, for these are indeed immortal and must submit to judgment.

[8] Cicero proved to be equally judicious and clever in following this method of treatment: after giving the palm to justice in all matters concerning the welfare of the state, he revealed, at the very end of his work,[6] the sacred abodes of immortal souls and the secrets of the heavens and pointed out the place to which the souls of those who had served the republic prudently, justly, courageously, and temperately[7] must proceed, or rather, must return. [9] In Plato's work these secrets had been disclosed by a man named Er, a Pamphylian by birth, a soldier by calling, who was supposed to be dead from wounds received in battle. But twelve days later, when he was about

---

[3] 110B–114C.

[4] 523A–526D.

[5] *Republic* x. 614B–621D. Cf. Proclus (Kroll), I, 168, who also discusses these passages from the *Republic, Phaedo,* and *Gorgias.*

[6] *De re publica* VI.9–26.

[7] Prudence, justice, courage, and temperance are the four cardinal virtues. See below, I.viii.3–4 and note.

to be burned on a pyre together with those who perished with him, he suddenly recovered the breath of life (or perhaps it had never left him) and made what one might call an official proclamation to the human race of all that he had seen and done in the days that elapsed between his two lives. Cicero, as if assured of the truth of this tale, deplored the ridicule it received at the hands of ignorant critics and yet, fearful of the unwarranted censure that was heaped upon Plato, preferred to have his account given by a man aroused from sleep rather than by one returned from the dead.[8]

CHAPTER II

[1] BEFORE CONSIDERING the words of *Scipio's Dream,* we must ascertain what sort of men Cicero says either ridiculed Plato's story or at least had no fear that the same thing might happen to them. He does not mean to leave the impression that they were an unlearned lot, but rather that they were men who concealed their fundamental ignorance by a display of apparent wisdom—the type of men, indeed, who were moved only to adverse criticism by reading such words as these. [2] Therefore we shall declare which group it was that, according to Cicero, indulged in superficial criticism, which of them went so far as to put his charges in writing, and finally what reply it is fitting to make to their objections, as far as they concern the present work. When these critics have been answered (a really simple matter) then any malicious attack, past or future, upon *Scipio's Dream*— surely Cicero never expected there would be any—will fall to the ground.

[3] The whole sect of Epicureans, consistently misapprehending the truth and continually branding as ridiculous things which are beyond their understanding, made sport of Plato's sacred scroll and majestic discourse on nature. In fact Colotes,[1] well known among the disciples of Epicurus because of his ready tongue, even wrote a book to vent his caustic criticisms. Those of his arguments, false though

[8] On the difference between Plato's *Republic* and Cicero's *Republic* and on Cicero's adoption of the setting of a dream rather than that of a myth such as Plato uses, cf. Favonius 1. Also cf. Macrobius' discussion of the purpose of the Platonic myths with that of Proclus (Kroll), II, 96–101.

[1] For further information about Colotes' attack upon Plato and details of his life, see Pauly, XI (1922), cols. 1120–22; W. Crönert, *Kolotes und Menedemos* (Leipzig, 1906).

they be, which do not apply to *Scipio's Dream*, the subject of this treatise, must be disregarded for the present; but we must follow up that cavil which, unless removed, will always discredit Cicero as well as Plato.[2] [4] He insists that philosophers should refrain from using fiction since no kind of fiction has a place with those who profess to tell the truth.[3] "If you wished to impart to us a conception of the heavenly realms and reveal the conditions of souls, why," he asks, "did you not do so in a simple and straightforward manner, instead of defiling the very portals of truth with imaginary character, event, and setting, in a vile imitation of a playwright?" [5] Since this censure, though directed against Plato's Er, nevertheless applies to our dreaming Scipio as well—in either case the author justified his choice of character as suited to the expression of his doctrines—we must resist this adversary and refute his pointless argument, so that by one stroke each character may retain his rightful dignity.

[6] Philosophy does not discountenance all stories nor does it accept all, and in order to distinguish between what it rejects as unfit to enter its sacred precincts and what it frequently and gladly admits, the points of division must needs be clarified. [7] Fables—the very word acknowledges their falsity[4]—serve two purposes: either merely to gratify the ear or to encourage the reader to good works. [8] They delight the ear as do the comedies of Menander and his imitators, or the narratives replete with imaginary doings of lovers in which Petronius Arbiter so freely indulged and with which Apuleius, astonishingly,[5] sometimes amused himself. This whole category of fables that promise only to gratify the ear a philosophical treatise avoids and relegates to children's nurseries. [9] The other group, those that

[2] Whittaker (*Macrobius*, p. 58) and Mras (pp. 236–37) have noted the similarity between Macrobius' defense of the use of myths and that of Proclus, and their replies to Colotes. Mras feels certain that Macrobius drew from Porphyry's lost commentary on Plato's *Republic* for this chapter. Proclus' indebtedness to Porphyry was acknowledged at the beginning of his argument. See also Boyancé, Chap. I, especially pp. 45–48.

[3] Cf. Proclus (Kroll), II, 105.

[4] *Fabula* derived from *fari*, "to tell." Cf. Varro VI.55.

[5] The reference is undoubtedly to Apuleius' great work, the *Golden Ass*, which abounds in romance and adventure. It is not surprising to find Macrobius expressing astonishment over such literary extravagances of Apuleius, for the latter was an eminent Platonist, author of two books on the life and philosophy of Plato and translator of Nicomachus' *Introductio arithmeticae* and the pseudo-Aristotelian treatise *De mundo*. Macrobius must have admired Apuleius' serious side but could hardly be expected to have any appreciation of the *Golden Ass*.

draw the reader's attention to certain kinds of virtue, are divided into two types. In the first both the setting and plot are fictitious, as in the fables of Aesop, famous for his exquisite imagination. The second rests on a solid foundation of truth, which is treated in a fictitious style. This is called the fabulous narrative (*narratio fabulosa*) to distinguish it from the ordinary fable; examples of it are the performances of sacred rites, the stories of Hesiod and Orpheus that treat of the ancestry and deeds of the gods, and the mystic conceptions of the Pythagoreans. [10] Of the second main group, which we have just mentioned, the first type, with both setting and plot fictitious, is also inappropriate to philosophical treatises. The second type is subdivided, for there is more than one way of telling the truth when the argument is real but is presented in the form of a fable. [11] Either the presentation of the plot involves matters that are base and unworthy of divinities and are monstrosities of some sort[6] (as, for example, gods caught in adultery, Saturn cutting off the privy parts of his father Caelus and himself thrown into chains by his son and successor), a type which philosophers prefer to disregard altogether;[7] or else a decent and dignified conception of holy truths, with respectable events and characters, is presented beneath a modest veil of allegory. This is the only type of fiction approved by the philosopher who is prudent in handling sacred matters.

[12] Therefore, since the treatises of Plato and Cicero suffer no harm from Er's testimony or Scipio's dream, and the treatment of sacred subjects is accomplished without loss of dignity by using their names, let our critic at last hold his peace, taught to differentiate between the fable and the fabulous narrative.

[13] We should not assume, however, that philosophers approve the use of fabulous narratives, even those of the proper sort, in all disputations. It is their custom to employ them when speaking about the Soul,[8] or about spirits having dominion in the lower and upper air, or about gods in general.[9] [14] But when the discussion aspires to treat of the Highest and Supreme of all gods, called by the Greeks the Good (*tagathon*) and the First Cause (*proton aition*), or to treat

[6] Cf. Proclus (Kroll), II, 106.
[7] Cf. Plato *Republic* II.377B–378D.
[8] Viz., the Neoplatonic Soul. See below, notes 10 and 13.
[9] Cf. Proclus (Kroll), II, 106.

of Mind or Intellect, which the Greeks call *nous*,[10] born from and originating in the Supreme God and embracing the original concepts of things, which are called Ideas (*ideai*),[11] when, I repeat, philosophers speak about these, the Supreme God and Mind, they shun the use of fabulous narratives. When they wish to assign attributes to these divinities that not only pass the bounds of speech but those of human comprehension as well, they resort to similes and analogies. [15] That is why Plato, when he was moved to speak about the Good, did not dare to tell what it was, knowing only this about it, that it was impossible for the human mind to grasp what it was. In truth, of visible objects he found the sun most like it, and by using this as an illustration[12] opened a way for his discourse to approach what was otherwise incomprehensible. [16] On this account men of old fashioned no likeness of the Good when they were carving statues of other deities, for the Supreme God and Mind sprung from it are above the Soul and therefore beyond nature.[13] It is a sacrilege for fables to approach this sphere.

[17] But in treating of the other gods and the Soul, as I have said, philosophers make use of fabulous narratives; not without a purpose, however, nor merely to entertain, but because they realize that a frank, open exposition of herself is distasteful to Nature,[14] who, just as she has withheld an understanding of herself from the uncouth senses of men by enveloping herself in variegated garments, has also desired to have her secrets handled by more prudent individuals through fabulous narratives. [18] Accordingly, her sacred rites are

---

[10] Macrobius is here referring to the two higher of the three well-known Neoplatonic hypostases. Readers who are not familiar with the Neoplatonic doctrines on the high origin of the human soul could hardly do better than to begin with Macrobius' brief discussion of the subject in a chapter (I.xiv) which has been called "as good a summary of the Plotinian trinity as was possible in Latin." For a full treatment of the Neoplatonic Supreme God, Mind, and Soul, see Whittaker, *Neo-Platonists*, pp. 53–70. I have adopted the standard practice of capitalizing *Soul* when the word refers to the member of the Neoplatonic trinity, and of using lower case when the word refers to human souls.

[11] Cf. Abelard *Epitome theologiae Christianae* (Migne, *Pat. Lat.*, CLXXVIII, 1701).

[12] *Republic* VI.508A–509B. Cf. Plotinus I.vii.1 and Proclus (Kroll), I, 276. It is a common practice of Neoplatonists to foist upon Plato philosophical tenets which originated in their own school.

[13] The Soul, the third Neoplatonic hypostasis, is permeated with Mind or *nous*, being an emanation from it; but since Soul generates the corporeal world, it represents a transitional stage between the intelligible realm and the corporeal realm. The Supreme God and Mind, being above the Soul, are therefore too far removed from the corporeal world to be described by worldly objects or attributes.

[14] Cf. Proclus (Kroll), II, 107.

veiled in mysterious representations so that she may not have to show herself even to initiates. Only eminent men of superior intelligence gain a revelation of her truths; the others must satisfy their desire for worship with a ritual drama which prevents her secrets from becoming common.[15] [19] Indeed, Numenius, a philosopher with a curiosity for occult things, had revealed to him in a dream the outrage he had committed against the gods by proclaiming his interpretation of the Eleusinian mysteries.[16] The Eleusinian goddesses themselves, dressed in the garments of courtesans, appeared to him standing before an open brothel, and when in his astonishment he asked the reason for this shocking conduct, they angrily replied that he had driven them from their sanctuary of modesty and had prostituted them to every passer-by. [20] In truth, divinities have always preferred to be known and worshiped in the fashion assigned to them by ancient popular tradition, which made images of beings that had no physical form, represented them as of different ages, though they were subject neither to growth nor decay, and gave them clothes and ornaments, though they had no bodies. [21] In this way Pythagoras himself, and Empedocles, Parmenides, and Heraclitus spoke of the gods, and Timaeus, their disciple, continued the tradition that had come down to him.

CHAPTER III

[1] AFTER THESE prefatory remarks, there remains another matter to be considered before taking up the text of *Scipio's Dream*. We must first describe the many varieties of dreams recorded by the ancients, who have classified and defined the various types that have appeared to men in their sleep, wherever they might be. Then we shall be able to decide to which type the dream we are discussing belongs.

[2] All dreams may be classified under five main types:[1] there is

[15] Cf. *ibid.*, 108. See Lobeck, p. 134; Victor Magnien, *Les Mystères d'Éleusis; leurs origines, le rituel de leurs initiations*, pp. 14–15.

[16] On Numenius' vulgarizing of mysteries, see K. S. Guthrie, *Numenius of Apamea* (London, 1917), p. 107.

[1] The elaborate classification and description of dreams forming this chapter was one of the most popular sections of the *Commentary* and caused the author to be regarded as one of the leading authorities on dreams during the Middle Ages. See the section on Macrobius' influence in the Introduction. The classification is of course not original; the bulk of it

the enigmatic dream, in Greek *oneiros,* in Latin *somnium;* second, there is the prophetic vision, in Greek *horama,* in Latin *visio;* third, there is the oracular dream, in Greek *chrematismos,* in Latin *oraculum;* fourth, there is the nightmare, in Greek *enypnion,* in Latin *insomnium;* and last, the apparition, in Greek *phantasma,* which Cicero, when he has occasion to use the word, calls *visum.*[2]

[3] The last two, the nightmare and the apparition, are not worth interpreting since they have no prophetic significance.[3] [4] Nightmares may be caused by mental or physical distress, or anxiety about the future: the patient experiences in dreams vexations similar to those that disturb him during the day. As examples of the mental variety, we might mention the lover who dreams of possessing his sweetheart or of losing her, or the man who fears the plots or might of an enemy and is confronted with him in his dream or seems to be fleeing him. The physical variety might be illustrated by one who has overindulged in eating[4] or drinking and dreams that he is either choking with food or unburdening himself, or by one who has been suffering from hunger or thirst and dreams that he is craving and searching for food or drink or has found it. Anxiety about the future would cause a man to dream that he is gaining a prominent

---

bears striking resemblances to the classification given by Artemidorus at the opening of his *Onirocriticon* and at times would serve as a free translation of the Greek work. There are, however, marked divergences between Macrobius and Artemidorus. So we must conclude either that their borrowings are independent of each other and go back ultimately to the same source, or that Macrobius has adopted the changes introduced by one or more intermediaries between himself and Artemidorus. Schedler (p. 85) believes Macrobius' immediate source to be Porphyry's lost commentary on Plato's *Timaeus;* Mras (p. 238) maintains that it is Porphyry's *Quaestiones Homericae;* Claes Blum (*Studies in the Dream-Book of Artemidorus,* pp. 57–60), argues that Posidonius is the ultimate source of both; Courcelle (p. 24) takes issue with Mras and feels that Macrobius' source here, as well as for the passage on Agamemnon's dream (1.vii.4–6), was Porphyry's lost commentary on Plato's *Republic.* For a critical comparison of the texts of Artemidorus and Macrobius and a discussion of the possible sources of Macrobius, Artemidorus, and Chalcidius, see Blum, pp. 53–60. Artemidorus' *Onirocriticon* is the acknowledged classic on the subject, being a main source of the leading dream books of the Middle Ages and exerting an influence even to the present. But in many instances the adoption of this venerable classification of dreams is to be traced to Macrobius' version rather than to Artemidorus. Cf. pseudo-Augustine *De spiritu et anima* xxv (Migne, *Pat. Lat.* XL, 798); John of Salisbury ii.xv.429A; Onulf *Vita Popponis* xxvii.

[2] Cicero *Academica* 1.40, ii.18, 77. Artemidorus 1.2 subordinates the *horama* and *chrematismos* to the *oneiros* and the *phantasma* to the *enypnion.*

[3] Cf. Artemidorus Introd. to Book iv.

[4] Cf. Cicero *De divinatione* 1.60, and for classical references on the effect of food on dreams, see note to this passage in Pease edition, "University of Illinois Studies in Language and Literature," Vol. VI, No. 2 (1920).

position or office as he hoped or that he is being deprived of it as he feared.[5]

[5] Since these dreams and others like them arise from some condition or circumstance that irritates a man during the day and consequently disturbs him when he falls asleep, they flee when he awakes and vanish into thin air.[6] Thus the name *insomnium* was given, not because such dreams occur "in sleep"—in this respect nightmares are like other types—but because they are noteworthy only during their course and afterwards have no importance or meaning.

[6] Virgil, too, considers nightmares deceitful: "False are the dreams (*insomnia*) sent by departed spirits to their sky."[7] He used the word "sky" with reference to our mortal realm because the earth bears the same relation to the regions of the dead as the heavens bear to the earth. Again, in describing the passion of love, whose concerns are always accompanied by nightmares, he says: "Oft to her heart rushes back the chief's valour, oft his glorious stock; his looks and words cling fast within her bosom, and the pang withholds calm rest from her limbs."[8] And a moment later: "Anna, my sister, what dreams (*insomnia*) thrill me with fears?"[9]

[7] The apparition (*phantasma* or *visum*) comes upon one in the moment between wakefulness and slumber, in the so-called "first cloud of sleep." In this drowsy condition he thinks he is still fully awake and imagines he sees specters rushing at him or wandering vaguely about, differing from natural creatures in size and shape, and hosts of diverse things, either delightful or disturbing. To this class belongs the incubus, which, according to popular belief, rushes upon people in sleep and presses them with a weight which they can feel.[10]

[8] The two types just described are of no assistance in foretelling the

---

[5] Cf. John of Salisbury II.xv.429A–B. On the influence of the Macrobian definition upon subsequent lexicography, see R. J. Getty, "Insomnia in the Lexica," *American Journal of Philology*, LIV (1933), 5, 11, 21.

[6] Cf. Artemidorus I.I, IV. Introd.

[7] *Aeneid* VI.896. For the Virgilian passages use has been made of the excellent translation of H. R. Fairclough in the Loeb Classical Library (New York, 1930). On a few occasions, as here, Macrobius has succumbed to his exegetical penchant and has distorted the obvious Virgilian meaning to suit his purpose. On such occasions it has been necessary to adapt Professor Fairclough's translation. Macrobius' other major work, the *Saturnalia*, deals largely with Virgil's poetry.

[8] *Ibid.* IV.3–5.

[9] *Ibid.* 9.

[10] Cf. John of Salisbury II.xv.429C.

future; but by means of the other three we are gifted with the powers of divination.

We call a dream oracular in which a parent, or a pious or revered man, or a priest, or even a god clearly reveals what will or will not transpire, and what action to take or to avoid.[11] [9] We call a dream a prophetic vision if it actually comes true. For example, a man dreams of the return of a friend who has been staying in a foreign land, thoughts of whom never enter his mind. He goes out and presently meets his friend and embraces him. Or in his dream he agrees to accept a deposit, and early the next day a man runs anxiously to him, charging him with the safekeeping of his money and committing secrets to his trust.[12] [10] By an enigmatic dream we mean one that conceals with strange shapes and veils with ambiguity the true meaning of the information being offered, and requires an interpretation for its understanding. We need not explain further the nature of this dream since everyone knows from experience what it is. There are five varieties of it: personal, alien, social, public, and universal. [11] It is called personal when one dreams that he himself is doing or experiencing something; alien, when he dreams this about someone else; social, when his dream involves others and himself; public, when he dreams that some misfortune or benefit has befallen the city, forum, theater, public walls, or other public enterprise; universal, when he dreams that some change has taken place in the sun, moon, planets, sky, or regions of the earth.[13]

[12] The dream which Scipio reports that he saw embraces the three reliable types mentioned above, and also has to do with all five varieties of the enigmatic dream. It is oracular since the two men who appeared before him and revealed his future, Aemilius Paulus and Scipio the Elder, were both his father,[14] both were pious and revered men, and both were affiliated with the priesthood. It is a prophetic vision since Scipio saw the regions of his abode after death and his future condition. It is an enigmatic dream because the truths revealed

---

[11] Cf. Artemidorus II.69; Philo Judaeus *De somniis* II.3; John of Salisbury II.xv.431A.

[12] Cf. Artemidorus I.2.

[13] Cf. Artemidorus I.2; John of Salisbury II.xv.429D.

[14] One his father by nature, the other his grandfather by adoption. The dreaming Scipio (commonly called Scipio the Younger or Scipio Aemilianus, destroyer of Carthage in 146 B.C. and founder of the Scipionic Circle) was the natural son of Aemilius Paulus, famous Roman general and Hellenophile, and the adopted son of Scipio Africanus, the oldest son of Scipio the Elder (conqueror of Hannibal).

to him were couched in words that hid their profound meaning and could not be comprehended without skillful interpretation.

It also embraces the five varieties of the last type. [13] It is personal since Scipio himself was conducted to the regions above and learned of his future. It is alien since he observed the estates to which the souls of others were destined. It is social since he learned that for men with merits similar to his the same places were being prepared as for himself. It is public since he foresaw the victory of Rome and the destruction of Carthage, his triumph on the Capitoline, and the coming civil strife. And it is universal since by gazing up and down he was initiated into the wonders of the heavens, the great celestial circles, and the harmony of the revolving spheres, things strange and unknown to mortals before this; in addition he witnessed the movements of the stars and planets and was able to survey the whole earth.

[14] It is incorrect to maintain that Scipio was not the proper person to have a dream that was both public and universal inasmuch as he had not yet attained the highest office but, as he himself admitted, was still ranked "not much higher than a private soldier."[15] The critics say that dreams concerning the welfare of the state are not to be considered significant unless military or civil officers dream them, or unless many plebeians have the same dream. [15] They cite the incident in Homer[16] when, before the assembled Greeks, Agamemnon disclosed a dream that he had had about a forthcoming battle. Nestor, who helped the army quite as much with his prudence as all the youth with their might, by way of instilling confidence in the dream said that in matters of general welfare they had to confide in the dream of a king, whereas they would repudiate the dream of anyone else.[17] [16] However, the point in Scipio's favor was that although he had not yet held the consulship or a military command, he—who himself was destined to lead that campaign—was dreaming about the coming destruction of Carthage, was witnessing the public triumph in his honor, and was even learning of the secrets of nature; for he excelled as much in philosophy as in deeds of courage.

[17] Because, in citing Virgil above as an authority for the unreliability of nightmares, we excerpted a verse from his description

[15] *Scipio's Dream* ii.1.
[16] *Iliad* ii.56–83.
[17] Cf. Artemidorus i.2; John of Salisbury ii.xv.429D.

of the twin portals of dreams, someone may take the occasion to inquire why false dreams are allotted to the gate of ivory and trustworthy ones to the gate of horn. He should avail himself of the help of Porphyry, who, in his *Commentaries*,[18] makes the following remarks on a passage in Homer[19] presenting the same distinction between gates: "All truth is concealed. [18] Nevertheless, the soul, when it is partially disengaged from bodily functions during sleep, at times gazes and at times peers intently at the truth, but does not apprehend it; and when it gazes it does not see with clear and direct vision, but rather with a dark obstructing veil interposed." [19] Virgil attests that this is natural in the following lines: "Behold—for all the cloud, which now, drawn over thy sight, dulls thy mortal vision and with dank pall enshrouds thee, I will tear away." [20] [20] If, during sleep, this veil permits the vision of the attentive soul to perceive the truth, it is thought to be made of horn, the nature of which is such that, when thinned, it becomes transparent. When the veil dulls the vision and prevents its reaching the truth, it is thought to be made of ivory, the composition of which is so dense that no matter how thin a layer of it may be, it remains opaque.[21]

CHAPTER IV

[1] NOW THAT we have discussed the types to which *Scipio's Dream* belongs, and before we examine the words of the dream itself, let us try to reveal its design and purpose, its *skopos,* as the Greeks call it.[1] Once again we must affirm, as we did at the opening of this discourse, that the purpose of the dream is to teach us that the souls of those who serve the state well are returned to the heavens after death and there enjoy everlasting blessedness.

[18] H. Schrader (*Porphyrii Quaestionum Homericarum reliquiae* [Leipzig, 1880–82], p. 352), following Schmidt and Gildersleeve, believes that Macrobius is referring to Porphyry's *De Homeri philosophia.* Mras (p. 238) believes that Porphyry's *Quaestiones Homericae* is meant.

[19] Odyssey XIX.562–67. Cf. Virgil *Aeneid* VI.893–96.

[20] *Aeneid* II.604–6.

[21] Cf. John of Salisbury II.xiv.428D. For other explanations of the puzzling Virgilian passage, see E. L. Highbarger, *The Gates of Dreams; an Archaeological Examination of Aeneid VI, 893–899,* and, by the same author, "Vergil's Nether World and Elysium; Addenda," *Proceed. Amer. Philol. Assoc.,* LXXVI (1945), xxxiii; Getty, "Insomnia in the Lexica," *American Journal of Philology,* LIV (1933), 12–14.

[1] Cf. Proclus (Kroll), II, 96.

[2] It was the following occasion, indeed, that impelled Scipio to relate his dream, which, he says, he had kept secret for a long time. When Laelius was deploring the fact that no statues of Nasica had been set up in public in recognition of his slaying a tyrant,[2] Scipio replied among other things: "Though for wise men the fullest reward for virtue is consciousness of the merit of their deeds, still that Divine Virtue does not long for statues held together with lead nor for triumphs with their withering laurels, but for rewards of a more substantial and enduring character." "What are they?" Laelius inquired. [3] Scipio then answered, "Grant me your indulgence since this is the third day of our holiday festival,"[3] together with other introductory words. Then he began to narrate his dream,[4] showing by words like the following that the rewards which he saw in the sky reserved for the outstanding men of public affairs were more substantial and lasting: [4] *That you may be more zealous in safeguarding the commonwealth, Scipio, be persuaded of this: all those who have saved, aided, or enlarged the commonwealth have a definite place marked off in the heavens where they may enjoy a blessed existence forever.*[5]

A little later, in describing the sort of place it was, Paulus said: *But, Scipio, cherish justice and your obligations to duty, as your grandfather here and I, your father, have done; this is important where parents and relatives are concerned, but is of utmost importance in matters concerning the commonwealth. This sort of life is your passport into the sky, to a union with those who have finished their lives on earth and who, upon being released from their bodies, inhabit that place at which you are now looking,* meaning the Milky Way.

[2] Publius Cornelius Scipio Nasica Serapio, member of the famous Cornelius Scipio family, was the leader of a group of senatorial conservatives who, with the assistance of their slaves and clients, murdered Tiberius Gracchus in a brawl. Nasica was so detested by the populace for his part in this attack that his life was in danger. To be kept safe, he was sent on a pretended mission to Asia, where he soon died.

[3] Cicero's *De re publica* is presented in the form of a dialogue which was supposed to have taken place during the Latin holidays in the winter of 129 B.C. at the home of Scipio. The conversation lasted three days, two books for each day.

[4] *Scipio's Dream* forms Chapters ix–xxvi of Book VI of Cicero's *De re publica*. Quotations from *Scipio's Dream* in the *Commentary* will be italicized. On the relation between *Scipio's Dream* and the rest of Cicero's *De re publica*, and on Macrobius' importance in preserving the text of *Scipio's Dream*, see Introduction, pp. 10-12.

[5] These words are spoken by Scipio's adoptive grandfather, Scipio the Elder, and the quotation following by Aemilius Paulus, his natural father. For the setting of this scene, see the opening paragraphs of *Scipio's Dream*.

[5] You must know that the place where Scipio thought he was in his dream is the Milky Way, called by the Greeks *galaxias*. We may be assured of this because in the first part of the dream Scipio uses these words: *From our lofty perch, dazzling and glorious, set among the radiant stars, he pointed out Carthage*. And a little later he spoke more clearly: *Furthermore, it was a circle of surpassing brilliance gleaming out amidst the blazing stars, which takes its name, the Milky Way, from the Greek word. As I looked out from this spot everything appeared splendid and wonderful*. About this Milky Way we shall have more to say later when we come to a discussion of the celestial circles.[6]

CHAPTER V

[1] THUS FAR our treatise has explained the following: what points of difference and similarity there are between Plato's *Republic* and Cicero's *Republic;* why Plato added to his work the testimony of Er, and Cicero, the dream of Scipio; what objections the Epicureans made to Plato's work and how this feeble cavil is refuted; in which treatises philosophers consider the use of fabulous narratives appropriate; and from which treatises they wholly exclude them. Then, of course, we included a classification of dreams and indicated which are significant and which are not; next we enumerated the various types of enigmatic dreams, to all of which that of Scipio was clearly related; and we also indicated whether Scipio was the proper person to have such a dream and what earlier opinions were expressed concerning the twin portals of dreams. In addition to all these matters we have shown what the design and purpose of the dream was and have clearly designated the region of the sky in which Scipio seemed to see and hear in his dream the things that he reported. Now we must discuss the words of *Scipio's Dream,* not all of them, but those that seem worth investigating.[1]

[6] I.xv.

[1] Macrobius omits treatment of about one quarter of Cicero's text, mostly introductory. His customary practice is to place the excerpted passage at or near the beginning of a chapter and to devote the remainder of the chapter to a discussion of it. Occasionally discussion of a passage is carried on beyond one chapter.

[2] First of all the passage about numbers[2] presents itself for consideration, in which Scipio's grandfather says: *When your age has completed seven times eight recurring circuits of the sun, and the product of these two numbers, each of which is considered full for a different reason, has rounded out your destiny, the whole state will take refuge in you and your name; the Senate, all good citizens, the Allies, and the Latins will look to you; upon you alone will the safety of the state depend; and, to be brief, as dictator you must needs set the state in order, if only you escape death at the hands of your wicked kinsmen.*

[3] Not without reason did he attribute fullness to numbers, for fullness properly belongs only to things divine and heavenly. It would not be correct to call any physical object full or perfect, for it is constantly rejecting part of its substance and seeking new additions.[3] (Even though metallic bodies are not subject to this state of flux, they must not be called perfect, but solid, *nasta*,[4] according to the Greeks.) [4] But this attribute of perfection is common to all numbers, for in the progress of our thought from our own plane to that of the gods they present the first example of perfect abstraction.[5] Moreover, those numbers particularly deserve to be called full or perfect (according

---

[2] In the passage which follows it becomes evident that Macrobius' work is really not a commentary on *Scipio's Dream*, but that he is compiling an encyclopedia and using excerpts from Cicero's work as an excuse for introducing lengthy discussions in various fields of learning and science. Thus the brief statement which follows, prophesying Scipio's death, serves Macrobius as a pretext for the elaborate discussion of Pythagorean arithmetic which occupies this and the next chapters. Pythagorean mathematics also received detailed treatment from many other classical and post-classical encyclopedists, e. g., Varro, Theo Smyrnaeus, Philo Judaeus, Chalcidius, Martianus Capella, Boethius, Cassiodorus, and Joannes Lydus. The two main divisions in Macrobius' arithmetical excursus contain basic Pythagorean doctrines: first, the explanation of the conception of the numerical origin of material objects (figurate numbers); second, a discussion of the virtues of the numbers in the sacred decad, a popular subject with the ancients, as witness the number of extant writings. The name given to a treatise of the latter sort was *Theologoumena arithmeticae*, a "Theology of Numbers." On Pythagorean arithmetic, see D'Ooge, especially Chap. vii and pp. 236–64; Heath, *Gr. Math.*, Chap. iii. F. E. Robbins, in "The Tradition of Greek Arithmology," *Classical Philology*, XVI (1921), 97–123, has made a study of the sources of a score of leading writers on Pythagorean number lore, including Macrobius, and has prepared a stemma of their possible lines of descent. On the survival of the Pythagorean doctrines in the Middle Ages, see V. F. Hopper, *Medieval Number Symbolism* (New York, 1938), Chap. vi.

[3] Cf. below, ii.xii.13–15.

[4] Following Bentley's emendation ναστά, in *Rheinisches Museum für Philologie*, XXXVI (1881), 325. The reading *vasta* of the MSS makes no sense.

[5] Explained in the following nine sections of this chapter.

to the interpretation that is essential to this treatise) which either bind bodies together,[6] or become bodies again, or form a single body; but the word body is used here as you conceive it through intelligence and not sense-perception. To avoid the offense of being obscure in all this discussion we must go back and clarify it by using simple examples.

[5] All physical bodies are bounded by surfaces, in which their extremities terminate. Moreover, although these termini are always around the bodies whose termini they are, they are nevertheless considered incorporeal.[7] For wherever body is said to exist, terminus is not yet understood; the concept of terminus is distinct from that of body. [6] Consequently the first transition from the corporeal to the incorporeal brings us to the termini of bodies; and these are the first incorporeality after corporeality, not pure nor entirely free from corporeality, for although they are naturally outside of bodies, they are not found except around bodies. Indeed, when you designate a whole body, the surface is also included in the name. But even if surfaces are not kept separate from bodies in the material realm, the intellect does distinguish between them. [7] As the terminus of a body is the surface, so the termini of the surface are lines, *grammai* in Greek; and lines terminate in points.[8] Now these are what are known as mathematical bodies,[9] about which geometricians dispute with skill and zeal. [8] When we consider the surface of one side of a body, we find that the number of its lines depends upon the form of the underlying body: whether it be triangular, quadrangular, or polygonal, its surface is enclosed by the same number of lines as it has angles. [9] At this point it would be well to keep in mind that all bodies have three dimensions: longitude, latitude, and altitude. Of the three we obtain one dimension by drawing a line (in longitude we do not have latitude); a surface, called by the Greeks *epiphaneia,* is marked by length and breadth and lacks thickness (we

---

[6] Explained below, i.vi.23–34.

[7] Cf. Nicomachus ii.vii.1–2: "The point, then, is the beginning of dimension, but not itself a dimension, and likewise the beginning of a line, but not itself a line; the line is the beginning of surface, but not surface; and the beginning of the two-dimensional, but not itself extended in two directions. Naturally, too, surface is the beginning of body, but not itself body" (D'Ooge trans.). Also cf. Cleomedes i.7.

[8] Cf. Euclid *Elementa* i.Definitiones; Theo Smyrnaeus 97, 111; Nicomachus ii.vi.7; Gellius i.xx; Philo Judaeus *De decalogo* 24–25; Chalcidius xxxii, xxxiii; Martianus Capella vi.708.

[9] Bodies, according to Macrobius, are either mathematical or material. See below, i.vi.35.

have indicated how many lines confine this surface); bodies acquire solidity by adding altitude to the other two dimensions (a solid
body is produced by filling the space enclosed by three dimensions,
and it is called *stereon,* an example being the cubical die). [10] If
you should wish to consider not the surface of one side, but all the
surfaces of a solid figure, which we may assume for the purpose of
illustration to be rectangular and equilateral, there are now not four
but eight angles to be reckoned with.[10] This you will recognize if
you imagine that above one quadrate (a surface such as was described above) you have placed another exactly like it, so that altitude, which was lacking in the plane, is now added: with the three
dimensions filled up a solid body is produced which geometricians
call a die or cube. [11] Hence it is apparent that the number eight
both is and is considered a solid body, if indeed one is represented by
a point, two by the drawing of a line[11] (which, as we said above, is
limited by two points), and four by points arranged at right angles
to each other, with lines extending between the points to form a
square. When these four are duplicated and made eight, forming
two equal squares, and one is superimposed upon the other, giving
the figure altitude, the result is a cubical figure, which is a solid
body.[12]

[12] Thus it becomes clear that numbers precede surfaces and
lines (of which surfaces consist), and in fact come before all physical
objects.[13] From lines we progress to numbers, to something more
essential, as it were, so that from the various numbers of lines we

[10] The reference of numbers to geometrical figures was very likely known to Pythagoras.
See D'Ooge, pp. 18, 55. The association by classical mathematicians of geometrical figures
with numbers is responsible for the meaning "number" being given to the word *figure,*
derived from Latin *figura.* Numbers consist of units, represented by points arranged in a
straight line (linear), in two dimensions (plane), or in three dimensions (solid). The
number two or any larger number may be arranged as linear; three becomes the first plane
number, if the points are arranged in triangular position, and any number above three may
be arranged as plane; four becomes the first solid number in a pyramid with a triangular
base, and any number above four may be solid. Macrobius chooses to regard four as a
plane number (quadrate), the first solid with which he deals being the cube, or eight. Cf.
Isidore of Seville III.vii.

[11] Following the reading *lineae ductum* of Eyssenhardt. I assume Jan's reading *lineae
punctum,* which makes no sense, to be a typographical error. Eyssenhardt offers no variant
readings here, and Jan lists only *ductum lineae* of R1. Cf. the reading *in lineae ductu* above,
I.v.9.

[12] Cf. Theo Smyrnaeus 104; Favonius 10; Chalcidius xxxiii.

[13] Cf. Theo Smyrnaeus 17–18; Nicomachus I.iv.2, I.vi.1; Plotinus VI.vi.9; Chalcidius liii;
pseudo-Bede *Mundi constitutio* (Migne, *Pat. Lat.,* XC, 906). See Inge, I, 85.

understand what geometrical figures are being represented. [13] But we have already remarked that surfaces with their lines are the first incorporeality after the corporeality of bodies and that they are nevertheless not to be separated from bodies on account of their indissoluble union with them. Therefore, whatever precedes surface is purely incorporeal; but we have shown that number is prior to surface and to lines; hence the first perfection of incorporeality is in numbers, and this is, as we previously stated, the common perfection and fullness of all numbers.[14] [14] The fullness of those numbers which form bodies or bind them together is a particular one, as we suggested above and will explain shortly; at the same time I shall not deny that there are other reasons for numbers being full.

[15] That the number eight produces a solid body has been demonstrated above. But this number has a special right to be called full, for in addition to its producing solid bodies it is also without doubt intimately related to the harmony of the spheres, since the revolving spheres are eight in number.[15] More about this later, however. [16] All numbers which, when paired, total eight are such that fullness is produced from their union. The number eight is either the sum of the two numbers that are neither begotten nor beget, namely, one and seven,[16] whose qualities will be discussed more fully in their proper place; or from the doubling of that number which is both begotten and begets, namely, four, since four comes from two and produces eight; or from three and five, one of which is the first uneven number of all, while the characteristics of the other will be treated later. [17] The Pythagoreans, indeed, called the number eight Justice[17] because it is the first number that may be divided into two equal even numbers and divided again into two more equal even numbers. It is also the product of equals: two times two times

[14] Macrobius has given us a rather full explanation of the Pythagorean doctrine that numbers underlie the entire creation.

[15] Because of numerical correspondence, eight was associated with the universe (seven planetary spheres and the celestial sphere). Cf. Theo Smyrnaeus 105; pseudo-Iamblichus 73, 75; Favonius 12. On this Pythagorean practice of numerical association, see Heath, *Gr. Math.*, pp. 67–69; D'Ooge, pp. 97–99.

[16] A number cannot be begotten if it is prime, and it cannot beget if as a factor it does not produce a number within the sacred decad. The Pythagoreans considered the numbers from one to ten basic and those above as repetitions. See D'Ooge, p. 267. Because seven was not begotten and is unable to beget it received the names Pallas Athena and Virgin. See below, I.vi.10–11, and note.

[17] This name is usually given to the number five, and occasionally to four, by the ancient authors who enumerate the Pythagorean epithets for the numbers of the decad.

two.[18] [18] Since it is the product of equal even numbers and may be divided equally, even down to the unit, which does not admit of division in mathematical computation, it deserves to receive the name Justice. And since it is clear, from what has previously been said, to what extent it depends both upon the fullness of its parts and upon its own fullness, it deserves to be called full.

CHAPTER VI

[1] FURTHERMORE, a reason patent to all persuades us that the number seven also deserves to be called full. But we cannot pass over this fact without first expressing admiration that of the two numbers which, when multiplied with each other, determine the life span of the courageous Scipio, the one is even, the other odd. Indeed, that is truly perfect which is begotten from a union of these numbers. An odd number is called male and an even female;[1] mathematicians, moreover, honor odd numbers with the name Father and even numbers with the name Mother.[2] [2] Hence Timaeus, in Plato's dialogue by the same name, says that the God who made the World-Soul intertwined odd and even in its make-up: that is, using the numbers two and three as a basis, he alternated the odd and even numbers from two to eight and from three to twenty-seven.[3] [3] The first cubes in either series arise from these: using the even numbers, two times two, or four, make a surface, and two times two times two, or eight, make a solid; again, using the odd numbers, thrice three, or nine, make a surface, and three times three times three, or twenty-seven, the first cube.[4] Accordingly we are given to understand that

---

[18] Cf. Theo Smyrnaeus 46; pseudo-Iamblichus 72; Martianus Capella VII.740.

[1] On the early Pythagorean association of odd with male and even with female, see D'Ooge, p. 90. Also see F. E. Robbins, "Arithmetic in Philo Judaeus," *Classical Philology,* XXVI (1931), 351.

[2] Cf. pseudo-Iamblichus 4–5: one, regarded as both odd and even, is male-female, and called Father and Mother.

[3] 35C. See below, I.vi.46.

[4] In the even series, two represents a line, four a quadrate, and eight (one quadrate superimposed upon another) a cube; in the odd series, three represents the first line, nine the first quadrate (points arranged thus: . . .), and twenty-seven becomes the first cube by superimposing two more quadrates of nine upon the first to form a cube whose sides are three. Cf. Nicomachus II.xv.2; pseudo-Iamblichus 2; Chalcidius xxxiii; Martianus Capella VII.740.

these two numbers, I mean seven and eight, which combine to make
up the life-span of a consummate statesman, have alone been judged
suitable for producing the World-Soul, for there can be no higher
perfection than the Creator.[5] [4] This, too, must be kept in mind, that
in affirming the dignity belonging to all numbers we showed that
they were prior to surfaces, lines, and all bodies; and besides we
learned a moment ago that numbers preceded the World-Soul, being
interwoven in it, according to the majestic account in the *Timaeus*,
which understood and expounded Nature herself. [5] Hence the
fact which wise men have not hesitated to proclaim is true, that the
soul is a number moving itself.[6]

Now let us see why the number seven deserves to be considered
full on its own merits.[7] That its fullness may be more clearly realized,
let us first examine the merits of the numbers whose sums make up
seven, then, at last, the capabilities of seven itself. [6] The number
seven is made up either of one and six, two and five, or three and
four. It would be well to treat these combinations separately; we
will confess that no other number has such a fruitful variety of
powers.

[7] In the first combination of one and six, one is called *monas*,
that is Unity, and is both male and female,[8] odd and even,[9] itself not
a number, but the source and origin of numbers.[10] [8] This monad,

---

[5] The use of the numbers seven and eight in the creation of the World-Soul will be explained later: I.vi.45–47.

[6] See below, I.xiv.19.

[7] The remaining portion of this chapter is largely arithmological, treating of the virtues
and powers of the numbers in the decad. Many arithmological treatises still survive, the
great majority being incorporated into works on other subjects. F. E. Robbins lists fourteen
authors in D'Ooge, pp. 90–91. See pp. 90–110 for a general discussion of arithmologies.
These treatises are marked above all by a lack of originality; many of them show very
close correspondence over extended passages. For detailed comparisons of texts, see Robbins,
"The Tradition of Greek Arithmology," *Classical Philology*, XVI (1921), 97–123, and the
numerological studies of W. H. Roscher. Robbins feels that the extant treatises probably go
back to a common ancestor.

[8] Cf. pseudo-Iamblichus 4.

[9] Cf. Theo Smyrnaeus 22; Chalcidius xxxviii. See Heath, *Gr. Math.*, p. 71; D'Ooge,
pp. 48–49.

[10] Cf. Professor Robbins's summary of Nicomachus' doctrine in D'Ooge, p. 116: "Just
as the point is not part of the line (for it is indimensional, and the line is defined as that
which has one dimension), but is potentially a line, so the monad is not a part of multitude
nor of number, though it is the beginning of both, and potentially both." Also cf. Theo
Smyrnaeus 19, 99; Chalcidius xxxviii.

the beginning and ending of all things, yet itself not knowing a beginning or ending,[11] refers to the Supreme God,[12] and separates our understanding of him (the One, without number) from the number of things and powers following; you would not be so rash as to look for it in a sphere lower than God. It is also that Mind,[13] sprung from the Supreme God, which, unaware of the changes of time, is always in one time, the present;[14] and although the monad is itself not numbered, it nevertheless produces from itself, and contains within itself, innumerable patterns of created things.[15] [9] Then, too, by giving a little thought to the matter, you will find that the monad refers to the Soul.[16] Indeed, the Soul is free from contamination with anything material, owing itself only to its Creator and to itself, and being endowed with a single nature; when it pours itself forth to animate the immense universe, it does not permit any division of its singleness. You see how the monad, sprung from the First Cause of things, everywhere undiminished and always indivisible, maintains the continuity of its powers even in regard to the Soul. [10] These remarks about the monad have been presented more briefly than the abundance of material suggested.

Be not disturbed over the fact that although the monad seems to surpass all numbers it is especially praiseworthy in conjunction with seven: the incorrupt monad is joined with no number more appro-

[11] Cf. pseudo-Iamblichus 3; Theo Smyrnaeus 18.

[12] The primeval Deity of the Neoplatonists was so far removed from the realm of mortals that the human mind could not begin to comprehend him. The Neoplatonists considered appellations and attributes inapplicable, for these would imply limitation. They taught that the Deity was "above existence" and "above goodness." Accordingly a popular designation for him was the "One." Association, as above, of the One with the monad is not original with the Neoplatonists but is frequently found in Neopythagorean writings, which in turn were probably influenced by the Stoics. See Inge, I, 83–85; D'Ooge, pp. 96, 238. Cf. Theo Smyrnaeus 100; pseudo-Iamblichus 3; Chalcidius xxxix.

[13] In Neoplatonic dogma the first emanation from the primeval One is Mind or pure Intellect. The association of Mind with the monad is likewise found among Neopythagoreans. See D'Ooge, pp. 96–97. Cf. Theo Smrynaeus 100; pseudo-Iamblichus 3, 6; Chalcidius xxxix.

[14] Cf. pseudo-Iamblichus 6.

[15] Cf. *ibid.* 3: the Neopythagorean doctrine that as the monad is the source of all numbers, so God is the source of the whole creation. See D'Ooge, p. 96; Inge, I, 84–85.

[16] The next Neoplatonic emanation after Mind is the Soul. Since this hypostasis is still spiritual, and separate from the material realm, it is still identified with the monad, for the Neoplatonists, like the Neopythagoreans, taught that the dyad represented the material realm of change and corruption. See Inge, I, 83–84; Whittaker, *Neo-Platonists,* pp. 53–54. Cf. Theo Smyrnaeus 100; pseudo-Iamblichus 8; Chalcidius ccxcv.

priately than with the Virgin.[17] [11] The reputation of virginity has
so grown about the number seven that it is called Pallas. Indeed, it
is regarded as a virgin because, when doubled, it produces no number
under ten, the latter being truly the first limit of numbers.[18] It is
Pallas because it is born only from the multiplication of the monad,
just as Minerva alone is said to have been born of one parent.[19]

[12] Six, which when joined with one makes seven, is a number
with various and manifold honors and abilities: first, because it is
the only number under ten that is equal to the sum of its parts.[20]
[13] We may divide it by two, three, or six, a half being three, a
third two, and a sixth one; the three added together make six. There
is further proof of the high regard in which this number is held,
but to avoid being tedious we shall take up only one of the many
functions of the number, chosen here because it emphasizes the dignity of the number seven equally with its own.

[14] Nature, in accordance with a definite numerical rhythm, has
established the normal term of nine months for human births, but
a cause arising out of the multiplication of the number six sometimes
requires a term of seven months. [15] To put it briefly and clearly:
the first two cubes of all numbers are eight (even) and twenty-seven
(odd), the odd being masculine and the even feminine, as we explained above. If these two together are multiplied by the number
six, the product is the number of days contained in seven months.
[16] Let the male and female numbers be joined together, meaning
eight and twenty-seven. They make thirty-five, which, multiplied

[17] Since seven "neither begets nor is begotten" and the monad "knows neither a beginning
nor ending," it is proper to join them. Cf. pseudo-Iamblichus 72. Each number in the Pythagorean decad had many epithets. For a comprehensive list, see Photius *Codex* 187. See also
D'Ooge, pp. 104–7.

[18] The decad embraces all numbers. See D'Ooge, pp. 99, 219. Cf. Theo Smyrnaeus 106;
pseudo-Iamblichus 80; Anatolius 29. For a comparison of the texts of Anatolius and
Macrobius, see G. Borghorst, *De Anatolii fontibus,* Chap. v.

[19] According to the myth, Pallas Athena sprang from the head of Zeus in full armor, and
was worshiped as the great virgin goddess. It was therefore fitting to associate her with the
number seven, which is neither begotten (prime) nor begets (as a factor it does not yield a
number within the decad). The ancients were impressed with the completeness of the
identification. See D'Ooge, p. 106. Cf. Theo Smyrnaeus 103; pseudo-Iamblichus 58, 71;
Philo Judaeus *De opificio mundi* 100; Anatolius 35; Favonius 8-9; Chalcidius xxxvi; Martianus Capella vii.738; Joannes Lydus ii.xii. Pythagoras is credited with naming seven
"Athena" in Stobaeus i.i.10.

[20] Such numbers were called perfect and merited special reverence. Twenty-eight is the
next one. Cf. Theo Smyrnaeus 45; Nicomachus i.xvi.1; pseudo-Iamblichus 42, 48; Chalcidius
xxxviii; Martianus Capella vii.736. See Heath, *Gr. Math.,* pp. 74–75; D'Ooge, p. 209.

six times, makes two hundred and ten, the number of days in seven months. Thus this number is so rich in its attributes that it marks the earliest complete development of the human fetus, as if it were judge of the proper time.[21] [17] A foreknowledge of the sex of the child may even be obtained from the uterus in that manner, according to Hippocrates.[22] The embryo moves either on the seventieth or the ninetieth day after conception. Multiply these numbers by three and you get in the one case a term of seven months, and in the other a term of nine.[23]

[18] So much for the first combination of numbers whose sum is seven. The second combination is two and five. Of these, two, the dyad, because it is first after the monad, is the first number.[24] It first departed from that single Omnipotence into the line of a perceptible body, and therefore refers to the errant spheres of the planets and the sun and moon, since these have been separated into a number from that which is called immovable (*aplanes* in Greek), and have been turned back in a counter motion.[25] Hence the number two is most

---

[21] Because six is a factor in the number of days in the first safe term of gestation and in the normal term, it received the epithet *zoogonetike*, "procreative." On this use of six as a factor, cf. pseudo-Iamblichus 51–52. The number seven is also procreative, being the number of months in the first safe gestation. Cf. *ibid.* 55; Photius *Codex* 187. The superstition, recorded in the Hippocratic writings and still surviving, that a baby born in the seventh or ninth month is safe but born in the eighth month is doomed is responsible for the number eight being regarded as unlucky. See Photius *Codex* 187; pseudo-Iamblichus 74; Aetius *Placita* v.xviii (Diels, pp. 427–29).

[22] Cf. pseudo-Hippocrates *De carnibus* xix; *De natura pueri*, ed. Kühn, I, 401.

[23] The discussion in this paragraph closely resembles that in pseudo-Iamblichus 64.

[24] Since the monad is the beginning of numbers, it cannot be a number, just as the point is the beginning of a line but is not a line. See Nicomachus ii.vi.3. Nicomachus belonged to a group that did not consider two a number, but three as the first number. See Heath, *Gr. Math.*, pp. 69–71.

[25] The monad, which Pythagoreans derived from *menein*, "to remain" (Theo Smyrnaeus 19; pseudo-Iamblichus 1), refers to the unchangeable and imperishable, the One, Mind, and Soul, as was stated above, and also refers to the celestial sphere, which, according to Macrobius (see below, i.xvii), shares in the divinity of the Soul. The celestial sphere, also called the fixed or immovable sphere because the stars appear to be fixed in it, deserves to be identified with the monad since it does not change. But the dyad, being the first increase of the indivisible monad, represents matter, change, and corruption (epithets applied to it by Pythagoreans: see pseudo-Iamblichus 8; Photius *Codex* 187). It refers to the corporeal realm, comprising everything below the celestial sphere. Inasmuch as the spheres of the seven planets revolve in a direction counter to that of the celestial sphere (another reason

appropriately joined with five since the former, by reason of its departure, refers to the errant spheres, as we have just pointed out, and the latter, by its numerical correspondence, refers to the zones of the celestial sphere.[26] [19] The possession of unusual powers came to the number five because it alone embraces all things that are and seem to be. (We speak of things intelligible as "being" and of things material as "seeming to be," whether they have a divine or a mortal body.)[27] Consequently, this number designates at once all things in the higher and lower realms. [20] There is the Supreme God; then Mind sprung from him, in which the patterns of things are contained; there is the World-Soul, which is the fount of all souls;[28] there are the celestial realms extending down to us; and last, the terrestrial realm; thus the number five marks the sum total of the universe. [21] These remarks, purposely and necessarily brief, are sufficient for the second combination that makes up the number seven.

Let us consider the abilities of the third pair, of three and four. [22] In geometry the smallest odd number of lines in a surface is three, in the triangle, and four, the smallest even number, in the quadrangle. [23] Moreover, we know, according to Plato (that is, according to the sanctuary of truth itself), that those bodies alone are closely held together which have a mean interposed between extremes to create a strong bond. When that mean is doubled the extremes are bound not only firmly but even indissolubly. Now the number three is the first to have a mean between two extremes to bind it together, and the number four is the first of all numbers to have two means.[29] [24] Borrowing the means from this number the Creator of the universe bound the elements together with an un-

---

for associating the dyad with the underlying spheres), they were called errant. In examining the diagram shown imagine yourself facing southward. The direction of the sun's apparent revolution is annual, in respect to the celestial sphere, and not diurnal. This classical scheme of a stationary earth, with seven planetary spheres revolving counter to the celestial sphere, is the one which prevailed throughout the Middle Ages and until the appearance of Copernicus' *De revolutionibus orbium coelestium* in 1543. On the division of opinion as to whether the spheres of Mercury and Venus were above or beneath the sun's, see below, i.xix.

[26] The celestial arctic and antarctic, north temperate and south temperate, and torrid zones. See below, ii.vii.1–6. Cf. pseudo-Iamblichus 32; Martianus Capella vii.735.

[27] The Platonic doctrine of the reality of ideas. See *Republic* v.478E–408A, x.596A–598C; *Phaedo* 76D–E, 102A–B. Cf. Plotinus iii.ii.1, iii.vi.7.

[28] Cf. Plotinus iii.ix.1; Porphyry *Sententiae* xxxviii. See below, i.xiv.8–10.

[29] *Timaeus* 32A–B. For commentators' explanations of the passage, see D'Ooge, p. 272.

breakable chain, as was affirmed in Plato's *Timaeus:*[30] in no other
way could the elements earth and fire, so opposed and repugnant
to each other and spurning any communion of their natures, be
mingled together and joined in so binding a union unless they were
held together by the two means of air and water. [25] For thus, in
spite of the utter diversity of these elements, the Creator harmonized
them so skillfully that they could be readily united. To each of them
he gave two qualities, one of which was of such sort that each element would find this quality related and similar to itself in the
element to which it adhered. [26] Earth is dry and cold, and water
cold and moist; but although these two elements are opposed, the
dry to the wet, they have a common bond in their coldness. Air is
moist and warm and, although opposed to water, the cold to the
warm, nevertheless has the common bond of moisture. Moreover,
fire, being hot and dry, spurns the moisture of the air, but yet adheres
to it because of the warmth in both. [27] And so it happens that each
one of the elements appears to embrace the two elements bordering
on each side of it by single qualities: water binds earth to itself by
coldness, and air by moisture; air is allied to water by its moisture,
and to fire by warmth; fire mingles with air because of its heat, and
with earth because of its dryness; earth is compatible with fire because of its dryness, and with water because of its coldness.[31] [28]
These different bonds would have no tenacity, however, if there
were only two elements; if there were three the union would be but
a weak one; but as there are four elements the bonds are unbreak-
able, since the two extremes are held together by two means.

This will be clearer if we cite a passage of the same purport taken
from Plato's *Timaeus:*[32] [29] "Divine Reason ordained that the universe should be so constructed as to be perceptible to sight and
touch. But it is obvious that nothing can be seen without the aid of
fire, nor touched unless tangible, nor is anything tangible without
earth. [30] Hence the Creator, endeavoring to compound the body
of the universe from fire and earth, saw that the two could not be
combined without some mean to cement them, and that the mean

[30] 32C.
[31] Cf. Theo Smyrnaeus 97; pseudo-Iamblichus 67; Chalcidius xxii, cccxviii; Martianus
Capella vii.738. See Duhem, I, 31. For survivals of the doctrine in the Middle Ages, see
Duhem, II, 481–85, V, 148; Thorndike, III, 130–31.
[32] 31B–32B.

which was best would bind itself as well as the extremes.[33] He also saw that one mean would be sufficient only to bind surfaces without altitude, but that when a third dimension had to be included in the union, two means were necessary to bind the whole. [31] Accordingly, he wove air and water into fire and earth, and thus a mutual attraction ran through the universe, linking together unlike elements by the similarities underlying their differences."

[32] A smiliar difference of density and weight exists between water and air as between air and fire, and again, the difference in lightness and rarity between air and water is the same as the difference between water and earth. Likewise, the difference in density and weight between earth and water is the same as between water and air, and the difference between water and air the same as between air and fire. Moreover, the difference of rarity and lightness between fire and air is the same as between air and water, and the difference between air and water is the same as between water and earth. [33] Not only are adjacent adhering qualities compatible, but the same uniformity is preserved in elements that are separated: as earth is to air so water is to fire; and wherever you begin, you will find the same mutual attraction. Thus they are linked together by that very feature which makes them uniformly different from each other.[34]

[34] So much by way of developing a proof that a plane cannot be firmly bound together except by the number three, nor a solid except by four. Hence the number seven possesses a dual power of binding, for both parts of it have inherited the primary links, three with one mean and four with two means. That is why Cicero, in another passage in *Scipio's Dream*,[35] says concerning the number seven, *It is, one might almost say, the key to the universe.*

[35] To continue, all bodies are either mathematical, the creatures of geometry, or such as are perceptible to sight or touch. The former possess three stages of development: the line grows out of the point,

---

[33] A portion of Plato's text is omitted in Macrobius' free translation: "And to effect this in the fairest manner is the natural property of proportion. For whenever the middle term of any three numbers, cubic or square, is such that as the first term is to it, so it is to the last term—and again, conversely, as the last term is to the middle, so is the middle to the first,—then the middle term becomes in turn the first and the last, while the first and last become in turn middle terms, and the necessary consequence will be that all the terms are interchangeable, and being interchangeable they all form a unity." (Bury's transl., *The Loeb Classical Library.*)

[34] Cf. pseudo-Iamblichus 67; Chalcidius xxi.　　[35] v.2

the surface out of the line, and the solid out of the surface; the latter, because of the adhesive qualities in the four elements, harmoniously grow together into firm bodily substances. [36] All bodies have three dimensions, longitude, latitude, and altitude, and the sum total gives us four terms, point, line, surface, and solid. Moreover, since all material bodies consist of four elements, earth, water, air, and fire, they must be separated by three interstices: one of these lies between earth and water, the second between water and air, and the third between air and fire. [37] The demarcation between earth and water is called Necessity by natural philosophers because it is believed to bind and solidify the clay of which bodies are made. Hence when Menelaus, in Homer's *Iliad*,[36] was invoking evil upon the Greeks, he said, "May all of you be resolved into earth and water," referring to the muddy substance of which human bodies were first made. [38] The demarcation between water and air is called Harmony, that is, a compatible and harmonious union: for this is the interval which unites the lower with the upper, reconciling incongruent factors. [39] The demarcation between air and fire is called Obedience; for whereas the muddy and heavy bodies are joined to the things above by Necessity, the things above associate with what is muddy by Obedience, with Harmony in the middle promoting a union of both.[37] [40] Complete bodies clearly consist, therefore, of four elements and their three interstices. And, you see, these two numbers, three and four, united by so many relationships, lend themselves to making both kinds of bodies (plane and solid) by reciprocal agreement.

[41] In addition to the fact that these two numbers exhibit a common disposition to form bodies, the Pythagoreans call the quaternary *tetraktys,* and so revere it among their secrets as pertaining to the perfection of the soul that they have made a religious oath from it: "By him who gave the quaternary number to our soul."[38]

[36] VII.99.

[37] Cf. pseudo-Iamblichus 67. Daniel of Morley repeats these names of the three interstices. See Thorndike, II, 176.

[38] The sacred tetrad of the Pythagoreans, represented by dots arranged in an equilateral triangle, thus:

    •

   • •

  • • •

 • • • •

Since the sum of the first four integers is equal to ten (the decad embracing all numbers), the tetrad was identified with the decad and was called perfect. It became the symbol of the elements of number, which in turn were regarded by Pythagoreans as the elements of all things. Cf. Theo Smyrnaeus 94; pseudo-Iamblichus 22; Porphyry *Vita Pythagorae* 20. See F. M. Cornford, "Mysticism and Science in Pythagorean Tradition," *The Classical Quarterly* XVII (1923), 1.

[42] The number three, indeed, marks the three divisions of the soul, the first being reason, *logistikon,* the second emotion, *thymikon,* and the third appetite, *epithymetikon.*[39] [43] Moreover, all wise men admit that the soul was also derived from musical concords. Among these an important one is the diapason, which consists of two others, the fourth and the fifth. The interval of the fifth is based on the ratio of three to two and the interval of the fourth on the ratio of four to three;[40] in one the first term is three and in the other four; this we shall discuss more fully in its proper place.[41] [44] Suffice it to say that the fourth and fifth are based upon these numbers. And from the fourth and fifth the concord of the diapason arises; whence Virgil, schooled in all of the arts,[42] when he wished to express that men were fully blessed in all respects, called them "O thrice and four times blest!"[43]

[45] These brief remarks have been concerned with the combinations of numbers whose sums are seven; we shall also have a few things to say about the number itself.[44] This number is now called

[39] Plato's tripartite soul. See *Republic* IX.580D–E, *et passim.* Cf. pseudo-Iamblichus 71; Joannes Lydus II.viii.

[40] If two strings of the same material, thickness, and tension, but differing in length in the ratio of three to two are vibrated, a tone interval of a fifth is produced; if the lengths are in the ratio of four to three, the interval is a fourth. Pythagoras is credited with the discovery of the numerical ratios of the fundamental musical concords. For an account of the discovery, see below, II.i.

[41] II.i.

[42] In Macrobius' day Virgil was admired not for the beauty of his poetry but for the erudition and perfection which were claimed for his works. Commentators expended great ingenuity upon demonstrating a profound or symbolic meaning where Virgil obviously had no such intention. Macrobius is one of the chief representatives of this group. Much of his *Saturnalia* is devoted to a defense and eulogy of Virgil, and he invariably remarks about his wisdom and perfection in the *Commentary.* See D. Comparetti, *Virgilio nel medio evo,* Chap. v. S. T. Collins, in *The Interpretation of Virgil with Special Reference to Macrobius,* p. 14, sees in Macrobius the culmination of a growing tendency to regard Virgil as omniscient and infallible. This tendency was to continue for at least a millennium. Dante seems to have had little appreciation of the exquisite poetry and imagination of Virgil. Rather he was concerned with the recondite meaning of even the insignificant lines of the *Aeneid* and regarded Virgil's wisdom and authority as oracular.

[43] *Aeneid* 1.94, a quotation of Homer *Odyssey* v.306. Pseudo-Iamblichus 26 quotes the Homeric passage as attesting to the virtues of three and four. Cf. pseudo-Iamblichus 18; Theo Smyrnaeus 100.

[44] The number seven receives the greatest attention from Macrobius, as it does in the arithmologies, mainly because it marks the lunar quarters, which, according to widespread ancient (and surviving) superstition were supposed to control menstruation, gestation, and the critical periods of diseases. See my article, "Moon Madness," *Annals of Medical History,* IX (1937), 250–54, 260–61. Classical documents bearing on the number have been exhaustively treated by W. H. Roscher, *Hebdomadenlehren der griechischen Philosophie und Ärzte.*

[*h*]*eptas,* the first letter no longer being in use;[45] but the ancients used to call it *septas,* the Greek word testifying to the veneration owing to the number.[46] It was by this number first of all, indeed, that the World-Soul was begotten, as Plato's *Timaeus* has shown.[47] [46] With the monad located on the apex, two sets of three numbers each descended on either side, on one the even, on the other the odd: that is, after the monad we had on one side two, four, and eight, and on the other three, nine, and twenty-seven;[48] and the mixture arising out of these seven numbers brought about the generation of the World-Soul at the behest of the Creator. [47] The fact that the origin of the World-Soul hinges upon seven steps is proof that this number has no mean ability; but in addition the Creator, in his constructive foresight, arranged seven errant spheres[49] beneath the star-bearing celestial sphere, which embraces the universe, so that they might counteract the swift motions of the sphere above and govern everything beneath.[50]

[48] The number seven motivates the moon, which is in the seventh planetary sphere, and regulates its course. Although it is possible to demonstrate this in many ways, let us begin with this proof. [49] The moon completes its circuit of the zodiac in almost twenty-eight days, for even though it consumes thirty days from the time it leaves the sun until it returns to it, it requires approximately twenty-eight days to make a complete circuit of the zodiac.[51] In the other

[45] The Ionic Greek dialect dropped the initial aspirate from writing about 800 B.C. According to Suidas *Lexicon: Σαμίων,* Athens officially adopted the Ionic alphabet in 403 B.C. and thereafter ceased to use the symbol H for the initial aspirate. So far the evidence of the inscriptions has corroborated Suidas' statement.

[46] Pythagoreans pointed to the resemblance between *septas,* "seven," and *septos,* "revered," as another proof of the number's virtue. Cf. pseudo-Iamblichus 57; Photius *Codex* 187; Philo Judaeus *De opificio mundi* cxxvii.

[47] 35B–C. Cf. Theo Smyrnaeus 103.

[48] This so-called lambda diagram was popular with the commentators on the *Timaeus* although it was probably not used by Plato. Plutarch (*De animae procreatione* xxix.1027D) states that Crantor (4th cent. B.C., first commentator on the *Timaeus*) used this figure, and implies that the master did not. For its later use see Theo Smyrnaeus 95; Chalcidius xxxiii.

[49] Mention that seven refers to the number of planets and planetary spheres is found in almost all of the arithmologies.

[50] Isidore of Seville III.xxxiv attributes this design to the countermotion of the planets, adding that if they did not thus retard the speed of the celestial sphere, the universe would collapse.

[51] Cf. Theo Smyrnaeus 103; pseudo-Iamblichus 60; Geminus 1.30.

two days it is catching up with the sun, which has gone on from that place where the moon last left it.[52] [50] The sun, you see, passes through one sign of the zodiac in a month's time. Let us suppose that the sun is in the first part of Aries when the moon leaves its conjunction with it or, as we say, "is born." After twenty-seven days and nearly eight hours the moon returns to the first part of Aries[53] but does not find the sun there, for it, meanwhile, has gone on, according to its own fixed course. Consequently we do not think of the moon as having yet returned to its starting point because our eyes saw it at that time not starting out from the first part of Aries, but leaving the sun. For two days, more or less, it pursues the sun, catches up with it, and then proceeds from it again, a new moon.[54] [51] The new moon is hardly ever born in the same sign twice in succession, except in Gemini where this sometimes happens because the sun consumes more than thirty-two days in the steep ascent of this sign.[55] On very rare occasions this happens in the other signs if the moon leaves its junction with the sun in the first part of a sign. [52] Seven is the source of this number of twenty-eight days, for if you add the numbers from one to seven, the total is twenty-eight.[56] [53] Twenty-eight, evenly divided into four quarters, marks the number of days required by the moon to complete its course out and back across the zodiac. From its northernmost point on the horizon the moon in seven days travels across the sky to the midpoint of its journey out, the ecliptic position;[57] in the following seven days it progresses from the midpoint to its southernmost limit; in the next seven days it turns back, ascending to the midpoint of its journey back; in the last seven it returns to its northernmost extremity. Thus it courses over the whole length and breadth of the zodiac in four seven-day periods.

[52] Cf. Cleomedes II.113–14; Martianus Capella VIII. 865.

[53] The average length of a lunar sidereal period is 27 days, 7 hours, 43 minutes, but it varies as much as 7 hours owing to perturbations.

[54] The average length of a lunar synodic period, the interval from one new moon to the next new moon, is 29 days, 12 hours, 44 minutes. The variation here is sometimes more than half a day.

[55] Cf. Cleomedes II.113; Martianus Capella VIII.848, 865.

[56] The second so-called perfect number, six being the first. See above, I.vi.12 and note. Cf. Nicomachus I.xvi.2; pseudo-Iamblichus 59.

[57] Cf. pseudo-Iamblichus 19. The moon's apparent path has an average inclination of 5°9' to the ecliptic. It therefore intersects the ecliptic twice during each revolution at points known as the lunar nodes.

[54] Following the same arrangement of seven-day periods the moon also regulates the phases of its light under a fixed law. In the first hebdomad it waxes to the appearance of a halved orb, and is then called half-moon; in the second hebdomad, by gathering its replenished fires it attains the full orb and is called full moon; in the third hebdomad it becomes halved again, when it wanes to the midpoint; in the last its light fades until it vanishes completely.[58] [55] Furthermore seven stages, which are called *phaseis* in Greek, mark the passage of a month: new moon, half-moon, gibbous, full moon, gibbous, half-moon, and conjunction, the latter being the stage at which the moon's light is completely invisible to us.[59] [56] The gibbous stage is intermediate between the first half and the full, as it is also between the full and the second half.

[57] The sun, too, upon which everything depends for life, varies its course in the seventh sign: it reaches the summer solstice in the seventh sign after leaving the winter solstice and reaches the autumn equinox in the seventh sign after leaving the spring equinox.[60]

[58] The three cycles of heavenly light also recur according to this number, the great, the intermediate, and the small cycles. The great cycle is the annual one by the sun; the intermediate is the monthly one by the moon; and the small is the daily one by the rising and setting of the sun. [59] Each of the three cycles has four divisions, and thus the number seven appears in the three cycles and the four divisions of each. These are the four parts: the first damp, the second hot, the third dry, and the last cold. [60] In the great cycle of the year the spring is damp, the summer hot, the autumn dry, and the winter cold. The intermediate cycle of the month is so regulated by the moon that the first hebdomad is damp, because the new moon regularly brings moisture;[61] the second, in which the moon waxes to take on a likeness of the sun, is hot; the third is dry, being farther removed from the first; and the fourth is cold as the moon's light

[58] Cf. Theo Smyrnaeus 103; pseudo-Iamblichus 59–60.

[59] Cf. pseudo-Iamblichus 60; Clemens Alexandrinus vi.xvi.143; Favonius 8; Chalcidius xxxvii; Martianus Capella vii.738; pseudo-Bede *Mundi constitutio* (Migne, *Pat. Lat.*, XC, 888).

[60] Cf. Theo Smyrnaeus 104.

[61] The many references in classical and popular literature to the moisture-producing powers of the moon originate in the fact that there is most radiation and hence the greatest deposit of dew on cloudless nights. The moon in any visible phase brings dew according to folk belief.

fades out. The third cycle, of dawn and sunset, is so arranged that the first quarter of the day is damp, the second hot, the third dry, and the fourth cold.[62]

[61] The ocean also observes this number in its ebb and flow. On the first day of the new moon its tide is higher than usual, it diminishes a little on the second day, on the third it is still lower than the second, decreasing until it reaches the seventh day. The eighth day corresponds to the seventh, the ninth to the sixth, the tenth to the fifth, the eleventh to the fourth, the twelfth to the third, the thirteenth to the second, and the fourteenth to the first. The third hebdomad is a repetition of the first, and the fourth of the second.[63]

[62] Again, seven is the number by which man is conceived, developed in the womb, is born, lives and is sustained, and passing through all the stages of life attains old age; his whole life is regulated by it.[64] To say nothing of the fact that nature has ordained that the uterus without seed be purged according to this number, as if by way of exacting a tribute every month from women not bearing a burden, this point must not be overlooked, that the sperm which within seven hours after emission has not escaped is pronounced effective. [63] Once the seed has been deposited in the mint where man is coined, nature immediately begins to work her skill upon it so that on the seventh day she causes a sack to form around the embryo, as thin in texture as the membrane that lies under the shell of an egg, enclosing the white. [64] Although this was surmised by natural scientists, Hippocrates himself, who cannot deceive nor be deceived, definitely proved it by experiment, and testifies in his book *On the Nature of the Child* [65] that the sperm expelled from the womb of a woman he had attended on the seventh day after conception had such a sack about it. For this woman, who begged him to end her pregnancy, he prescribed vigorous jumping. He says that on the

[62] On the quadripartition of the annual, monthly, and daily cycles according to the four elements, see *Introductio in Claudii Ptolemaei opus De effectibus astrorum*, ascribed to Porphyry, Chap. i; Oribasius *Compendium medicinae* ix.iii; Joannes Lydus ii.ix; Byrhtferth, p. 10.

[63] This paragraph corresponds so closely to the text of pseudo-Iamblichus 60 as to be almost a translation of it. Cf. pseudo-Bede *Mundi constitutio* (Migne, *Pat. Lat.*, XC, 885).

[64] Cf. Aristotle *De generatione animalium* iv.x.777B; pseudo-Iamblichus 70–71; Gellius iii.x.7–9; pseudo-Galen, ed. Kühn, IX, 908; Clemens Alexandrinus vi.xvi.143. Classical authors commonly assigned the discovery of the importance of the number seven in the climacterics of human life to the Chaldeans, meaning the astrologers.

[65] Pseudo-Hippocrates *De natura pueri*, ed. Kühn, I, 386.

seventh day the seventh leap sufficed for expelling the seed with a sack such as we have described above.[66] So much for Hippocrates' statement.

[65] Strato the Peripatetic and Diocles of Carystus assign the stages in the development of the embryo to seven-day periods as follows: on the second hebdomad drops of blood appear on the surface of the aforementioned sack; on the third hebdomad they work their way into the humor within; on the fourth hebdomad this humor coagulates so that there is a curdling intermediate between flesh and blood, as it were, both liquid and solid; and occasionally, indeed, on the fifth hebdomad a human shape is being molded in the substance of the humor, no larger than a bee in fact, but in such a manner that on that small scale all the limbs and the distinct contour of the whole body stand out. [66] We added the word *occasionally* because it is an established fact that when the limbs are delineated in the fifth hebdomad the child is born in the seventh month. When the child is to be born in the ninth month, however, the limbs distinctly appear in the sixth hebdomad in the case of a girl, and in the seventh in that of a boy.[67]

[67] The seventh hour after birth determines whether the offspring will live or has been doomed in the womb to breathe only this short time. Those that are doomed before birth are not able to continue breathing beyond this number of hours; it is understood that the child that can breathe beyond the seventh hour will live, unless perchance some other cause, as is quite possible, should snatch it away.[68] [68] Moreover, after seven days it casts off the remnants of the umbilical cord, after two weeks its eyes begin to move towards light, and after seven weeks it freely turns its pupils and whole face to moving visible objects. [69] After seven months the teeth begin to

---

[66] This paragraph corresponds closely to the text of pseudo-Iamblichus 61–62. Cf. Philo Judaeus *De opificio mundi* cxxiv.

[67] This paragraph is a translation of pseudo-Iamblichus 62–63. For a comparison of texts, see W. H. Roscher, *Die hippokratische Schrift von der Siebenzahl*, pp. 92–97. Cf. Theo Smyrnaeus 104; Gellius III.x.7; pseudo-Galen, ed. Kühn, IX, 908; Favonius 9–10. Honorius of Autun *De philosophia mundi* IV.xv (Migne, *Pat. Lat.*, CLXXII, 90) quotes this paragraph. On the survival in the Middle Ages of the belief that fetuses formed in the fifth hebdomad are born in the seventh month and those formed in the seventh hebdomad are born in the ninth month, see Thorndike, III, 237.

[68] Cf. pseudo-Iamblichus 64–65. The correspondence is very close throughout the remainder of this chapter.

appear in the jaws,[69] and after fourteen months the child sits up
without fear of falling.[70] After thrice seven months its babbling
takes the form of words,[71] and at twenty-eight months it stands
firmly and walks.[72] After five times seven months it begins to refuse
the nurse's milk unless suckling is prolonged by unbroken habit.[73]
[70] After seven years the teeth that first appeared yield their place to
new ones better adapted to chewing solid foods.[74] By the seventh
year, too, the child speaks plainly.[75] Hence it is said that seven vowel
sounds were invented by nature,[76] although Latin, by pronouncing
the same letter now long and now short, prefers to reckon them as
five instead of seven. But if you count vowel sounds and not merely
letters, Latin also has seven. [71] By the fourteenth year the child
reaches the age of puberty. Then the generative powers begin to
show themselves in the male, and the menses in the female.[77] The
strength of manhood, as it were, is released from the tutelage of
boyhood. Girls, however, because of the early age at which they
marry, are free two years earlier, according to law. [72] After thrice
seven years a beard covers the cheeks.[78] This year also marks the
limit of increasing stature.[79] After four times seven years the body
ceases to grow broader.[80] At the thirty-fifth year the man attains the
full vigor of his physical powers; no one is able to increase his

[69] *Ibid.* 65. Cf. Theo Smyrnaeus 104; Gellius III.x.12; Chalcidius xxxvii; Favonius 9;
Martianus Capella VII.739.
[70] Pseudo-Iamblichus 65.
[71] *Ibid.*
[72] *Ibid.*
[73] *Ibid.*
[74] *Ibid.* Cf. Theo Smyrnaeus 104; Philo Judaeus *De opificio mundi* ciii; Chalcidius
xxxvii; Favonius 9.
[75] Pseudo-Iamblichus 65. Cf. Philo Judaeus *Legum allegoria* i.x.
[76] Pseudo-Iamblichus 65. Cf. Philo Judaeus *Legum allegoria* i.xiv; *De opificio mundi*
cxxvi; Chalcidius xxxvii. Macrobius has in mind the Greek alphabet with its seven vowel
sounds: a, i, u, and long and short e and o.
[77] Pseudo-Iamblichus 65–66. Cf. Theo Smyrnaeus 104; Philo Judaeus *Legum allegoria*
i.x; Chalcidius xxxvii; Favonius 9; Martianus Capella VII.739.
[78] Cf. Theo Smyrnaeus 104; Philo Judaeus *De opificio mundi* ciii; Chalcidius xxxvii;
Favonius 9; Martianus Capella VII.739. Pseudo-Iamblichus 65 differs, assigning the beard
to the second hebdomad.
[79] Pseudo-Iamblichus 66. Cf. Theo Smyrnaeus 104; Philo Judaeus *Legum allegoria* i.x.
According to Chalcidius xxxvii, Favonius 9, and Martianus Capella VII.739, the fourth
hebdomad marks the limit of increasing stature.
[80] Pseudo-Iamblichus 66. Cf. Theo Smyrnaeus 104.

strength later.[81] With pugilists it has become the rule that those who
have already gained the victor's crown expect no further increase in
strength, whereas those who have not gained such honor by this time
quit the ranks.[82] [74] At the forty-second year the man still retains
his full vigor, experiencing no lessening of his powers unless he has
been injured. From the sixth to the seventh hebdomads of years a
decline does set in, it is true, but imperceptibly, so that it does not
betray the change by evidence of weakness. On this account some
states observe the custom of not drafting a man for military service
after his forty-second year,[83] while in a greater number retirement
is granted at the age of forty-nine.

[75] And now we must call attention to the fact that the number
seven multiplied by itself produces the age which is properly considered and called perfect, so that a man of this age, as one who has
already attained and not yet passed perfection, is considered ripe in
wisdom[84] and not unfit for the exercise of his physical powers. [76]
When the decad, which has the highest degree of perfection of all
numbers, is joined to the perfect number seven, and ten times seven
or seven times ten years are reached, this is considered by natural
philosophers the goal of living, and terminates the full span of human life.[85] When anyone exceeds this age he is retired from active
duty and devotes himself solely to the exercise of his wisdom; his
whole occupation is in persuading others, and he is honored by
release from other obligations. From the seventh to the tenth hebdomads of years each man's duties vary according to his physical
capacities.[86]

[77] The number seven also marks the members of the body.
There are seven within, which the Greeks call the dark members:

---

[81] Pseudo-Iamblichus 66. Cf. Chalcidius xxxvii; Martianus Capella vii.739.

[82] Pseudo-Iamblichus 66.

[83] Ibid.

[84] Cf. Philo Judaeus De opificio mundi ciii.

[85] Pseudo-Iamblichus 66–67. Cf. Philo Judaeus De opificio mundi ciii.

[86] With the above ten hebdomads in a man's life cf. the elegiac verses of the early
Athenian lawgiver, Solon, quoted by Philo Judaeus De opificio mundi civ. Another popular scheme, also based on hebdomads, presented seven ages of man. These, as ascribed
to the physician Hippocrates and quoted by Philo (ibid. cv), are: little child, child, lad,
young man, man, elderly man, and old man. Cf. Jaques's speech on the seven ages of
man in Shakespeare, As You Like It, II, vii, 140ff., beginning with the words, "All the
world's a stage." For the history of the idea of the ages of man, see F. Boll, Die Lebens-
alter (Leipzig and Berlin, 1913).

the tongue, the heart, the lungs, the liver, the spleen, and two kidneys.[87] There are seven others, each with its own veins or ducts, whose function it is to receive and expel food and air: the pharynx, the esophagus, the stomach, the bladder, and the three principal intestines: one of these is called the *dissiptum*,[88] which separates the stomach from the lower intestines; another is the middle intestine,[89] which the Greeks call the *mesenteron;* and the last, which the ancients called the *hira,* is considered the most important of the intestines, and passes off the waste products of the food.[90] [78] Regarding the air and food, with the introduction and expulsion of which the aforementioned organs and their vascular appendages are occupied, this observation has been made: life without air is not sustained beyond the seventh hour and without food beyond the seventh day.[91] [79] There are also seven tissues in the body, filling all the region from the interior to the surface: marrow, bone, sinew, vein, artery, flesh, and skin. So much for the inner parts. [80] There are also seven visible parts of the body: the head, the trunk, two arms, two legs, and the generative organ.[92] Those which are divided also consist of seven parts: in the arms, the upper arm, the elbow, the forearm, the palm, and the three joints of the fingers; in the legs, the thigh, the knee, the shin, the foot proper, and again the three joints of the toes. [81] Since nature has located the senses and their functions in the head, the citadel of the body, the operations of the senses are performed through seven openings: the mouth, two eyes, two nostrils, and two ears.[93] Hence it is only right that this number,

[87] Pseudo-Iamblichus 67. Cf. Theo Smyrnaeus 104; Philo Judaeus *Legum allegoria* 1.12; Anatolius 36; Chalcidius xxxvii; Martianus Capella vII.739.

[88] The duodenum.

[89] The ileum.

[90] The large intestine and rectum. Pseudo-Iamblichus 68 lists the following seven: pharynx, esophagus, stomach, duodenum, ileum, bladder, rectum. He places the bladder just before the rectum probably because the bladder is close to the rectum in the human body. The *hira* of Macrobius clearly refers to more than the rectum. On Macrobius' medical knowledge (only his *Saturnalia* treated), see Max Neuburger, "Die Medizin im Macrobius und Theodoretus," *Janus,* XXVIII (1924), 155–72.

[91] Pseudo-Iamblichus 68. Cf. Hippocrates, ed. Kühn, I, 442; Gellius III.x.15.

[92] Pseudo-Iamblichus 68. Philo Judaeus *De opificio mundi* cxviii and Martianus Capella vII.739 omit the generative organ and instead have two divisions of the trunk (chest and abdomen). Anatolius 36 substitutes the neck.

[93] Pseudo-Iamblichus 68. Cf. Theo Smyrnaeus 104; Philo Judaeus *De opificio mundi* cxix; Anatolius 36; Clemens Alexandrinus vI.xvi.144; Chalcidius xxxvii; Martianus Capella vII.739. Favonius 8 has seven sense organs, substituting tactual sense throughout the body for one nostril.

the regulator and master of the whole fabric of the human body, should also indicate whether a patient will recover or not.[94] What is more, all bodies have seven motions: forward, backward, to the left or right, upward or downward, and rotating.[95] [82] The number seven is distinguished for having so many functions, whether exercised in the combinations amounting to seven or by itself, that it is deservedly considered and called full. This, I believe, will suffice to explain why the numbers eight and seven are called full on various grounds.

[83] This, then, is the meaning of the passage in *Scipio's Dream*:[96] when Scipio has reached his fifty-sixth year, a fateful sum for him, all hope of public safety will rest with him, and a dictatorship will be due him in order to recover by his strength and valor the security of the general welfare if only he succeeds in escaping the wicked plots of his kinsmen. By *eight times seven recurring circuits of the sun* Cicero means fifty-six years, a year being a circuit and recurrence of the sun: a circuit because the sun goes around the zodiac every year; a recurrence because it traverses the same signs every year by fixed law.

CHAPTER VII

[1] NOW SOME MEN wonder about the reason for the admission of uncertainty in the grandfather's words, *if only you escape death at the hands of your wicked kinsmen*. They want to know how a divine soul, long since returned to the heavens and here especially professing a knowledge of the future, could possibly be in doubt about whether or not his grandson would be able to escape his

[94] Ancient physicians as well as Pythagoreans agreed that seven was the most important number in determining the critical days of diseases. References on this subject are legion: e.g., pseudo-Iamblichus 68; Theo Smyrnaeus 104; Gellius III.x.14; Philo Judaeus *De opificio mundi* cxxv; Clemens Alexandrinus VI.xvi.145; Anatolius 35; Chalcidius xxxvii. A lengthy treatise on this subject, ascribed to Galen (ed. Kühn, IX, 900–41), had great influence on the medicine of the Middle Ages. For a discussion of the classical documents, see W. H. Roscher, *Hebdomadenlehren der griechischen Philosophie und Ärzte*, pp. 60–86, and *Die hippokratische Schrift von der Siebenzahl*, pp. 88–91. For survivals of this belief in the Middle Ages, see Thorndike, Indexes: "Critical Days."

[95] Cf. Plato *Timaeus* 34A; pseudo-Iamblichus 55; Philo Judaeus *De opificio mundi* cxxii; Anatolius 36; Chalcidius cxxi; Martianus Capella VII.736; Joannes Lydus II.xii. Sometimes the rotary motion is omitted: Plato *Timaeus* 43B; Nicomachus II.vi.4; pseudo-Iamblichus 47; Philo Judaeus *Legum allegoria* I.iv; Macrobius *Saturnalia* VII.ix.3.

[96] Quoted above, I.v.2.

enemies. But these men are not mindful of the fact that all portents and dreams conform to the rule that their announcements, threats, or warnings of imminent adversity are always ambiguous. [2] Consequently we surmount some difficulties by caution and others we escape by entreaty and propitiation; still others are inevitable, being turned away by no skill or powers. When the deity admonishes, we may escape by vigilance and caution; sacrifice and propitiation can avert threatened disaster; but never do divine announcements go unfulfilled. [3] You will then ask: "But how are we to distinguish so as to know whether to beware, to pray, or passively to wait upon fate?" In the present work it will be fitting merely to acquaint the reader with the sort of ambiguity that is purposely used in prophecies, in order that he may cease to wonder about the uncertainty admitted above; nevertheless one may seek in the Creator's own work the signs by which he may solve the riddle, if the divine will does not prevent; for, in the words of Virgil, springing from the innermost depths of his knowledge, "The Fates forbid us to know more." [1]

[4] Even commonplace examples teach us that when a prediction about the future is made, it is always clothed in doubt, but in such a way that the diligent inquirer—"unless divinely opposed," as we say —may find clues to the information he is seeking concealed in the prophecy. Take an instance from Homer.[2] A dream sent from Zeus, as it is related, encouraged King Agamemnon by an outright promise of victory to engage in battle with the enemy at a future date. He, as one following a divine prophecy, went into battle, but was scarcely able to return to camp, leaving most of his men dead on the field. [5] Must we say that the deity had sent him a deceitful vision? Not so, but because the Fates had already decreed such disaster for the Greeks, there was a hint concealed in the words of the dream which, if carefully heeded, could have enabled him at least to avoid calamity, and perhaps even to conquer. [6] The divine command was to lead out the whole army, but he, thinking only of the command to fight, did not attend to the order to lead out the whole army and overlooked Achilles, who at that time was still smarting from a recent insult and had withdrawn his soldiers from battle. The king went forth to battle and sustained the defeat which was owing him, and

[1] *Aeneid* III.379–80.
[2] *Iliad* II.5ff.

thus absolved the deity from blame of falsehood by not following all of his commands.[3]

[7] Virgil, who closely copies the Homeric perfection throughout his work, was no less careful when he came to a similar point: Aeneas, though fully instructed by the Delian oracle in choosing the region that was destined by fate for his kingdom, slipped into error by the oversight of one word. [8] It is true that the name of the region which he was obliged to seek was not expressly given, but when he was told to seek the ancient origin of his forebears—Crete and Italy had produced the ancestors of his race on either side—there was something in the words that clearly indicated and, so to speak, pointed a finger at Italy. For since Teucer had come from Crete and Dardanus from Italy, the divine voice, by addressing them as "long-suffering Dardanians," [4] clearly suggested Italy, from which Dardanus had come, calling them by the name of that ancestor whose place of origin they had to seek.[5]

[9] The prediction about Scipio's death is likewise an announcement of a certainty; the doubt expressed for the sake of procuring ambiguity is nullified by a phrase contained in the opening of the dream. The declaration of Scipio's grandfather, *When your age has completed seven times eight recurring circuits of the sun, and the product of these two numbers . . . has rounded out your destiny,* was really a divine announcement that he could not avoid death at the hands of his kinsmen.[6] The reason that his grandfather related all the other events in Scipio's life in their sequence without being obscure, and seemed vague about death alone, is one of the following: either deference is shown to human melancholy and fear; or it is fitting to conceal this in particular, other things being more readily

---

[3] Synesius viii and Proclus (Kroll), I, 115, defend Zeus on the same grounds. Mras (p. 251) and Claes Blum (*Studies in the Dream-Book of Artemidorus*, p. 57) feel that Porphyry was the source of Macrobius and Proclus. There is brief mention of this defense in an extant fragment of his *Quaestiones Homericae*, commenting on the passage in the *Iliad* (*Porphyrii Quaestionum Homericarum reliquiae*, ed. Schrader, p. 23). Mras believes that this work was Macrobius' source, but Courcelle (p. 23) favors the supposition that Porphyry's lost commentary on Plato's *Republic* was the source.

[4] *Aeneid* iii.94.

[5] Aeneas' oversight is also noted by Servius in his comment on this passage (Servius, I, 358).

[6] The mystery of Scipio the Younger's death was never solved. One theory placed the blame upon his widow, Sempronia, and his mother-in-law, Cornelia, mother of the Gracchi. See Appian *Bella civilia* 1.20.

expressed in oracles than the end of life; or it is necessary to have some obscurity in prophetic utterances.

CHAPTER VIII

[1] WE HAVE CONSIDERED only a part of the grandfather's statement; let us now take up the remainder. *That you may be more zealous in safeguarding the commonwealth, Scipio, be persuaded of this: all those who have saved, aided, or enlarged the commonwealth have a definite place marked off in the heavens where they may enjoy a blessed existence forever. Nothing that occurs on earth, indeed, is more gratifying to that supreme God who rules the whole universe than the establishment of associations and federations of men bound together by principles of justice, which are called commonwealths. The governors and protectors of these proceed from here and return hither after death.*

[2] After revealing to Scipio the time and manner of his death, it was fitting for the grandfather to introduce next the subject of the rewards that good men should expect after death. In contemplation of such rewards men's thoughts have been so far removed from fear of imminent death as even to be incited to a yearning for it because of the splendor of the prospect of blessedness and a celestial abode. But first it will be necessary to explain a few matters about the blessedness which is reserved for the protectors of commonwealths, so that we may afterwards clear up the whole passage which we have just excerpted for discussion.

[3] Virtues alone make one blessed and only through them is one able to attain the name.[1] Hence those who maintain that virtues are found only in men who philosophize openly affirm that none are blessed except philosophers. Properly assuming wisdom to be an understanding of divine things, they say that only those men are wise who search for heavenly truths with acuteness of mind and lay hold of them by sagacious and painstaking inquiry and pattern after them as far as they are able. In their opinion it is here alone that the virtues are exercised, and they attribute four functions to the virtues:[2]

[1] Cf. Plotinus 1.ii.1.
[2] The four kinds of goodness, according to Socrates and Plato. See Plato *Republic* iv. 427E. These came to be known as the Four Cardinal Virtues. Saint Ambrose is said to

[4] prudence, that is, to despise the world and all that is in the world in contemplation of what is divine, and to direct all the attention of the soul to divine things alone; temperance, to abstain from everything that the habits of the body seek, as far as nature will permit;[3] courage, for the soul not to be terrified as it withdraws from the body, so to speak, under the guidance of philosophy, and to have no dread of the dizzy heights of the complete ascension to the celestial realms; justice, to accept the only way to this mode of life, namely, obedience to each virtue.[4]

Now according to the limitations of so stringent a classification the rulers of commonwealths would be unable to attain blessedness. [5] But Plotinus, chief with Plato among the professors of philosophy, in a treatise *On the Virtues,*[5] arranges the grades of the virtues according to a proper and natural classification. In his scheme each of the above four virtues embraces four types: the first, political virtues; the second, cleansing virtues; the third, virtues of the purified mind; and the fourth, the exemplary virtues.

[6] Man has political virtues because he is a social animal. By these virtues upright men devote themselves to their commonwealths, protect cities, revere parents, love their children, and cherish relatives;

---

have been the first to adapt the Platonic classification to Christian theology. According to the Roman Catholic Church these are the natural virtues, as distinguished from the theological virtues, Faith, Hope, and Charity. Occasionally the two groups are combined to form the Seven Cardinal Virtues. W. H. V. Reade (*Cambr. Med. Hist.* V, 790) credits Macrobius with transmitting the fourfold classification of virtues to the Middle Ages. Henry, in an appendix "On the Four Virtues of Macrobius" (pp. 248–50), has gathered the passages which medieval writers drew from the *Commentary.* See also Byrhtferth, p. 92; Thorndike, I, 674–75; Manitius, III, 177.

[3] Quoted with acknowledgement by Abelard *Theologia Christiana* ii (Migne, *Pat. Lat.,* CLXXVIII, 1185).

[4] Cf. Cicero *De finibus* 1.42–53 and *Tusculanae disputationes* iii.36–37; Plotinus i.ii.1; Porphyry *Sententiae* xxxii.2–3.

[5] Plotinus i.ii. Macrobius' rare citations of his authorities have been under suspicion, this one in particular. Petit, who was the first to call attention to the unreliability of his references, argues (p. 67) that Macrobius was here drawing upon Porphyry and not Plotinus. Linke (pp. 245–46) and Schedler (p. 88) agree with him, the latter going so far as to maintain that wherever Plotinus is cited as Macrobius' source, Porphyry was the actual source. Mras (p. 251) feels that Porphyry was Macrobius' main source but that he also used Plotinus. Henry's attitude is directly opposed to Schedler's and about as extreme. He admits (pp. 161, 191) that some of Macrobius' discussion is found in Porphyry and not in Plotinus, but he insists that Porphyry was used merely to supplement Plotinus. The most recent investigator, Courcelle, is inclined (p. 22) to emphasize the importance of Porphyry but he does not deny that Macrobius also used Plotinus here. On the place of political virtues in Plotinus' system, see Whittaker, *Neo-Platonists,* pp. 91–95.

by these they direct the welfare of the citizens, and by these they safeguard their allies with anxious forethought and bind them with the liberality of their justice; by these "They have won remembrance among men." [6] [7] To have political prudence[7] one must direct all his thoughts and actions by the standard of reason, and wish for or do nothing but what is right, and have regard for human affairs as he would for divine authority. In prudence we find reason, understanding, circumspection, foresight, willingness to learn, and caution. To have political courage, one must exalt his mind above all dread of danger, fear nothing except disgrace, and bear manfully both adversity and prosperity. Courage endows one with magnanimity, confidence, composure, nobleness, constancy, endurance, and steadfastness. To have political temperance, one must strive after nothing that is base, in no instance overstepping the bounds of moderation but subduing all immodest desires beneath the yoke of reason. Temperance is accompanied by modesty, humility, self-restraint, chastity, integrity, moderation, frugality, sobriety, and purity. To have political justice, one must safeguard for each man that which belongs to him.[8] From justice comes uprightness, friendship, harmony, sense of duty, piety, love, and human sympathy. [8] By these virtues the good man is first made lord of himself and then ruler of the state, and is just and prudent in his regard for human welfare, never forgetting his obligations.

The virtues of the second type, known as the cleansing virtues, are found in the man who is capable of attaining the divine. They release the minds only of those who have resolved to cleanse themselves from any contamination[9] with the body, and by an escape from mortal things, as it were, to mingle solely with the divine.[10] These are the virtues of men of leisure, who have withdrawn from active service in the state. We mentioned above the nature of each

---

[6] Virgil *Aeneid* vi.664.

[7] The bulk of the remainder of this chapter is quoted with acknowledgement by Vincent of Beauvais in *Speculum doctrinale* iv.ix.

[8] Cf. Cicero *De finibus* v.65; Porphyry *Sententiae* xxxii.2.

[9] Following Eyssenhardt, who adopts the reading *corporis contagione;* Jan reads *corporis cogitatione.*

[10] Quoted with acknowledgement by Abelard in *Theologia Christiana* ii (Migne, *Pat. Lat.*, CLXXVIII, 1185). Cf. Porphyry *Sententiae* xxxii.3. Porphyry reports that Plotinus, the founder of the Neoplatonic school, on four occasions during the six years of their association attained to a complete ecstatic union with God.

of these virtues when we were speaking of the virtues of philosophers, those which they, indeed, regard as the only virtues.

[9] The third type includes the virtues of the purified and serene mind, completely and thoroughly cleansed from all taint of this world. In that estate it is the part of prudence not to prefer the divine as though there were any choice, but to know it alone, and to fix one's attention upon it as if there were nothing else; it is the part of temperance not to restrain earthly longings but to forget them completely; it is the part of courage to ignore the passions, not to suppress them, so that one "knows not how to be angry, has longing for nothing";[11] it is the part of justice to be so attached to the divine heavenly Mind as to keep an everlasting covenant with it by imitating it.[12]

[10] The fourth type comprises the virtues that are present in the divine Mind itself, the *nous,* from the pattern of which all the other virtues are derived. For if we believe that there are ideas of other things in the Mind, then with much greater assurance must we believe that there are ideas of the virtues. There the divine Mind itself is prudence; it is temperance because it always looks back upon itself with unremitting attention; it is courage because it is always the same and is never changed; it is justice because, by eternal law, it never turns from constant application to its work.[13]

[11] These are the four types of the four virtues, which above all else are most clearly distinguished from one another in regard to the passions. These, as we know, are: "Fears and desires, griefs and joys." [14] The first type of virtues mitigates the passions, the second puts them away, the third has forgotten them, and to the fourth they are anathema.

[12] Now if the function and office of the virtues is to bless, and, moreover, if it is agreed that political virtues do exist, then political virtues do make men blessed. And so Cicero is right in claiming for the rulers of commonwealths a place *where they may enjoy a blessed existence forever.* In order to show that some men become blessed

---

[11] Juvenal *Satirae* x.360.

[12] Cf. Porphyry *Sententiae* xxxii.4.

[13] Cf. *ibid.* 5.

[14] Virgil *Aeneid* vi.733. The fourfold division of the "unreasoning passions," according to the Stoics. Cf. Cicero *Tusculanae disputationes* iii.7, iv.11–14; Horace *Epistulae* i.vi.12; Philo Judaeus *De vita Mosis* ii.139; Servius, II, 103.

by the exercise of virtues at leisure and others by virtues exercised in active careers, he did not say with finality that nothing is more gratifying to that supreme God than commonwealths, but added a qualification, *nothing that occurs on earth is more gratifying.* His purpose was to distinguish those who are primarily concerned with divine matters from the rulers of commonwealths, whose earthly achievements prepare their way to the sky.

[13] What could be more accurate, what more guarded than his definition of the term commonwealths as *the associations and federations of men bound together by principles of justice?* Indeed there have been bands of slaves and of gladiators that might be called associations and federations, but they were not bound together by principles of right. The name "just" can be applied only to that group of men which in its entirety consents in obedience to the laws.

CHAPTER IX

[1] HIS WORDS, *The governors and protectors of these commonwealths proceed from here and return hither,* must be interpreted in the following manner. Philosophers whose views are correct do not hesitate to agree that souls originate in the sky; moreover, this is the perfect wisdom of the soul, while it occupies a body, that it recognizes from what source it came. [2] Hence, in a diatribe both witty and pungent a famous quotation was used seriously: "From the sky has come to us the saying, 'Know thyself.' "[1] Indeed, this is said to have been the advice of the Delphic oracle.[2] To one desiring to know by what path blessedness is reached the reply is, "Know thyself."[3] The maxim was inscribed on the front of the temple at Delphi.[4] [3] A man has but one way of knowing himself, as we have just remarked: if he will look back to his first beginning and origin and "not search for himself elsewhere."[5] In this manner the soul, in the very cognizance of its high estate, assumes those virtues by which it is raised

---

[1] Juvenal *Satirae* xi.27.

[2] Cf. Xenophon *Cyropedia* vii.ii.20.

[3] Cf. Porphyry *Sententiae* xxxii.8, and quotation from him in Stobaeus *Florilegium* xxi.26–28; Adelard 16–17.

[4] Cf. Pausanias *Descriptio Graeciae* x.xxiv.i. Macrobius (*Saturnalia* i.vi.6) says that it was inscribed on the doorpost of the temple. See Sir J. G. Frazer, *Pausanias' Description of Greece* (London, 1913), V, 348–49.

[5] Persius *Satirae* i.7.

aloft after leaving the body and returns to the place of its origin; in fact, a soul that is permeated with the pure and subtle stuff of the virtues does not become defiled or burdened with the impurities of the body, nor does it seem to have ever left the sky which it has always kept in sight and thought. [4] But when a soul allows the habits of its body to enslave it and to change the man somehow to a beast, it dreads leaving the body, and at the very last moment "with a moan it passes indignant to the Shades below." [6] [5] Such a soul does not readily leave the body at death, since "not all the plagues of the body quit it utterly," [7] but it either hovers about its corpse or it goes to seek lodging in a new body, in beast as well as man, and chooses the beast best suited to the sort of conduct it willfully adopted in the man. [8] It prefers to endure anything in order to avoid the sky which it forsook through negligence, deceit, or rather betrayal. [6] But the rulers of commonwealths and other wise men, by keeping in mind their origin, really live in the sky though they still cling to mortal bodies, and consequently have no difficulty, after leaving their bodies, in laying claim to the celestial seats which, one might say, they never left.

With good reason and not in vain flattery did the men of antiquity enroll certain founders of cities and men distinguished in public service in the number of the gods. Hesiod, affirming his belief in the divine lineage of heroes, numbers the early kings among the gods and, in witness of the power they once exercised, assigns to them the task of ruling human affairs in the sky as well. [7] For fear that it might annoy someone if we should quote the original words [9] of the Greek poet, we shall offer them in translation: "These are the hero-gods by the will of supreme Jupiter, formerly men, now with the heavenly deities watching over human affairs, generous and munif-

<hr/>

[6] Virgil *Aeneid* xii.952 (the closing words of the poem).

[7] *Ibid.* vi.736–37. Cf. Servius, II, 103–4.

[8] Cf. Plato *Phaedo* 81D–82A; Plotinus iii.iv.2. Mras (p. 253) believes that Macrobius is adopting Plotinus' attitude in preference to Porphyry's because, according to Augustine *De civitate Dei* x.xxx, Porphyry denied that human souls entered into beasts. But Courcelle (p. 22) points out that Augustine's statement is based upon Porphyry's *De regressu animae* and that in his *Peri Stugos* Porphyry accepts Plotinus' view. Courcelle accordingly feels that Macrobius may have been following Porphyry here too. Cf. Vincent of Beauvais *Speculum naturale* xxiii.lxxv.

[9] *Opera et dies* 121–26. The Latin translation used by Macrobius is a very free one. This passage is cited in Plato *Republic* v.469A, in *Cratylus* 398A, and by Platonists and Neoplatonists, as Mras (p. 253) has noted.

icent, having now also gained the authority of kings." [8] Virgil is in agreement with this, too, for although he consigns his heroes to the underworld in accordance with his plan, he does not deprive them of the sky, but grants them an "ampler ether" and states[10] that "they know their own sun and stars of their own," thus giving evidence of his twofold training, the poet's imagination and the philosopher's accuracy. [9] If, as Virgil declares, even the more trivial things in which men indulged during life occupy them after death—"The selfsame pride in chariot and arms that was theirs in life, the selfsame care in keeping sleek steeds, attends them when hidden beneath the earth" [11]—then much more surely do the former rulers of cities retain in the sky their interest in ruling men.[12]

[10] These souls are believed to be received into the outermost sphere of the universe, the so-called fixed sphere, a name that is appropriate if, indeed, they started out from there. The starry portion of the universe affords habitation for those souls not yet overtaken by a longing for a body; and leaving here they slip down into bodies.[13] The deserving souls are allowed to return here.[14] Therefore, what was told to Scipio in his dream while standing in the Milky Way, a part of the fixed sphere, was quite correct: *The governors and protectors of these commonwealths proceed from here and return hither.*

CHAPTER X

[1] LET US PASS on to what follows. *At this point, though I was greatly dismayed, not at the fear of dying but rather at the thought of being betrayed by relatives, I nevertheless asked whether he and my father Aemilius Paulus and the others whom we think of as dead were really still living.*

[2] Even in chance happenings and in fictitious narratives the seeds of the virtues implanted in us become manifest; these you may now see shining forth from Scipio's heart, though he is only dreaming. In a single incident he exercises equally well all his political

---

[10] *Aeneid* vi.640–41.
[11] *Ibid.* 653–55.
[12] Cf. John of Salisbury iii.x.496A.
[13] Cf. below, i.xii.2–3, 13; Plotinus iii.iv.6; Porphyry, quoted by Stobaeus (ii.388).
[14] Cf. Plotinus i.vi.8; Porphyry *De abstinentia* i.30.

virtues.[1] [3] In that he does not falter when his death is predicted, he displays courage. In that he is dismayed at the thought of betrayal at the hands of relatives and shudders more at the prophecy of someone else's crime than at that of his own doom, he gives evidence of piety and extreme love for his kin. His conduct also reflects his sense of justice, which safeguards for each man what belongs to him. Because he does not regard his own judgments as the criterion of truth and spurns opinion, which in less cautious minds is mistaken for knowledge, and because he seeks more accurate information, he undoubtedly shows prudence. [4] When complete blessedness and a place in the sky are promised to those in whose class Scipio knows he belongs, and when he nevertheless suppresses his yearning to hear about such things so that he may ask whether his grandfather and father are still living, what is this but temperance? By this time it was clear that Scipio had been transported in his dream to those regions which were destined for him.

[5] Furthermore, Scipio's question brings up the subject of the immortality of the soul. This is the purport of his interrogation. We are of the opinion that the soul perishes with a man's last breath and has no further existence—did he not say, *whom we think of as dead?* —surely that which is dead has ceased to exist any longer. Consequently Scipio wanted to learn from his grandfather whether he and his father Aemilius Paulus and the others were really living. [6] This question, as it concerned his grandfather and father, came from a solicitous son, and as it concerned the others, came from a wise man bursting into nature's secrets. Let us look into the grandfather's reply.

"Of course these men are alive," he said, *"who have flown from the bonds of their bodies as from a prison; indeed, that life of yours, as it is called, is really death."* [7] If it is death to pass into the lower regions and life to be in the heavens, you will easily discern what must be considered the soul's death and what its life by determining what place is meant by the lower regions, so that the soul, while it is shunted off here, should be believed to be dead, and while it is far removed from here should be thought of as enjoying life and truly flourishing.

[8] Inasmuch as the whole discussion which the ancients provoked

[1] See above, I.viii.7.

in trying to solve this question is obscured by their refusal to be explicit, we, because of our love of brevity, have excerpted out of the mass of material those points which will serve to extricate us. [9] Before the zeal of philosophers for the study of natural science grew to such vigorous proportions, those who were responsible for establishing religious rites among different races insisted that the lower regions were nothing more than the mortal bodies themselves,[2] shut up in which souls suffered a horrible imprisonment in vile darkness and blood. [10] They called the body the tomb of the soul, the vaults of Pluto, and the infernal regions; everything that fable taught us to believe was in the lower regions they tried to assign to us ourselves and to our mortal bodies. The river Lethe was to them nothing more than the error committed by the soul in forgetting its former high estate before it was thrust into a body,[3] and in thinking that its sole existence was in a body. [11] Similarly, they thought that Phlegethon was merely the fires of our wraths and passions,[4] that Acheron was the chagrin we experienced over having said or done something, even to the point of becoming melancholy, as is the way with human beings, that Cocytus was anything that moved us to lamentation or tears,[5] and that Styx was anything that plunged human minds into the abyss of mutual hatred.[6] [12] The description of the punishments, they believe, originated in human experience;[7] and the vulture "gnawing at the deathless liver,"[8] they would have us understand is nothing more than the pangs of a conscience prying into our insides as though they were guilty of offense, and incessantly tearing at our very vitals with the chastisement of a sense of guilt, and like the vulture clinging to the "liver that grows anew,"[9] always stirring up cares that are ready to subside, never relenting with a feeling of pity. This is the rule, that "no guilty man is acquitted who has himself for judge";[10] one cannot escape his own decision in regard to himself. [13] Those who have food set before them and

---

[2] See below, i.xi.
[3] See below, i.xii.8–11.
[4] Cf. Porphyry, quoted in Stobaeus i.1012. Johannes Scottus xiii.1 cites Macrobius.
[5] Cf. Stobaeus i.1012.
[6] Cf. ibid.
[7] Cf. ibid. 1022; Lucretius De rerum natura iii.978–1023.
[8] Virgil Aeneid vi.598.
[9] Ibid. 600.
[10] Juvenal Satirae xiii.2–3.

yet are tortured with hunger and wasting away from starvation are really, they say, the men whom a longing to acquire more and more compels to overlook their present wealth, men affluent yet needy, suffering the evils of poverty amidst their plenty, not knowing how to take stock of their possessions because of a lust for possessing. [14] They "hang outstretched on spokes of wheels"[11] who are reckless about the future, who never govern their actions by reason nor solve their problems by recourse to the virtues. They entrust themselves and all their business to fortune, and so are always whirled about by chance and accident.[12] [15] They "roll a huge stone up a hill,"[13] consuming their lives in futile and tedious efforts, the dark stone ever wavering and seeming ready to fall back on their heads, who strive for the arduous places of power and the accursed sovereignty of an autocrat, destined never to reach their goal without fear,[14] and compelling their subjects to "hate, provided that they fear."[15] These men always seem to obtain the end they merited; and the cosmogonists had good reason to expect this.

[16] Take the case of Dionysius,[16] that ruthless tyrant of Syracuse. Wishing to show a former servant of his, who thought that the tyrant's life was the only truly blessed one, how really wretched it was and how constantly he was in fear of threatening danger, he arranged a banquet and had a sword unsheathed and let down by a slender horsehair attached to the hilt, with the point poised over the flatterer's head. Costly viands lay before him and all the splendor of the Sicilian court, but when in the face of death he begged to be released, Dionysius said, "Such is the life that you suppose is blessed. This is the sort of death we always see before us. Consider when a man can be happy who never ceases to fear."

[17] If what the cosmogonists maintain is correct, and "each of us suffers his own punishment,"[17] and if we believe that the infernal regions are in our very bodies, what other attitude must we adopt than that the "death" of the soul occurs when it is plunged into the

---

[11] Virgil *Aeneid* vi.616–17.
[12] See Lobeck, pp. 798–99.
[13] Virgil *Aeneid* vi.616.
[14] Cf. Cicero *Tusculanae disputationes* iv.35.
[15] Cicero *De officiis* i.97; Suetonius *Tiberius* lix.
[16] Cf. Cicero *Tusculanae disputationes* v.61–62; Plutarch *Dion* ix.
[17] Virgil *Aeneid* vi.743.

lower regions of the body, but that it "lives" when it escapes to the upper world after leaving the body?

CHAPTER XI

[1] WE MUST also mention the additions that have been made to these beliefs by the philosophers, a more exacting group in the search for truth. Both the followers of Pythagoras and later those of Plato declared that there are two deaths, one of the soul, the other of the creature, affirming that the creature dies when the soul leaves the body, but that the soul itself dies when it leaves the single and individual source of its origin and is allotted to a mortal body.[1] [2] The first assertion is obvious and is recognized by all; the second is apprehended only by the wise, all others believing this to be the soul's life. Consequently most people fail to understand why we sometimes call the god of death magnificent[2] and sometimes ruthless:[3] the complimentary name refers to the first death, that of the creature, and is witness that the soul is released and restored to the real riches of its origin and to its natural freedom; concerning the second death, which is commonly thought of as life, we testify by our use of a dread word that the soul is being thrust from the radiance of its immortal state into the shades of death, as it were.

[3] For a creature to have existence, it is necessary that a soul be confined in the body;[4] for this reason the Greek words for body are *demas,* that is a "bond," and *soma,* a *sema,* as it were, being a "tomb" of the soul.[5] Thus you see that Cicero, by the words *those who have flown from the bonds of their bodies, as if from a prison,*

---

[1] Literally: "is dispersed in a mortal frame." Macrobius frequently emphasizes that the soul loses its indivisibility when it comes into the material world. Cf. below, I.xii.6; Plotinus I.viii.11.

[2] Dis, the god of the lower world, is here identified with the Latin *dis,* meaning "rich." By a remarkable coincidence it was also possible to identify Pluto with the Greek *ploutos,* meaning "riches." Plato derives Pluto's name thus in *Cratylus* 403A.

[3] For instance, Virgil *Georgicon* IV.492.

[4] The attitude that the body is the confinement of the soul is frequently expressed by Pythagoreans and Platonists. See Plato *Phaedo* 62B; Cicero *Tusculanae disputationes* 1.74; Philo Judaeus *De somniis* 1.138; Plotinus IV.viii.1,3; Athenaeus *Deipnosophistae* 157C; Porphyry *Sententiae* viii; Proclus (Diehl) 64B.

[5] *Demas* is here identified with *dema,* "bond." Plato (*Cratylus* 400C) is of the opinion that the identification of *soma* with *sema* is Orphic. Cf. *Georgias* 493A. There is no etymological connection between the words of either pair.

means both that the body serves as fetters and that it is a tomb, being the prison of the entombed.

[4] The Platonists, however, did not believe that the lower regions referred to mortal bodies, but that they were more extensive; they called a definite part of the universe the "abode of Dis," meaning the lower regions. As to what constituted its boundaries they had rather different views, embracing three sets of opinions.

[5] Some of them divided the universe into two parts, active and passive.[6] They said that that part was active which, since it was immutable, imposed causes and laws of change upon the rest. The part which suffered the changes was passive. [6] They declared that the immutable part of the universe extended from the outer sphere, which is called the *aplanes,* the fixed sphere, down to the beginning of the moon's sphere, and that the changeable part extended from the moon to the earth;[7] that souls were living while they were in the immutable part but died when they fell into the region subject to change, and that accordingly the area between the moon and the earth was known as the infernal regions of the dead. The opinion that the moon is the demarcation of life and death and that souls falling from there towards the earth die and that those rising from there to the heavens are returning to life has some merit. The realm of the perishable begins with the moon and goes downwards. Souls coming into this region begin to be subject to the numbering of days and to time. [7] Natural philosophers called the moon the ethereal earth[8] and its inhabitants lunar people, but their reasons for doing so are too numerous for us to take up here.[9] There is no doubt

[6] Cf. Aristotle *De generatione et corruptione* i.6; *De caelo* i.iii; *Physica* iii.ii–iii, viii.5, *et passim.*

[7] Schedler (p. 47) and Whittaker (*Macrobius,* p. 65) assume that Macrobius is referring to the Aristotelians as the first group. P. Capelle (*De luna, stellis, lacteo orbe animarum sedibus,* pp. 8–10) has pointed out that the opinion that the region between the earth and moon is changeable and full of corruption and the region between the moon and celestial sphere is unchangeable and pure is Pythagorean and is found much earlier than Aristotle. There seems to be a fusion here. See below, i.xxi. 33–34. Cf. Philo Judaeus *De monarchia* i.1 and *De somniis* 1.34; Plutarch *De genio Socratis* xxii; Stobaeus 1.906; Daniel of Morley *Philosophia* (cited by Thorndike, II, 176).

[8] This appellation is ascribed to Orpheus in Proclus (Diehl) 292B, and to the Egyptians by Porphyry, according to Proclus (Diehl) 45D (cf. 154A, 227D, 283B). It was used by Pythagoreans, according to Simplicius *In Aristotelis De caelo commentaria* 229B. See also Lobeck, p. 500. Pseudo-Bede *Mundi constitutio* (Migne, *Pat. Lat.,* XC, 888) quotes Macrobius.

[9] See below, i.xix.10.

that the moon is the builder and affords the increase of mortal bodies, so that some bodies, at the renewal of her light, experience an increase and diminish again when she wanes. A lengthy statement about this obvious phenomenon would be tedious,[10] so let us proceed to the other opinions about the boundaries of the infernal regions.

[8] A second group[11] preferred to divide the universe into three successions of the four elements: in the first rank were arranged earth, water, air, and fire, the last being a purer form of air touching upon the moon. In the rank above this the four elements were again found, but of a more refined nature, so that the moon now stood in the place of earth—we just remarked that natural philosophers called the moon the "ethereal earth"—water was in the sphere of Mercury, air in the sphere of Venus, and fire in the sun itself. The elements of the third rank were thought of as reversed in order, so that earth now held last position and with the other elements drawn inwards the lowest and highest extremities ended in earth; thus the sphere of Mars was considered fire, the sphere of Jupiter air, the sphere of Saturn water, and the *aplanes,* the fixed sphere, earth.[12] The men of old handed down the tradition that the Elysian fields were in this sphere, destined for the pure souls. [9] The soul, when it was dispatched to a body, descended from these fields through the three ranks of the elements to the body by a threefold death. This is the second opinion among Platonists about the death of the soul when it is thrust downwards into a body.

[10] The third group of Platonists[13]—you remember we said there were three divisions of opinion here—like the first group divide the universe into two parts, but not in the same way. These would have the sky, which is called the fixed sphere, as one part, and the seven so-called errant spheres and what is between them and the earth, and the earth itself, as the second part. [11] According to this sect, which is more devoted to reason, the blessed souls, free from all bodily

---

[10] References to this matter are very common in classical literature: e.g., Aristotle *Partes animalium* iv.v; Cicero *De divinatione* ii.33 and *De natura deorum* ii.50; Horace *Satirae* ii.iv.30; Pliny ii.221, xi.149; pseudo-Iamblichus 60; Gellius xx.viii.

[11] Pythagoreans, according to Proclus (Diehl) 154A. Taylor (p. 259) suggests that it is a late Pythagorean view since it follows the Alexandrian order of the planets.

[12] Cf. Proclus (Diehl) 154A–B.

[13] The Neoplatonists.

contamination, possess the sky;[14] but the soul that from its lofty pinnacle of perpetual radiance disdains to grasp after a body and this thing that we on earth call life, but yet allows a secret yearning for it to creep into its thoughts,[15] gradually slips down to the lower realms because of the very weight of its earthy thoughts.[16] [12] It does not suddenly assume a defiled body out of a state of complete incorporeality, but, gradually sustaining imperceptible losses and departing farther from its simple and absolutely pure state, it swells out with certain increases of a planetary body: in each of the spheres that lie below the sky it puts on another ethereal envelopment,[17] so that by these steps it is gradually prepared for assuming this earthy dress. Thus by as many deaths as it passes through spheres, it reaches the stage which on earth is called life.[18]

CHAPTER XII

[1] AT THIS POINT we shall discuss the order of the steps by which the soul descends from the sky to the infernal regions of this life. The Milky Way girdles the zodiac, its great circle meeting it obliquely so that it crosses it at the two tropical signs, Capricorn and Cancer.[1] Natural philosophers named these the "portals of the sun"[2] because the solstices lie athwart the sun's path on either side, checking farther progress and causing it to retrace its course across the belt beyond whose limits it never trespasses. [2] Souls are believed to pass through these portals when going from the sky to the earth and

---

[14] Cf. Plotinus III.iv.6, IV.iii.17; Porphyry *Sententiae* xxix, and quoted in Stobaeus II.388; Iamblichus, quoted in Stobaeus I.906.

[15] *Cogitatio*, "thinking" about the lower realms = *contagio*, "defilement." This chapter contains several examples of the use of false etymology and chance resemblance of words to strengthen an argument, a practice dear to Pythagoreans, Platonists, and Neoplatonists.

[16] Cf. Plotinus IV.iii.12, 15, III.ii.4, I.viii.4.

[17] See below, I.xii.14.

[18] The last three sentences are quoted with acknowledgement by Albertus Magnus in *Summa theologica* II.xii.q.72.m.4.art.3.

[1] Actually the crossing is at Gemini and Sagittarius. Macrobius is following Porphyry (*De antro nympharum* xxviii), whose error results from his attempt to make the portals of souls correspond with Homer's description of the doors of the Ithacan cave (*Odyssey* XIII.109–12). A glossator of Bede *De natura rerum* xviii (Migne, *Pat. Lat.*, XC, 234) calls attention to Macrobius' error.

[2] Porphyry (*De antro nympharum* xxviii) cites Homer (*Odyssey* XXIV.12) as the author of the name. Cf. Macrobius *Saturnalia* I.xvii.63; Helpericus of Auxerre *De computo* ii (Migne *Pat. Lat.*, CXXXVII, 25).

returning from the earth to the sky. For this reason one is called the portal of men and the other the portal of gods: Cancer, the portal of men, because through it descent is made to the infernal regions; Capricorn, the portal of gods, because through it souls return to their rightful abode of immortality, to be reckoned among the gods.[3]
[3] This is what Homer with his divine intelligence signifies in his description of the cave at Ithaca. Pythagoras also thinks that the infernal regions of Dis begin with the Milky Way,[4] and extend downwards, because souls falling away from it seem to have withdrawn from the heavens. He says that the reason why milk is the first nourishment offered to the newborn infant is that the first movement of souls slipping into earthly bodies is from the Milky Way.[5] Now you see, too, why Scipio, when the Milky Way had been shown to him, was told that the souls of the blessed *proceed from here and return hither.*

[4] So long as the souls heading downwards still remain in Cancer they are considered in the company of the gods, since in that position they have not yet left the Milky Way. But when in their descent they have reached Leo, they enter upon the first stages of their future condition. Since the first steps of birth and certain primary traces of human nature are found in Leo, and, moreover, since Aquarius is in opposition to Leo, setting just as it is rising, the festival in honor of the dead [6] is celebrated when the sun is in Aquarius, that is, in a sign contrary and hostile to human life.[7] [5] The soul, descending from the place where the zodiac and the Milky Way intersect, is protracted in its downward course from a sphere, which is the only divine form, into a cone,[8] just as a line is sprung from a point and passes from this indivisible state into length; from its point, which is a monad, it here comes into a dyad, which is its first protraction.[9]

[3] Cf. Porphyry *De antro nympharum* xx, xxii. Albertus Magnus (*Summa theologica* II.xii.q.72.m.4.art.3) quotes most of this paragraph.
[4] On the Pythagorean view that the Milky Way is the place of souls, cf. Porphyry *De antro nympharum* xxviii; Proclus (Kroll), II, 129; Heraclides Ponticus, cited in Stobaeus I.906. See also Capelle, *De luna, stellis, lacteo orbe animarum sedibus,* Chap. III, and A. B. Cook, *Zeus,* II, 37-45.
[5] Cf. Porphyry *De antro nympharum* xxviii; Proclus (Kroll), II, 129-30.
[6] The Parentalia, February 13-21.
[7] Probably because Saturn, direst of the planets, is lord of Aquarius. See below, I.xxi.26. Cf. Suetonius *Domitianus* xvi.1, and note in Mooney edition; Ptolemy *Tetrabiblos* I.xvii.38.
[8] The course described by the soul, as it descends from the indivisible point of its origin to the rounded form it assumes in the material realms, would be a cone. Cf. below, I.xiv.8.
[9] Cf. above, I.vi.18.

[6] This is the condition that Plato called "at once indivisible and divisible" when he was speaking in the *Timaeus*[10] about the construction of the World-Soul. Souls, whether of the world or of the individual, will be found to be now unacquainted with division if they are reflecting on the singleness of their divine state, and again susceptible to it when that singleness is being dispersed through the parts of the world or of man.[11]

[7] When the soul is being drawn towards a body in this first protraction of itself it begins to experience a tumultuous influx of matter rushing upon it. This is what Plato alludes to when he speaks in the *Phaedo*[12] of a soul suddenly staggering as if drunk as it is being drawn into the body; he wishes to imply the recent draught of onrushing matter by which the soul, defiled and weighted down, is pressed earthwards.[13] [8] Another clue to this secret is the location of the constellation of the Bowl of Bacchus[14] in the region between Cancer and Leo, indicating that there for the first time intoxication overtakes descending souls with the influx of matter;[15] whence the companion of intoxication, forgetfulness, also begins to steal quietly upon souls at that point. [9] Now if souls were to bring with them to their bodies a memory of the divine order of which they were conscious in the sky, there would be no disagreement among men in regard to divinity; but, indeed, all of them in their descent drink of forgetfulness, some more, some less. Consequently, although the truth is not evident to all on earth, all nevertheless have an opinion, since opinion is born of failure of the memory.[16] [10] Truth is more accessible to those who drank less of forgetfulness because they more easily recall what they previously knew above.[17] That is why in Greek the word for reading[18] means "knowledge regained": when

---

[10] 35A.

[11] Cf. Plotinus i.i.8, iv.ii.1; Porphyry *Sententiae* v.

[12] 79C.

[13] Cf. Plotinus i.vi.5, iv.viii.1; Synesius v.

[14] Actually the constellation Crater is located between Corvus and Hydra. Cf. Aratus *Phaenomena* 448. But if during an evening in the spring the observer faces south and looks almost overhead, he will see how the souls, passing through the descending portal of Cancer, by veering slightly to the left, would go by Crater.

[15] See Lobeck, p. 736.

[16] Cf. Adelard 10.

[17] The doctrine that learning is merely recollection occurs frequently in Plato: e.g., *Phaedo* 72E, 76B; *Phaedrus* 249C; *Meno* 81D–86A. Cf. Cicero *Tusculanae disputationes* 1.57–58.

[18] *Anagnosis*. Macrobius is quoted in pseudo-Bede *Mundi constitutio* (Migne, *Pat. Lat.*, XC, 901).

we are learning the truth we are relearning those things that we naturally knew before the influx of matter intoxicated our souls as they approached their bodies. [11] Moreover, this is the matter which, imprinted with ideas, has fashioned the whole mass of the universe that we see everywhere about us. The highest and purest part of it, upon which the heavenly realm depends for sustenance and existence, is called nectar and is believed to be the drink of the gods, whereas the lower and more turbid portion is believed to be the drink of souls; this is what the ancients meant by the river Lethe.[19] [12] Members of the Orphic sect believe that material mind is represented by Bacchus himself, who, born of a single parent, is divided into separate parts.[20] In their sacred rites they portray him as being torn to pieces at the hands of angry Titans and arising again from his buried limbs alive[21] and sound, their reason being that *nous* or Mind, by offering its undivided substance to be divided, and again, by returning from its divided state to the indivisible, both fulfills its worldly functions and does not forsake its secret nature.

[13] By the impulse of the first weight the soul, having started on its downward course from the intersection of the zodiac and the Milky Way to the successive spheres lying beneath, as it passes through these spheres, not only takes on the aforementioned envelopment in each sphere by approaching a luminous body,[22] but also acquires each of the attributes which it will exercise later. [14] In the sphere of Saturn it obtains reason and understanding, called *logistikon* and *theoretikon;* in Jupiter's sphere, the power to act, called *praktikon;* in Mars' sphere, a bold spirit or *thymikon;* in the sun's sphere, sense-perception and imagination, *aisthetikon* and *phantastikon;* in Venus' sphere, the impulse of passion, *epithymetikon;* in Mercury's sphere, the ability to speak and interpret, *hermeneutikon;* and in the lunar sphere, the function of molding and

---

[19] Cf. Plotinus iv.iii.26; Synesius v.

[20] Cf. Macrobius *Saturnalia* i.xviii.15; Proclus (Diehl) 53C, 184E. See Lobeck, pp. 557, 711, 736; F. M. Cornford, *From Religion to Philosophy* (London, 1912), pp. 209–10; J. E. Harrison, *Prolegomena to the Study of Greek Religion* (Cambridge, England, 1922), pp. 489–90.

[21] Following Eitrem's reading *vivus et integer, Nordisk Tidsskrift for Filologi,* III (1915), 55. The MSS read *unus et integer.*

[22] On the development of this theory from the writings of Plato and Aristotle, see R. C. Kissling, "The OXHMA-ΠNEYMA of the Neo-Platonists and the *De Insomniis* of Synesius of Cyrene," *Amer. Journ. of Philol.,* XLIII (1922), 318–20.

increasing bodies, *phytikon*.[23] [15] This last function, being the farthest removed from the gods, is the first in us and all the earthly creation; inasmuch as our body represents the dregs of what is divine, it is therefore the first substance of the creature. [16] The difference between terrestrial and supernal bodies (I am speaking of the sky and stars and the other components) lies in this, that the latter have been summoned upwards to the abode of the soul and have gained immortality by the very nature of that region and by copying the perfection of their high estate; but to our terrestrial bodies the soul is drawn downwards, and here it is believed to be dead while it is shut up in a perishable region and the abode of mortality.

[17] Be not disturbed that in reference to the soul, which we say is immortal, we so often use the term "death." In truth, the soul is not destroyed by its death but is overwhelmed for a time; nor does it surrender the privilege of immortality because of its lowly sojourn, for when it has rid itself completely of all taint of evil and has deserved to be sublimated, it again leaves the body and, fully recovering its former state, returns to the splendor of everlasting life. [18] The distinction between the soul in life and in death, which the learning and wisdom of Cicero drew forth from the sanctuaries of philosophy, is now, I believe, perfectly clear.[24]

CHAPTER XIII

[1] SCIPIO, encouraged in his dream both by the prospect of the sky which is allotted as a reward to the blessed and by the promise of immortality, had his glorious and splendid expectations corroborated upon seeing his father; he had asked whether he was still living, apparently being yet in doubt. [2] Hereupon he began to wish for death that he might really live. Not content with having wept at the sight of his parent whom he had believed dead, as soon

[23] A Neoplatonic doctrine which became very popular in the Middle Ages. Cf. Servius, II, 482–83; Proclus (Diehl) 260A–B, 348A; Isidore of Seville v.xxx.8; Bede *De temporibus* iv (Migne, *Pat. Lat.*, XC, 281); Byrhtferth, p. 130; Dante *Paradiso* xviii, xxi. See Lobeck, pp. 932–34. For other survivals, see Thorndike, I, 708, II, 203, 584, 744, III, 415.

[24] Schedler (p. 52) and Cumont (pp. 119–20) believe that Porphyry was the source for Chapters x–xii. Cumont thinks that Macrobius' source was Porphyry's *De regressu animae*, but Courcelle (pp. 29–31) argues that it was rather his *Peri Stugos*.

as he was able to speak out he desired first of all to convince him that nothing was closer to his heart than to remain henceforth with him. He did not, however, determine by himself to carry out his desires without consulting his father. One action betokens his prudence, the other his piety.

Now let us consider the words of his question and his father's advice.[1] [3] *"I pray you, most revered and best of fathers, since this is truly life, as I hear Africanus tell, why do I linger on earth? Why do I not hasten hither to you?" "You are mistaken," he replied, "for until that God who rules all the region of the sky at which you are now looking has freed you from the fetters of your body, you cannot gain admission here.* [4] *Men were created with the understanding that they were to look after that sphere called Earth, which you see in the middle of the temple.[2] Minds have been given to them out of the eternal fires you call fixed stars and planets, those spherical solids which, quickened with divine minds, journey through their circuits and orbits with amazing speed. Wherefore, Scipio, you and all other dutiful men must keep your souls in the custody of your bodies and must not leave this life of men except at the command of that One who gave it to you, that you may not appear to have deserted the office assigned you."*

[5] This doctrine and precept are Plato's, who in his *Phaedo*[3] lays down the rule that a man must not die of his own volition. And yet in the same dialogue he also says that philosophers ought to seek after death, and that philosophy is itself a meditation upon dying.[4] These statements seem to be contradictory but are really not, for Plato acknowledged two deaths in a man. Now I am not here repeating what was said above, that there are two deaths, one of the soul, the other of the creature; rather he is maintaining that there are, as well, two deaths of the creature, that is, of man, one afforded by nature and the other by the virtues. [6] The man dies when the soul leaves the body in accordance with the laws of nature; he is also said to

---

[1] The bulk of the remainder of this chapter is quoted with acknowledgement by Abelard in *Theologia Christiana* ii (Migne, *Pat. Lat.*, CLXXVIII, 1193–94) and in *Sic et non* clv (*ibid.*, 1605–6).

[2] Use of the word explained below, i.xiv.2.

[3] 62ff.

[4] 64A, 67D. Cf. Hugh of Saint Victor *Eruditio didascalica* ii.i (edition by Buttimer [Washington, D. C., 1939]).

die when the soul, still residing in his body, spurns all bodily allure-
ments under the guidance of philosophy, and frees itself from the
tempting devices of the lusts and all the other passions.[5] This is the
death which, as we pointed out above,[6] proceeds from the second
type of those virtues which befit only philosophers. [7] This is the
death which Plato is saying wise men ought to seek; but the other
death, which nature ordains for all, he forbids us to force, or to
cause, or to hasten,[7] teaching us to wait upon nature and showing
us why this is imperative by borrowing terms from everyday use.
[8] He says that those who are committed to prison by the authority
in power should not run away before that authority which shut them
up permits them to leave; that we do not escape the penalty by steal-
ing away but rather aggravate it. He also adds that the gods are our
masters, who govern us with care and forethought, and that it is
wrong, moreover, to remove, against their will, any of their possessions from the place in which they have set them.[8] Just as the man
who takes the life of another man's slave will be liable to punishment, so he who seeks to end his own life without the consent of his
master will gain not freedom but condemnation.[9]

[9] Plotinus develops more fully the principles of Plato's doctrine.[10] He says that the soul, after departing from the man, should

---

[5] Cf. Porphyry *Sententiae* ix.

[6] i.viii.8.

[7] Vincent of Beauvais (*Speculum doctrinale* v.cxvi) quotes with acknowledgement this paragraph up to this point.

[8] Cf. *Phaedo* 62B–C.

[9] Cumont, p. 114, believes that Macrobius did not consult the *Phaedo* but obtained this material indirectly.

[10] Here again Macrobius has been accused of misrepresenting his source. The similarity of some of his statements (not found in Plotinus) to material in Porphyry has led some scholars to conclude that he derived the Plotinian doctrines from Porphyry. See Petit, pp. 75, 79; Linke, p. 246; Schedler, p. 97; Cumont, pp. 114–19. Mras (pp. 257–58) and Henry (pp. 167–81) feel that Macrobius used Porphyrian material to supplement Plotinus' arguments. Courcelle (pp. 25–28) admits that Macrobius probably had the text of Plotinus before him, but usually he sides with Cumont against Henry in assuming that the *De regressu animae* of Porphyry was Macrobius' main source on suicide. That Courcelle is correct in maintaining that Macrobius did not use Plato's *Phaedo* here, but rather a work by Porphyry—probably his lost commentary on the *Phaedo*—and that Henry is mistaken, seems quite clear. Courcelle's reasons here are convincing and throughout his volume he has given evidence to show that the late Latin encyclopedists were not consulting the original works of Plato, but were rather using late commentaries on him. See the summary of Courcelle's arguments in the section on Sources in the Introduction. Without realizing that Macrobius was falsifying his sources, John of Salisbury (ii.xxvii.471C) cites Plotinus as his authority for doctrines which he has taken from this passage.

be found to be free of all bodily passions, but that the man who violently expels it from his body does not permit it to be free. Anyone who, weary of indigence, or because of fear or hatred—all these are considered passions—takes his life into his own hands, defiles his soul by the very act of forcibly expelling it, even if it was free from these taints before.[11] He adds that death ought to be the soul's release from the body and not its bondage; that the soul that has been expelled by force is bound more tightly about the body. [10] Indeed, this accounts for the fact that ejected souls for a long time hover about their bodies,[12] or their place of burial, or the ground into which the hand [13] was thrown. But souls which in this life free themselves from the chains of the body by the philosopher's death, even while the body remains intact, find their way to the sky and stars. Thus he shows that of the voluntary deaths only that one is commendable which is obtained, as we said, in the philosopher's manner and not by the sword, by contemplation[14] and not by poison. [11] He also says that death occurs naturally only when the body leaves the soul and not when the soul leaves the body.[15]

Now it is a well-known fact that a definite and fixed reckoning of numbers associates souls with bodies.[16] As long as these numbers hold out, the body continues to be animated, but when they run out, that secret power by which the association was maintained slips away; and this is what is known as fate or the allotted span of years. [12] The soul itself does not fail—for, to be sure, it is immortal and everlasting—but the body collapses, its course of numbers having run out; the soul does not become weary with its service, but merely leaves its office, the body, when it can no longer be animated. Hence the words of that most learned bard: "I shall fulfill the number and rejoin the shades." [17] [13] This is therefore the truly natural death, when the span of numbers runs out and brings on the end for the

[11] Cf. Plotinus i.ix.

[12] Cf. Porphyry De abstinentia ii.47.

[13] Before bodies were cremated it was customary to cut off some member (os resectum), usually a finger, and to bury it after the cremation. This seems to have been a relic of inhumation. See W. H. Roscher, Ausführliches Lexikon der griechischen und römischen Mythologie (Leipzig, 1890–94), II, col. 235.

[14] Prudentia, as defined above, i.viii.4.

[15] Cf. Plotinus i.ix.

[16] Cf. Philo Judaeus De somniis i.138.

[17] Virgil Aeneid vi.545.

body, and not when life is wrested from a body still capable of carrying on.

The difference between death by nature and by volition is an important one. [14] When the soul is deserted by the body it can retain nothing corporeal in itself if it has conducted itself chastely while it was in this life; but when it is violently thrust from the body, since in departing its bonds are broken and not released, the very compulsion becomes the occasion of passion, and it is tainted with evil even while it is breaking the bonds.[18] [15] Another reason for not ending one's own life Plotinus adds to those above: inasmuch as it is agreed, he says, that the rewards above are bestowed upon souls in proportion to the degree of perfection attained by each in this life, it behooves us not to hasten the end of life since improvement upon our attainments is still possible.[19] [16] This is quite true, indeed, for in the esoteric discourses about the return of the soul the remark is made that delinquents in this life are like those who stumble on level ground and are able to rise again without difficulty, whereas the souls that depart from this life with the pollution of sin upon them must be likened to those who have fallen into a deep abyss from which they cannot be recovered. We must therefore use the span of life allotted us in order to get a greater opportunity of purification.

[17] But you will say that one who is already completely purified should take his life into his hands since there is no reason for him to linger, for further improvement is not required of one who has already attained his goal. On the contrary, the very act of summoning death ahead of time in the hope of enjoying blessedness ensnares a man in a net of passion, since hope is a passion as well as fear;[20] this man also incurs the other penalties discussed above. [18] This explains why Aemilius Paulus forbade his son, hoping for a truer life, to hasten to him; he did not want Scipio's rash yearning for freedom and resurrection to bind him and hold him back the more because of his passion.

Furthermore, he did not tell him that he could not die unless a natural death overtook him, but that he could not gain admission

---

[18] Cf. Porphyry *De abstinentia* 1.38.

[19] Cf. Plotinus 1.ix.

[20] Cf. *ibid.* On the Stoic division of the passions see above, 1.viii.11, and note.

there: [19] *for until God . . . has freed you from the fetters of your body, you cannot gain admission here.* He who had already been received into heaven knew that admission to a habitation in the sky was open only to the completely pure. It is equally true that death which does not come naturally must be feared, and that we must not anticipate the time decreed by nature. [20] These statements by Plato and Plotinus about suicide, which we have just reported here, will clear up any difficulty in the words with which Cicero prohibits it.

CHAPTER XIV

[1] NOW LET US take up the passage immediately following the one just discussed. *Men were created with the understanding that they were to look after that sphere called Earth, which you see in the middle of the temple. Minds have been given to them out of the eternal fires you call fixed stars and planets, those spherical solids which, quickened with divine minds, journey through their orbits and circuits with amazing speed.*

[2] Why, in referring to the earth, he calls it a sphere set in the middle of the universe, we shall discuss rather fully when we come to the nine spheres.[1] His designation of the universe as the *temple* of God was appropriate, too, and was for the edification of those who think that there is no other god except the sky itself and the celestial bodies we are able to see. In order to show, therefore, that the omnipotence of the Supreme God can hardly ever be comprehended and never witnessed, he called whatever is visible to our eyes the temple[2] of that God who is apprehended only in the mind, so that those who worship these visible objects as temples might still owe the greatest reverence to the Creator, and that whoever is inducted into the privileges of this temple might know that he has to live in the manner of a priest.[3]

In the above passage we are also informed in words that cannot be mistaken that such divinity is present in the human race that we

---

[1] I.xxii.
[2] Cf. Varro VII.7, who derives *templum* from *tueri*, "to gaze at." See also Boyancé, pp. 115–19.
[3] Cf. Porphyry *Ad Marcellam* xvi, xix.

are all of us ennobled by our kinship with the heavenly Mind. [3] Attention must be drawn to the fact that Paulus is using the word *animus* in both its proper and improper senses. The proper meaning of *animus* is of course "mind," which no one denies is more divine than soul, but sometimes we also assume for the word the meaning "soul." [4] Accordingly, when he says, *Animi have been given to them out of those eternal fires,* he wants us to understand "mind," which is the essence that we alone have in common with the sky and stars. But when he says, *Your animus must be kept in the custody of your body,* he is then referring to the soul, imprisoned in the confines of the body, to which the divine Mind is not subject.

[5] Now let us explain, in accordance with the teachings of cosmogonists, how *animus,* meaning "mind," is common to us and the stars.[4] [6] God, who both is and is called the First Cause, is alone the beginning and source of all things which are and which seem to be.[5] He, in a bounteous outpouring of his greatness, created from himself Mind. This Mind, called *nous,* as long as it fixes its gaze upon the Father, retains a complete likeness of its Creator, but when it looks away at things below creates from itself Soul.[6] [7] Soul, in turn, as long as it contemplates the Father, assumes his part, but by diverting its attention more and more, though itself incorporeal, degenerates into the fabric of bodies. Thus it has purest reason, *logikon,* from Mind from which it springs; moreover, out of its own nature it takes on the first beginnings of sense-perception and growth, *aisthetikon* and *phytikon.* But of these the first, *logikon,* which is received at birth from Mind, inasmuch as it is truly divine, is suitable only for the divine; the other two, *aisthetikon* and *phytikon,* are apart from the divine and hence conform with the mortal.[7] [8] Soul, creating and fashioning bodies for itself—on that account the creation, which men who really know about God and Mind call *nous,* has its beginning in Soul—out of that pure and clearest fount of Mind from whose abundance it had drunk deep at birth, endowed those divine or

---

[4] Cf. Plato *Timaeus* 41D–42E, and see Whittaker, *Neo-Platonists,* pp. 23–24. H. F. Stewart (*Cambr. Med. Hist.,* I, 573) calls the passage that follows "as good a summary of the Plotinian trinity as was possible in Latin." The view that stars are animated beings was held by Tycho Brahe and Kepler. See Thorndike, I, 457.

[5] Cf. above, i.vi.19, and note.

[6] Cf. Plotinus v.ii.1, v.i.7; Porphyry *Sententiae* xxx, xxxi.

[7] Cf. Plotinus v.ii.1. On the Neoplatonic emanations, see Whittaker, *Neo-Platonists,* pp. 53-70.

ethereal bodies, meaning the celestial sphere and the stars which it was first creating, with mind; divine minds were infused into all bodies which had smooth spherical shapes,[8] and that is the reason why he said, when he was speaking about the stars, *which are quickened with divine minds*. [9] Soul, degenerating as it came into the lower regions and to the earth, discovered that the frailty of the mortal realm made it incapable of sustaining the pure divinity of Mind. Human bodies, on the other hand, were found to be capable of sustaining, with difficulty, a small part of it, and only they, since they alone seemed to be erect—reaching towards heaven and shunning earth, as it were—and since only the erect can always gaze with ease at the heavens;[9] furthermore, they alone have in their heads a likeness of a sphere,[10] the shape which we said was the only one capable of containing mind. [10] Man alone was endowed with reason, the power of mind, the seat of which is in the head; but he was also given the other two faculties of sense-perception and growth, since his body is mortal. [11] Accordingly, man possesses reasoning power and perceives and grows, and solely by his reasoning power has deserved precedence over the other animals, which, because they are always bent forward and have difficulty in looking upwards, have drifted away from the heavens,[11] and which, because they have not received in any part of their bodies a likeness of divine shapes, have been allotted no share of mind and consequently lack reasoning power; only two faculties belong to them, sense-perception and growth. [12] If there is any suggestion of reasoning power in them it is really not reasoning power but memory, and not memory mingled with reason but merely attendant upon the dull perceptions of the five senses. We shall not discuss this point further since it has nothing to do with the present work. [13] A third class of terrestrial bodies is that of the trees and vegetation, which lack both reasoning power and sense-perception; because the faculty of growth alone remains in these, they are said to be alive in this respect alone.[12]

---

[8] Cf. Plato *Timaeus* 33B, 34B.

[9] Cf. Plato *Cratylus* 396B–C; *Republic* ix.586A; *Timaeus* 90A; Aristotle *De partibus animalium* ii.x.656A, iv.x.686A, *et passim*.

[10] Cf. Plato *Timaeus* 44D, 73C–D; Chalcidius ccxxxi.

[11] Cf. Plato *Timaeus* 91E.

[12] Aristotle's classification of life into the reasoning, sensitive, and vegetative. See *De anima* ii.ii–iii.

[14] This classification was also used by Virgil. He assigned Soul to the world, and in order to bear witness to its purity he also called it Mind. He says that the sky, the lands, the seas, and the stars "are sustained by an inward breath," [13] referring here to Soul just as in another passage he uses the word soul to mean "breath": ". . . insofar as fire and breath avail." [14] In order to affirm the excellence of the World-Soul he declared that it was Mind, saying that "Mind motivates the universe"; to show that all life in the universe is derived from and is animated by Soul he adds, "Thence comes the race of men and of beasts," and all the rest of the creation; to affirm that Soul always retains the same vigor but is restricted in the exercise of its powers in living creatures because of the grossness of their bodies, he adds, ". . . insofar as it is not hindered by an injurious bodily frame," and by other mortal frailties.[15]

[15] Accordingly, since Mind emanates from the Supreme God and Soul from Mind, and Mind, indeed, forms and suffuses all below with life, and since this is the one splendor lighting up everything and visible in all, like a countenance reflected in many mirrors arranged in a row,[16] and since all follow on in continuous succession, degenerating step by step in their downward course, the close observer will find that from the Supreme God even to the bottommost dregs of the universe[17] there is one tie, binding at every link and never broken. This is the golden chain of Homer which, he tells us, God ordered to hang down from the sky to the earth.[18]

[16] By the words of Paulus it becomes clear that of all the creatures on earth man alone has a common share in Mind, that is *animus,* with the sky and the stars. And that is why he said, *Minds have been given to them out of the eternal fires you call fixed stars and planets.* [17] He did not infer, however, that we were animated by those celestial and eternal fires—indeed, fire, even if it is divine, is nevertheless corporeal, and we could not be animated by a body,

---

[13] *Aeneid* vi.724–26. Cf. Servius, II, 102.

[14] *Aeneid* viii.403.

[15] *Ibid.* vi.726–32. Cf. pseudo-Bede *Mundi constitutio* (Migne, *Pat. Lat.,* XC, 901).

[16] Plotinus i.i.8 uses the same figure. W. H. V. Reade (*Cambr. Med. Hist.,* V, 790) says that it was through Macrobius that this doctrine and figure were transmitted to the Middle Ages.

[17] That is, the earth. See below, i.xxii.6.

[18] *Iliad* viii.19. For Proclus' use of the cord as a symbol, see σειρά in the indexes of the Diehl and Kroll editions.

even if it were divine—but rather by that which animates those very bodies which are and seem to be divine, that is, by that part of the World-Soul which we said consists of pure Mind. [18] And so after saying, *Minds have been given to them out of the eternal fires you call fixed stars and planets,* he presently added, *which are quickened with divine minds,* so as clearly to distinguish between the corporeal portion of the stars, the *eternal fires,* and the Soul-portion, the *divine minds;* he also shows that from the stars the power of mind comes into our souls.

[19] It is interesting to note that this discussion of Soul embraces the opinions of all who are known to have made pronouncements about the soul. Plato said that the soul was an essence moving itself;[19] Xenocrates, a number moving itself;[20] Aristotle called it entelechy;[21] Pythagoras and Philolaus, harmony;[22] Posidonius, idea;[23] Asclepiades, a harmonious functioning of the five senses;[24] Hippocrates, a subtle spirit diffused through every part of the body;[25] Heraclides Ponticus, light;[26] Heraclitus the philosopher, a spark of starry essence;[27] Zeno, a spirit grown into the body;[28] Democritus, a spirit implanted in the atoms having such freedom of movement that it permeated the body.[29] [20] Critolaus the Peripatetic stated that it was composed of a fifth essence;[30] Hipparchus called it fire;[31] Anaximenes, air;[32] Empedocles[33] and Critias,[34] blood; Parmenides, a mix-

---

[19] Cf. *Phaedrus* 245; Plutarch *De animae procreatione in Timaeo* iii.1013C; Aetius *Placita* IV.ii.5 (Diels, p. 386).

[20] Cf. Cicero *Tusculanae disputationes* 1.20; Plutarch *op. cit.* i.1012D; Stobaeus 1.794; Aetius *op. cit.* IV.ii.4 (Diels, p. 386); Adelard 23.

[21] Cf. *De anima* ii.1; Cicero *Tusculanae disputationes* 1.22; Stobaeus 1.796.

[22] Cf. above, I.vi.43; below, II.ii.1; Aristotle *De anima* I.iv.407B; Lucretius *De rerum natura* III.100.

[23] Cf. Plutarch *op. cit.* xxii.1023B.

[24] Cf. Stobaeus 1.796; Aetius *op. cit.* IV.ii.8 (Diels, p. 387).

[25] Cf. *De morbo sacro* xix; Tertullian *De anima* xv.

[26] Cf. Tertullian *op. cit.* ix; Stobaeus 1.796; Aetius *op. cit.* IV.ii.6 (Diels, p. 388).

[27] Cf. Aristotle *De anima* I.ii.405A; Themistius *De anima* I.ii; Stobaeus 1.282; Tertullian *op. cit.* v; Vincent of Beauvais *Speculum historiale* III.xxxii.

[28] Cf. Tertullian *op. cit.* v; Cicero *Tusculanae disputationes* 1.19.

[29] Cf. Aristotle *De anima* I.ii.404A; Themistius *op. cit.* I.ii; Cicero *Tusculanae disputationes* 1.22.

[30] Cf. Tertullian *op. cit.* v.

[31] Cf. *ibid.*

[32] Cf. Themistius *op. cit.* I.ii; Stobaeus 1.796.

[33] Cf. Cicero *Tusculanae disputationes* 1.19; Tertullian *op. cit.* v.

[34] Cf. Aristotle *De anima* I.ii.405B; Themistius *op. cit.* I.ii.

ture of earth and fire;[35] Xenophanes, one of earth and water;[36] Boethos, of air and fire;[37] and Epicurus, a mixture of heat, air, and breath.[38] The acceptance of the soul's incorporeality has been as general as the acceptance of its immortality.

[21] Now let us see what is meant by the two terms mentioned together in the phrase *which you call fixed stars and planets.* These two words [*sidera* and *stellae*] are not synonymous as are the words *ensis* and *gladius;*[39] *stellae* refers to the solitary planets, the five errant ones and the others which, belonging to no constellation, are borne along by themselves,[40] whereas *sidera* refers to the stars which, with many others, make up their respective constellations, as for instance Aries, Taurus, Andromeda, Perseus, and Corona, and the various other figures that are supposed to be visible in the heavens. Likewise, among the Greeks *aster* and *astron* do not have the same meaning, *aster* signifying a lone star and *astron* a group of stars, which form a constellation or *sidus.*[41]

[22] In speaking of the stars as *spherical solids,* he is not merely describing the lone stars but the stars in constellations as well. All stars, even if they differ somewhat in magnitude, are identical in shape. Both words are needed to describe a solid sphere: the word *solid* would not suffice unless roundness were inferred, nor the word *spherical* unless a solid ball were inferred, since the one word overlooks the shape and the other the solidity of a starry body. [23] We use the word sphere in this instance with reference to the bodies of the stars, which are all of this shape.[42] In addition, the word sphere has another application, referring to the *aplanes,* the greatest

---

[35] Cf. Stobaeus 1.796; Aristotle *Metaphysica* 1.iii.984B.

[36] Cf. pseudo-Plutarch *De vita et poesi Homeri* ii.93; Stobaeus 1.294.

[37] See Pauly, III (1899), cols. 601–2.

[38] Cf. Lucretius *op. cit.* iii.269–81; Stobaeus 1.798. Courcelle (p. 31) believes that Macrobius may have drawn this list of philosophers' views on the soul from Porphyry's lost *De regressu animae.* Manegold of Lautenbach paraphrases Macrobius' paragraph on the soul. See Manitius, III, 176.

[39] Cf. Quintilian *Institutio oratoriae* x.i.11.

[40] About one-tenth of the 1022 stars catalogued by Ptolemy were ἀμόρφωτοι, i.e., not included in his forty-eight constellations.

[41] Cf. Isidore of Seville iii.lix; Honorius of Autun *De imagine mundi* i.lxxxix (Migne, *Pat. Lat.,* CLXXII, 142). Macrobius does not conform with the classical distinction between *aster* and *astron.* See L. Edelstein, "The Philosphical System of Posidonius," *Amer. Journ. of Philol.,* LVII (1936), 297–98.

[42] Cf. Stobaeus 1.516, 536; Aetius *op. cit.* ii.xiv.1 (Diels, pp. 343–44).

sphere, and the seven underlying spheres in which the five errant planets and the two brilliant planets[43] run their courses.

[24] The words *circus* and *orbis* have their own distinct meanings, and indeed they vary on different occasions. Cicero used the word *orbis* to mean "circle" when he spoke of the *orbis lacteus,* the "Milky Circle," and later used *orbis* in reference to the spheres when he spoke of the *nine spheres or globes.*[44] The word *circus* refers to the great circles that girdle the outermost sphere, as we shall see in the following chapter; one of these is the Milky Circle, about which he used the expression *a circle . . . gleaming out amidst the blazing stars.*[45] [25] But none of the above meanings of *circus* and *orbis* apply to the words at the opening of this chapter. Rather by the word *orbis* he means one complete revolution of a star, or the distance covered by the star in the sphere in which it is traveling until it returns to its starting point; the word *circus* here refers to the boundary lines encircling the spheres and marking the limits within which the sun and moon veer in their courses, and within which the lawful deviation of the errant planets is confined.

[26] The errant planets were thus named by the ancients because they are borne along in their own course, moving from west to east in a contrary direction to that of the greatest or celestial sphere;[46] moreover, they all have similar movements and travel at the same rate of speed, and yet they do not all complete their orbits in the same amount of time. [27] He described their speed as *amazing,* for although it is the same for all and none can accelerate or retard its speed, the time required for their revolutions varies. The explanation, the differences in the distances traversed, will be given shortly.[47]

CHAPTER XV

[1] AFTER TELLING his son about the nature of the stars and the starry minds of men, Paulus again urged Scipio to reverence the gods and to be upright in his dealings with men; again he reminded him

---

[43] It is common practice with classical authors to distinguish between the sun and moon and the other five planets.

[44] *Scipio's Dream* iv.1.

[45] See above, 1.iv.5.

[46] Cf. Cicero *De divinatione* 1.17, and see note to this passage in Pease edition, p. 103.

[47] 1.xxi.5–6.

of the reward, pointing out the Milky Way, the recompense for virtuous conduct and the meeting place of blessed men, with this comment: *Furthermore, it was a circle of surpassing brilliance gleaming
out amidst the blazing stars, which takes its name, the Milky Way,
from the Greek word.* [2] In designating the Milky Way, the word
orbis here has the same meaning as *circus*. The Milky Circle, indeed,
is only one of the circles that girdle the celestial sphere: there are
besides it ten others, which will be discussed fully when the proper
time comes. It is the only one of the circles visible to the eye, the
others being apprehended in the mind and not seen.[1]

[3] Concerning this Milky Way many men have expressed different views, some offering fabulous explanations of its existence,[2]
others natural ones; we shall say nothing about the fabulous explanations and shall take up only those that seem essential to its nature.
[4] Theophrastus said that the Milky Way was a seam where the two
hemispheres of the celestial sphere were joined together,[3] and that
accordingly, where the rims met, a greater brilliance was evident.
[5] Diodorus said it was fire of a condensed and concentrated sort,
pressed together into one belt with crooked boundaries, its difference
in consistency being responsible for its being massed together; as a
result it became visible, whereas the rest of the celestial fire did not
present its light to our eyes since it was diffused by the extreme
subtlety of its nature.[4] [6] Democritus' explanation was that countless stars, all of them small, had been compressed into a mass by their
narrow confines, so that the scanty spaces lying between them were
concealed; being thus close-set, they scattered light in all directions
and consequently gave the appearance of a continuous beam of
light.[5] [7] Posidonius, whose definition more nearly conforms with
prevailing opinion, says that the Milky Way is a stream of stellar
heat[6] which crosses the zodiac obliquely; inasmuch as the sun never
passes beyond the boundaries of the zodiac and has left the remain-

---

[1] Cf. Geminus v.11.

[2] See Hyginus *Astronomica* II.43; Philo Judaeus *De providentia* II.89; Porphyry *De antro nympharum* xxviii; Stobaeus I.574.

[3] Cf. Philo Judaeus *De providentia* II.89; Achilles *Isagoge in Arati Phaenomena* xxiv; pseudo-Bede *Mundi constitutio* (Migne, *Pat. Lat.*, XC, 896).

[4] See Diels, p. 230.

[5] Cf. Achilles *op. cit.* xxiv; Stobaeus I.576; Aetius *Placita* III.i.6 (Diels, p. 365); Aristotle *Meteorologica* I.viii.345A.

[6] Cf. Stobaeus I.576; Aetius *op. cit.* III.i.8 (Diels, p. 366).

ing portion of the sky without a share in its heat, the purpose of the Milky Way, lying athwart the path of the sun, is to temper the universe with its warmth. We have already indicated where this intersects with the zodiac.[7]

So much for the Milky Way. [8] Now there are ten other circles, as we have said, one of which is the zodiac, the only one of these ten that was able to acquire breadth, for a reason which we shall explain. [9] The great circles of the celestial sphere are incorporeal lines which are apprehended in the mind as having length only and lacking breadth;[8] but in the case of the zodiac the fact that it contained the signs made breadth necessary.[9] [10] Two lines, therefore, bound the amount of space occupied by this belt with its spreading signs; in addition, a third one drawn through the middle is called the ecliptic[10] since, when both the sun and moon are pursuing their courses along the same line at the same time, it is inevitable that one should suffer eclipse: a solar eclipse occurs if the moon comes directly under the sun, and a lunar eclipse occurs if the moon is diametrically opposite the sun.[11] [11] The sun can be eclipsed only on the thirtieth day of the moon, and the moon can never experience an eclipse except on the fifteenth day of its cycle.[12] It so happens that when the moon is situated on the ecliptic in a position diametrically opposite the sun and the earth's cone is moving along the ecliptic, the usual brilliance of the moon is obliterated; and again the moon, in coming under the sun, by thrusting itself directly into line, shuts off the light of the sun from our eyes.[13] [12] In an eclipse the sun suffers no loss, but we are deprived of its light, whereas the moon, at the time of its eclipse, suffers by not receiving the sun's beams, with which it gives radiance to the night.[14] Virgil, who was well trained in all of the arts, was aware of this when he spoke of "The sun's many eclipses, the moon's many labors."[15] Although three lines are required to

[7] I.xii.I.
[8] Cf. Theo Smyrnaeus 133; Chalcidius lxviii.
[9] Cf. Chalcidius lxix.
[10] Cf. Cleomedes I.18, II.115; pseudo-Iamblichus 19; pseudo-Bede *Mundi constitutio* (Migne, *Pat. Lat.*, XC, 896).
[11] Cf. Theo Smyrnaeus 194–96; Chalcidius lxxxvii–lxxxviii.
[12] Cf. Geminus x.6, xi.4; Stobaeus I.538; Isidore of Seville III.lvii–lviii.
[13] Cf. Pliny II.47.
[14] Cf. Cleomedes II.95; Helpericus of Auxerre *De computo* xx (Migne, *Pat. Lat.*, CXXXVII, 35).
[15] *Georgicon* II.478.

bound and divide the zodiac, the men of antiquity, the authors of our vocabulary, wished it to be spoken of as one circle.

There are five other circles, called parallels.[16] [13] The middle and greatest of these is the equinoctial;[17] the two close to the poles and therefore small are called the septentrional[18] and the austral;[19] midway between the equinoctial and the polar circles are the two tropics, greater than the polar circles and smaller than the middle circle. These mark the limits of the torrid zone on either side.

[14] In addition, there are two others, called the colures, which are so called because they do not make complete circles.[20] Crossing the celestial north pole and proceeding in different directions, they intersect each other at the northern vertex and divide each of the five parallels into four equal parts, intersecting the zodiac so that one of them crosses at Aries and Libra and the other at Cancer and Capricorn; but they are not believed to extend to the south pole.[21]

[15] The two that remain to complete the number given above are the meridian and the horizon.[22] These are not fixed on the celestial sphere but vary with the location of the observer or inhabitant. [16] The meridian is the point which the sun reaches when it is directly over one's head, that is at midday. Because the roundness of the earth makes the aspect of localities different, the same part of the sky is not over the heads of all men; so all will not be able to have the same meridian, but each people have their own meridian directly overhead. [17] Similarly, each individual, as he looks about him, has his own horizon.[23] The horizon is a circular boundary that marks the apparent junction of the sky and the earth, and since our eyes cannot see to the ends of the earth, as much as each one beholds by looking about him in all directions is for him his individual boundary of that portion of the sky above

---

[16] Cf. Theo Smyrnaeus 130; Cleomedes i.11–12; Geminus v.1–11; Chalcidius lxv; Martianus Capella viii.818–22; Isidore of Seville iii.xliii; Honorius of Autun De philosophia mundi ii.xiii (Migne, Pat. Lat., CLXXII, 60–61).

[17] Celestial equator.

[18] Celestial arctic circle.

[19] Celestial antarctic circle.

[20] From the Greek kolouros, meaning "dock-tailed."

[21] Cf. Geminus v.49–50; Theo Smyrnaeus 132; Martianus Capella viii.823; Honorius of Autun De philosophia mundi ii.xiv (Migne, Pat. Lat., CLXXII, 61).

[22] Cf. Theo Smyrnaeus 131–33; Geminus v.54–67; Chalcidius lxvi; Honorius of Autun De philosophia mundi ii.xv (Migne, Pat. Lat., CLXXII, 61).

[23] Cf. Theo Smyrnaeus 133; Aristotle Meteorologica ii.vii.365A.

the earth. [18] This horizon, which each one's vision circumscribes for himself, cannot extend beyond three hundred and sixty stades[24] in diameter, for vision does not exceed one hundred and eighty stades in any one direction. When it reaches this point it fails since what is beyond is concealed from us by the roundness of the earth. So this number, doubled for two opposite directions, gives us three hundred and sixty stades, the amount of space included in anyone's horizon.[25] As much of this space as you lose behind you by proceeding forwards is gained from the space ahead, and so the horizon always changes as you progress in any direction.[26] [19] This prospect about which we have been speaking is obtained on land only on a perfectly flat plain, or on sea at a moment of tranquillity.[27] Do not be influenced by the fact that we can often see a mountain at a very great distance or that we can see into the upper reaches of the sky, for it is one thing when a lofty object presents itself to our eyes and another when our gaze stretches out over a flat surface; it is here only that the circle of the horizon lies. Let these words suffice about the matter of the circles girding the celestial sphere.

CHAPTER XVI

[1] LET US PROCEED to the passage that follows: *As I looked out from this spot, everything appeared splendid and wonderful. Some stars were visible which we never see from this region, and all were of a magnitude far greater than we had imagined. Of these the smallest was the one farthest from the sky and nearest the earth, which shone forth with borrowed light. And, indeed, the starry spheres easily surpassed the earth in size.*

[2] In the words *As I looked out from this spot*, he is affirming what we already noted above, that Scipio's meeting with his father and grandfather in his dream took place in the Milky Way. Next

---

[24] About thirty-five miles, if we assume that he is using Eratosthenes' stade here, as he does elsewhere. On the number of feet in a stade, see below, 1.xx, note 17. Macrobius should have completed his list of celestial circles by discussing the celestial horizon (ὁρίζων θεωρητός). Instead he confuses it with the visible horizon (ὁρίζων αἰσθητός). Greek writers on astronomy clearly distinguish between the two or else omit the visible horizon.

[25] Cf. Macrobius *Saturnalia* VII.xiv.15; pseudo-Bede *Mundi constitutio* (Migne, *Pat. Lat.*, XC, 907); Honorius of Autun *De imagine mundi* II.xxv (Migne, *Pat. Lat.*, CLXXII, 149).

[26] Cf. Cleomedes 1.21.

[27] Cf. pseudo-Bede *Mundi constitutio* (Migne, *Pat. Lat.*, XC, 897).

he reports that two things about the stars particularly aroused his admiration, the newness of some and the great size of all of them.

First of all let us discuss the matter of newness. [3] In adding the words *which we never see from this region,* he adequately explains why some of the stars are not visible to us. Our abodes lie in such a position that certain stars can never be seen by us because that portion of the sky in which they move can never appear to us who live here. [4] This quarter of the earth, which is inhabited by all the people with whom we can have any contact, verges towards the north pole, and the spherical shape of the earth causes the south pole to be plunged into the depths.[1] Although the celestial sphere is always revolving around the earth from east to west, the polar axis which holds the Great Bear, since it is above us, will always be visible to us, however much it turns in the swirl of the heavens; and it will always display "the Bears that shrink from the plunge 'neath Ocean's plain."[2] [5] The south pole, on the other hand, once buried from our sight, as it were, by the location of our abodes, will never show itself to us, nor the stars with which it is undoubtedly adorned. And this is what Virgil, knowing nature's ways full well, meant when he said, "One pole is ever high above us, while the other, beneath our feet, is seen of black Styx and the shades infernal."[3]

[6] Now since the roundness of the earth has caused this contrast in the regions of the heavens, making them either always or never visible to us living in this latitude, he who is in the sky will surely see the whole of the heavens; for there is no portion of the earth to obstruct his view inasmuch as all of it scarcely occupies the space of a point in comparison with the size of the heavens. [7] To one who never had the opportunity on earth of seeing the stars in the south polar region, when first they came into view with the obstruction of the earth removed, there was just cause for astonishment.[4] His remark, *Some stars were visible which we never see from this region,* indicates that he fully understood the reason why he had never seen them before; that he meant the earth

[1] Cf. Cleomedes 1.21; Theo Smyrnaeus 130.
[2] Virgil *Georgicon* 1.246.
[3] *Ibid.* 241–42. Chalcidius lxvi quotes the second line in the same connection.
[4] Cf. Cicero *Tusculanae disputationes* 1.45.

by the words *this region* he showed by the gesture he used while speaking.

[8] Now let us consider the meaning of the words *all were of a magnitude far greater than we had imagined*. He himself showed why men never imagined the true magnitude of the stars when he added: *And, indeed, the starry spheres easily surpassed the earth in size*. [9] In truth, how could a man—unless he were one whom a training in philosophy had raised above man, or rather, had made a man in the true sense of the word—ever suspect that one star was greater than the whole earth, when single stars as a rule scarcely seem able to match the light of one torch? The true magnitude of the stars will then be recognized when it is proven that each of them is larger than the whole earth. This you may test in the following manner. [10] Geometricians define the point as that space which, on account of its incomprehensible minuteness, cannot be further divided into parts; in fact it is not even considered a part but is said to be merely a symbol.[5] Astronomers have shown us that the earth occupies the space of a point in comparison with the size of the orbit in which the sun revolves.[6] Furthermore, we know how much smaller the sun is than its own orbit. By very obvious calculations of space, the diameter of the sun is found to be one two hundred and sixteenth part of the measurement of the circle in which it moves.[7] [11] Since the sun's dimensions are a definite part of the full extent of its orbit and the earth in comparison with the sun's orbit is but a point which cannot even be a part, there can be no hesitation in agreeing that the sun is greater than the earth, if a part is greater than that which on account of its minuteness is not even large enough to be called a part.

[12] Now it is certain that the orbits of the more remote stars are greater than the sun's orbit if that which contains is greater than that which is contained, since the arrangement of the heavenly spheres is such that each lower one is entirely encompassed by the one above it. Hence the sphere of the moon, being farthest from the celestial sphere and closest to the earth, he called the *smallest*,

[5] Cf. Aristotle *Topica* VI.iv.141B; Nicomachus II.vii.1; pseudo-Iamblichus 1.

[6] A frequently repeated assertion: e.g., Aristarchus *De magnitudinibus et distantiis solis et lunae* Hypothesis 2; Euclid *Phaenomena* i; Theo Smyrnaeus 120, 128; Cleomedes 1.56; Geminus XVI.29; Chalcidius lix, lxiv; Stobaeus 1.448; Martianus Capella VI.584.

[7] See below, I.xx.30.

because the earth itself fades into a point, as it were, being the last. [13] If, as we said, the orbits of the more remote stars are greater than the sun's orbit and, moreover, if each star is of such size as to be considered a part in comparison with the measurement of its orbit, then, surely, each star is larger than the earth, which we said is only a point in comparison with the sun's circuit, which in turn is smaller than the circuits of the more remote stars.[8] A later discussion will indicate the truth of his statement about the moon's light being borrowed.[9]

CHAPTER XVII

[1] SCIPIO LOOKED about him everywhere with wonder, and when his eyes lighted on the earth, he fell into pleasant reveries. Hereupon his grandfather's admonition recalled him to the upper realms, and in the following words he pointed out to him the order of the spheres, beginning with the celestial sphere: [2] *The whole universe is comprised of nine circles, or rather spheres. The outermost of these is the celestial sphere, embracing all the rest, itself the supreme god, confining and containing all the other spheres. In it are fixed the eternally revolving movements of the stars.* [3] *Beneath it are the seven underlying spheres, which revolve in an opposite direction to that of the celestial sphere. One of these spheres belongs to that planet which on earth is called Saturn. Below it is that brilliant orb, propitious and helpful to the human race, called Jupiter. Next comes the ruddy one, which you call Mars, dreaded on earth. Next, and occupying almost the middle region, comes the sun, leader, chief, and regulator of the other lights, mind and moderator of the universe, of such magnitude that it fills all with its radiance. The sun's companions, so to speak, each in its own sphere, follow—the one Venus, the other Mercury—and in the lowest sphere the moon, kindled by the rays of the sun, revolves.* [4] *Below the moon all is mortal and transitory, with the exception of the souls bestowed upon the human race by the benevolence of the gods.*

[8] Aristotle *De caelo* II.xiv.298A; *Meteorologica* I.iii.339B; Cleomedes II.97. Macrobius makes no mention of the moon's size. This may be an indication that he (or his source) was familiar with the figures of Hipparchus and Ptolemy for the size and distance, figures which differ only slightly from actuality.

[9] I.xix.9–10.

Above the moon all things are eternal. Now in the center, the ninth of the spheres, is the earth, never moving and at the bottom. Towards it all bodies gravitate by their own inclination.

[5] In this passage we have an accurate description of the universe from top to bottom; the whole "body" of the universe, so to speak, is represented, the *to pan* of the Greeks,[1] for he begins with the words, *The whole universe is comprised.* . . . Virgil, indeed, spoke of the universe as a great body:

And mingles with its great body.[2]

[6] By alluding to obscure points that need elucidation, Cicero has left us in this passage many problems to discuss. With reference to the seven underlying spheres he says: *Which revolve in an opposite direction to that of the celestial sphere.* [7] In saying this, he is directing us to inquire whether the celestial sphere revolves, and whether the seven spheres are controlled by it and yet go counter to it; whether the order of the spheres which he offers is approved by Plato; how it happens, if the seven truly underlie the celestial sphere, that the planets of all these are said to light up the zodiac when the zodiac is a single belt situated at the top of the celestial sphere; what causes the differences in duration of the courses of the planets through this same zodiac (all of these things Cicero necessarily affirms when he sets forth the order of the spheres); lastly, what causes all weights to *gravitate towards the earth,* as he says.

[8] That the celestial sphere revolves is taught to us by the nature, force, and plan of the World-Soul, whose eternity consists in motion.[3] Now motion never leaves what life has not abandoned, nor does life depart from that in which motion is still present.[4] Therefore, the body of the celestial sphere, which the World-Soul fashioned to participate in its immortality, in order that it should never cease functioning, is always in motion and does not know how to rest, since Soul itself, by which the sphere is impelled, is never at rest.[5] [9] Inasmuch as the essence of Soul, which is incorporeal, is

---

[1] Cf. Plotinus iii.iii.6, *et passim.*
[2] *Aeneid* vi.727.
[3] Cf. Plato *Timaeus* 36E.
[4] Cf. Plato *Phaedrus* 245C.
[5] Cf. Plotinus ii.ii.1.

in motion and, moreover, Soul created before all other things the body of the celestial sphere, without doubt the faculty of motion was first passed on to the body of the celestial sphere from the realm of incorporeality; and this force, undiminished and intact, does not leave that which it first began to move. [10] And so, indeed, the celestial sphere is compelled to turn with a rotary motion because it must always be in motion and there is no place beyond to which it can proceed;[6] its motion is perpetually within itself. It moves where it is able and where there is space; its motion is rotary since the only progress of a sphere embracing all spaces and regions is in revolutions.[7] As a result it always seems to be pursuing Soul, which moves about its vast immensity. [11] Shall we say, therefore, that it never finds it, since it is always pursuing it? Rather, it is always finding it because it is omnipresent and everywhere complete.[8] Why, then, does the sphere not rest if it has found what it was seeking? Because Soul does not know rest. The sphere would rest if it should ever find Soul resting, but since the latter, leading the chase, is ever pouring itself into the universe, body is ever commingling with it.[9] Let these few statements concerning the secret of the rotary motion of the celestial sphere, gleaned from the many things Plotinus said on the subject, suffice.

[12] When Cicero called the outermost sphere, whose revolutions we have just explained, the *supreme god*,[10] he did not mean to imply the First Cause and All-Powerful God, since this sphere, the sky, is the creation of Soul, and Soul emanates from Mind, and Mind from God, who is truly the Supreme.[11] Indeed, he called it *supreme* with respect to the other spheres lying beneath, as witness the words immediately following, *confining and containing all the other spheres;* he called it *god* because it is immortal and divine and is full of the reason imparted to it by that purest Mind,[12] and also because it produces and itself contains all the virtues which follow that omnipotence of the original Head. [14] The ancients called it

[6] Cf. *ibid.*
[7] Cf. *ibid.;* Porphyry *Sententiae* xxx.1.
[8] Cf. Plotinus ii.ii.1.
[9] Cf. *ibid.*
[10] Cf. the attitude of Adelard of Bath, cited by Thorndike, II, 41.
[11] Cf. above, i.vi.18, and note.
[12] Cf. Chalcidius xciii, cv.

Jupiter, and to cosmogonists Jupiter is the soul of the world.[13] Hence Virgil's words, "With Jove I begin, ye Muses; of Jove all things are full."[14] This sentiment, borrowed by other poets, originated with Aratus,[15] who, in introducing the subject of the stars, saw that he would have to begin with the celestial sphere, the abode of the stars; hence he said that he had to begin with Jupiter.[16] [15] So also Juno is called his sister and wife, for she is air:[17] she is called sister because the air is made of the same seeds as the sky, and she is called wife because air is subordinate to the sky.

[16] Attention must be called to this fact, too, that some authorities maintain that, with the exception of the two brilliant luminaries and of the five errant planets, the stars move only with the celestial sphere, being fixed in it. Other authorities maintain (a position closer to the truth) that these stars have their own motions in addition to their revolutions in the celestial sphere, but that, because of the vast dimensions of the celestial sphere, ages past belief are consumed in a star's completion of its individual orbit. So these movements are imperceptible to us because our brief moment of time is not sufficient to detect them.[18] [17] Hence Cicero, acquainted with all the better schools of thought, made allowance for either opinion when he said, *In it are fixed the eternally revolving movements of the stars,* calling the stars *fixed* and yet not denying that they have their own movements.

CHAPTER XVIII

[1] NOW LET US inquire whether on the basis of reliable evidence those seven underlying spheres really do move, as he says, *in an opposite direction to that of the celestial sphere.*[1] [2] That the sun and moon and the five errant planets, so called because they wander,

---

[13] Cf. Macrobius *Saturnalia* i.xviii.15.

[14] *Eclogae* iii.60.

[15] *Phaenomena* 1.

[16] Cf. *Scholia in Caesaris Germanici Aratea,* Eyssenhardt edition of Martianus Capella (Leipzig, 1866), p. 379. Johannes Scottus (Chap. ccclxv) cites this passage.

[17] ἀήρ (air) is an anagram of ἥρα (Hera). Cf. Plato *Cratylus* 404C; Diogenes Laertius *Vitae philosophorum* vii.147; Macrobius *Saturnalia* i.xv.20, iii.iv.8.

[18] See below, ii.xi.9–12.

[1] The bulk of this chapter is quoted in a gloss on Bede *De temporum ratione* xvi (Migne, *Pat. Lat.,* XC, 363–65).

progress in their own motion from west to east in addition to their apparent motion from east to west, which results from their being dragged along by the diurnal rotation of the celestial sphere, has been considered incredible and impossible by the ignorant and learned alike; but to the diligent inquirer the truth will be so clear that not only will he accept it in his mind but he will be able to confirm it with his eyes as well. [3] Still, that we may direct our discussion to those who stubbornly deny this truth, come, you who pretend that this is not clear to you, let us examine all the proposals which your position maintains, causing your disbelief, and those which truth itself prompts.

[4] Shall we say that the errant planets and the two brilliant orbs are fixed in the celestial sphere like the other stars and give no indication of any motion of their own but are merely borne on by the sweep of the celestial sphere's rotation? Or shall we say that they also have motions of their own? Again, if they have motions of their own they either follow the path of the celestial sphere from east to west, moving both independently and in the same direction as it, or else they move in an opposite direction, from west to east. One of these, it seems to me, must be the case.

Let us now see which of them can be proven true. [5] If the planets were fixed they would never leave their positions and would always be in the same signs, as in the case of the other stars. Among the fixed stars the Pleiades, for example, never disperse their existing configuration, nor do they leave the near-by Hyades, nor stray from the vicinity of Orion. The union of the two Bears is never dissolved. The Dragon, slipping between them, always remains in their embrace. [6] But the planets are seen now in one region of the sky and now in another, and often, although two or more have come together in close proximity, they later leave the place in which they were seen together and in time separate from each other. Therefore, we may be sure, as our eyes attest, that the planets are not fixed in the celestial sphere. Consequently they have motions of their own; and no one will be able to deny what his eyes verify.[2]

[7] We must ask next whether they move from east to west or go in the opposite direction by their own independent motion. Here, too, the proof is perfectly obvious and, again, our eyesight will

[2] Cf. Cleomedes 1.16.

confirm it. Let us consider the order of the signs which we see mark the divisions of the zodiac, and let us begin with any sign in the sequence. [8] If Aries is in the ascendant,[3] Taurus is the next to follow, and after it Gemini, Cancer, and so on. Now if the planets were progressing from east to west, they would not move from Aries into Taurus, which is behind Aries, nor from Taurus into Gemini, still farther behind, but would move forward from Gemini into Taurus and from Taurus into Aries in the same direction as the rotation of the celestial sphere. [9] But since they recede from the first sign into the second, and from the second into the third, and so on, into the signs behind, and since the signs, moreover, are fixed in the celestial sphere, we may be sure that these planets move not with the celestial sphere, but in the opposite direction.[4]

To prove our case conclusively, let us call attention to the moon's course, more noticeable because of its brilliance and the short duration of its cycle. [10] About the second day after the new moon has left the sun it becomes visible at sunset, a neighbor of the sun, so to speak, which it just left. After sunset it stays on the border of the sky and then shortly sets. On the third day it sets later than on the second, and day by day it withdraws farther from the setting sun, until at sunset on the seventh day it is seen in the middle of the sky. After another seven days it is just rising when the sun is setting. [11] Thus in half a month it has traversed half the sky or one hemisphere, going from the west to the east. Then, after another seven days, it finds itself at sunset at the top of the hidden hemisphere, the proof of this being that it does not become visible until the middle of the night. After another seven days it overtakes the sun again and both rise together until, passing beneath the sun, it becomes new again and gradually goes off into the east.[5]

[12] The sun also moves from west to east, although its pace is much slower than the moon's, crossing only one sign in the time that the moon takes to traverse the whole zodiac; nevertheless, it affords our eyes clear proof that it also has its own motion. [13]

---

[3] That is, rising on the eastern horizon.
[4] Cf. Theo Smyrnaeus 147; Cleomedes 1.16, 18; Chalcidius lxxiv.
[5] Cf. Geminus xii.11–13.

Let us suppose that the sun is in Aries, which, because it is the equinoctial sign, makes the hours of the day and night equal. When it is setting in this sign we presently see Libra or the claws of Scorpio rising. Taurus is seen near the western horizon, for the Pleiades and Hyades, the brighter constellations of Taurus, set shortly after the sun. [14] In the following month the sun has gone back into the sign behind Aries, that is Taurus, and so we do not see the Pleiades or any other constellation of Taurus during that month. A sign that rises with the sun and sets with it is of course never visible, and even near-by constellations are concealed by it. [15] The Dog Star, because it is near Taurus, is not visible at that time, being hidden by the sun's neighboring light; hence Virgil's remark, "The snow-white Bull with gilded horns ushers in the year, and the Dog fades away, retiring before his confronting star." [6] This does not mean that when Taurus and the sun are in conjunction, the Dog Star, which is near Taurus, is beginning to set; rather he says it "fades away" when Taurus is holding the sun, because it is becoming invisible, with the sun so close by. [16] When the sun is setting in Taurus, Libra is seen so much higher in the sky that the whole of Scorpio is above the horizon, while Gemini is seen near the western horizon. A month later Gemini is no longer seen, which means that the sun has gone into it. After leaving Gemini it recedes into Cancer, and then at sunset Libra is seen in the zenith. [17] And so it becomes evident that the sun has crossed three signs, Aries, Taurus, and Gemini, and has receded through half a hemisphere. Three months later, after crossing through the three following signs, Cancer, Leo, and Virgo, it is found in Libra, again making day and night equal. When it is setting in this sign, Aries is rising, the sign in which the sun set six months before.[7]

[18] Now we have preferred to deal with the setting rather than the rising sun because the signs which lie behind are seen after sunset; and when we point out that the sun recedes to the signs which are still seen after its setting, we are demonstrating that the sun must be moving in a direction counter to that of the celestial sphere. [19] These observations about the sun and moon will also

---

[6] *Georgicon* 1.217–18.
[7] Cf. Geminus XII.5–10.

suffice to clarify the backward motion of the other five planets, which move in the same manner into the signs behind, in the opposite direction to that of the rotation of the celestial sphere.[8]

CHAPTER XIX

[1] NEXT WE MUST say a few things about the order of the spheres, a matter in which it is possible to find Cicero differing with Plato, in that he speaks of the sphere of the sun as the fourth of seven, occupying the middle position, whereas Plato says that it is just above the moon, that is, holding the sixth place from the top among the seven spheres. [2] Cicero is in agreement with Archimedes and the Chaldean system; Plato followed the Egyptians, the authors of all branches of philosophy, who preferred to have the sun located between the moon and Mercury even though they discovered and made known the reason why others believed that the sun was above Mercury and Venus.[1]

Those who hold the latter opinion are not far from a semblance of truth; indeed, their misapprehension arose from the following cause. [3] From the sphere of Saturn, the first of the seven, to the sphere of Jupiter, the second from the top, there is so much space intervening that the upper planet completes its circuit of the zodiac

---

[8] Cf. Cleomedes 1.18.

[1] From the surviving lists of the order of the planets it appears that the order that placed Mercury and Venus above the sun prevailed in the early period and that the other order was adopted later or gradually superseded the earlier one. Plato's order (*Timaeus* 38D; *Republic* x.616E) was moon, sun, Venus, Mercury. This is also given by Aristotle (*Metaphysica* xi.viii.1073B) and Chrysippus (Stobaeus 1.448). Eratosthenes deviated from the Platonic order by inverting the positions of Mercury and Venus (Theo Smyrnaeus 142; Chalcidius lxxiii). Macrobius adopts the Platonic order (1.xix.7–10), but a little later (1.xxi.27) gives Plato's order as moon, sun, Mercury, Venus—another bit of evidence in support of those who hold that he did not read the *Timaeus*. Still later (ii.iii.14), in explaining why Platonists rejected Archimedes' figures for the distances of the planets, he gives the correct Platonic order. The other order, which placed Mercury and Venus beneath the sun, seems to have grown more popular after the second century b.c. It is the one given by Cicero in *Scipio's Dream* iv.2 and *De divinatione* ii.91, and in Geminus 1.27; Cleomedes 1.3; Vitruvius ix.5; Ptolemy ix.1. I should not hesitate to speak of Plato's order as the early one and of Ptolemy's as the late one were it not for the fact that Ptolemy (ix.1) refers to the infrasolar order· as the early one and the supra-solar order as the late one. He says that he prefers to go back to the old order because he cannot see that the contention of later writers (possibly Eratosthenes), that Mercury and Venus must be above the sun because their transits have never been observed, is valid, for Mercury and Venus could be traveling in different planes. For further discussion of the Platonic and Ptolemaic orders, see Taylor, pp. 192–94; Boyancé, pp. 59–65.

in thirty years, the lower one in twelve.[2] Again, the sphere of Mars is so far removed from Jupiter that it completes its circuit in two years.[3] [4] Venus is so much lower than Mars that one year is sufficient for it to traverse the zodiac. But the planet Mercury is so near Venus and the sun so near Mercury that these three complete their revolutions in the same space of time, that is, a year more or less.[4] On this account Cicero called Mercury and Venus the *sun's companions*, for they never stray far from each other in their annual periods. [5] The moon, moreover, lies so much farther below these that what they accomplish in a year it does in twenty-eight days. Hence there was no disagreement among the ancients regarding the correct order of the three superior planets, the vast distances between them clearly arranging them, nor about the location of the moon, which is so much lower than the rest. But the proximity of the three neighboring planets, Venus, Mercury, and the sun, was responsible for the confusion in the order assigned to them by astronomers, that is, with the exception of the skillful Egyptians, who understood the reason, here outlined.

[6] The sphere in which the sun journeys is encircled by the sphere of Mercury, which is above it, and by the higher sphere of Venus as well. As a result, when these two planets course through the upper reaches of their spheres, they are perceived to be above the sun, but when they pass into the lower tracts of their spheres they are thought to be beneath the sun. [7] Those who assigned to them a position beneath the sun made their observations at a time when the planets' courses seemed to be beneath the sun, which, as we noted, sometimes happens; indeed, this position is more notice-

---

[2] The sidereal period of Saturn is 29.46 years, and of Jupiter 11.86 years.
[3] The sidereal period of Mars is 687 days.
[4] The orbits of Venus and Mercury are within the earth's orbit and so these planets appear to swing back and forth with respect to the sun. They never go very far from the sun's position in the sky and are seen during the same year as morning and evening stars. The greatest apparent distance of Venus from the sun (maximum elongation) is 48 degrees of celestial arc and of Mercury 28 degrees. At the beginning of a solar year Mercury and Venus might appear ahead of the sun as morning stars and at the end of the year might be behind as evening stars, or vice versa. So Macrobius, who is using a geocentric orientation, says that their revolutions consume "a year more or less." The revolutions of Venus and Mercury are actually 225 and 88 days respectively. Macrobius' figures for the duration of the five planets' revolutions are the same as those regularly found in the classical handbooks. See Geminus 1.24–30; Cleomedes 1.16–17; Theo Smyrnaeus 136; Chalcidius lxx.

able since we get a clearer view at that time. When Mercury and Venus are in their upper regions, they are less apparent because of the sun's rays.[5] As a result, the false opinion has grown stronger, and this order has received almost universal acceptance.[6]

[8] Nevertheless, accurate observations have disclosed the true order; and in addition to the evidence of our eyes, we may be further assured by the fact that the moon, which has no light of its own but borrows it from the sun, necessarily lies beneath the source of its light. [9] The reason why the moon has to borrow its light while all the other planets shine forth with their own radiance is the following. The other planets are located above the sun in the purest ether, where everything, whatever it be, is natural and spontaneous light;[7] all this light, with its fire, lies so directly above the sphere of the sun that the zones of the celestial sphere that are farthest from the sun are subject to perpetual cold, as we shall explain later.[8] [10] The moon, on the other hand, because it alone is beneath the sun, in the lowest sphere and near the transitory realms devoid of their own light, could have no light except from the sun above it, whose radiance it reflects.[9] Moreover, since the earth is the lowest part of the whole universe and the moon is the lowest limit of the ether, the moon has been given the name "ethereal earth." [10] [11] The moon cannot be stationary like the earth because nothing re-

[5] The reason given is incorrect. Venus and Mercury are less brilliant when they are nearing superior conjunction because of their greater distance from us. Greatest brilliancy of Venus is attained 36 days before or after inferior conjunction, at which time she is 2½ times as brilliant as at superior conjunction.

[6] Ptolemy's authority, and not Macrobius' reason, was probably responsible for the acceptance of the "false opinion." That his authority was even at this early date beginning to exert its weighty influence and was causing the downfall of the Platonic order may be inferred from a statement in Proclus (Diehl) 258A–C. For my interpretation of Macrobius' meaning in this paragraph, see Appendix A.

[7] Following those who derived *aither*, "ether," from *aithesthai*, "to blaze." See pseudo-Aristotle *De mundo* ii.392A. This derivation is acceptable to modern etymologists. See E. E. Boisacq, *Dictionnaire étymologique de la langue grecque* (Heidelberg, 1938), p. 23; L. Meyer, *Handbuch der griechischen Etymologie* (Leipzig, 1901), II, 91. Vitruvius (ix.i.16) explains that the flames of fire rise and hence the ether above the sun is scorched and set afire.

[8] ii.vii. The ancient cosmography which Macrobius is following conceives of the region of fire as marked by the belt of the zodiac, which lies directly above the apparent annual path of the sun. The motions of the visible planets, with the exception of Venus, are confined to the zodiac. Polar regions, remote from the fire of the zodiac, are stiff with cold.

[9] Cf. Geminus ix.1–2; Cleomedes ii.101; Stobaeus 1.558.

[10] Cf. above, i.xi.7, and note.

mains stationary in a revolving sphere except the center; now the earth is the center of the mundane sphere; therefore it alone stands still.[11]

[12] Again, why does the earth merely become bright without reflecting light when the sun shines upon it, whereas the moon, like a mirror, reflects the light that it receives?[12] Because the earth is the residue of air and water, in themselves condensed and compact, and is therefore compressed by the immensity of its load[13] and does not suffer any light to penetrate beyond its surface. The moon, on the other hand, although it too is a bottommost limit, marks the end of the region of purest light and ethereal fire; consequently, though of a denser substance than the other celestial bodies, it is still much purer than the earth,[14] and it permits the light to penetrate to such a degree that it sends it forth again, but with no heat, so far as we can tell. [13] Indeed, when a ray of light reaches us directly from its starting point, the sun, it carries with it the essence of fire from which it springs. But when it is poured into the body of the moon and is reflected, it gives forth light but no heat. So also with the mirror: when it reflects the brilliance of a flame set at a distance, it returns only the image of the flame without the heat.[15]

[14] Enough has already been said about the position that Plato and his authorities assigned to the sun, and about the authorities that Cicero followed in placing the sun in the fourth sphere, and the reason behind their difference of opinion, and why Cicero said that the moon was *in the lowest sphere, kindled by the rays of the sun.* Now we must also tell why Cicero, when he wished the sun to have the fourth place among the seven spheres, did not simply say the "middle position" (the fourth number is of course not *almost the middle* among seven, but is the middle), but instead said, *Next, and occupying almost the middle region, comes the sun.* [15] The additional word qualifying his statement was not idle, for in his system the sun will hold the middle position in respect to number but not to space. If its position is between the three upper and the three lower spheres, it is surely the middle one in number, but if the

[11] See below, i.xxii.3.
[12] Cf. pseudo-Bede *Mundi constitutio* (Migne, *Pat. Lat.*, XC, 888).
[13] See below, i.xxii.5–7.
[14] Being the transition from ether to air. Cf. below, i.xxi.33; Cleomedes 1.17.
[15] Cf. Plutarch *De facie in orbe lunae* xvi.929E.

dimensions of the whole area occupied by the seven spheres are clearly perceived, the region of the sun is not found to be in the middle since it is farther removed from the top than the bottom is from it; the proof of this may be briefly stated. [16] Saturn, the highest planet, passes through the whole zodiac in thirty years, the sun, the middle one, in a year, and the moon, the lowest, in less than a month. The difference between the sun's orbit and Saturn's is as the difference between thirty and one, but the difference between the moon's orbit and the sun's is as the difference between twelve and one. [17] From this it is clearly seen that the sun does not make an equal division of all the space from the top of the universe to the bottom.[16] Because Cicero was referring to the numerical position of the sun, he called it *middle,* which it truly is, but because of the distances involved, he qualified his statement with the word *almost.*

[18] We must remember that the names Saturn, Jupiter, and Mars have nothing to do with the nature of these planets but are fictions of the human mind, which "numbers the stars and calls them by name."[17] Hence, he does not say, "That planet which is Saturn," but rather, *which on earth is called Saturn,* and *that brilliant orb, called Jupiter,* and *the one which you call Mars.* In each instance he indicates that these names are not chosen in accordance with nature but are convenient designations applied by men.[18]

[19] When he calls Jupiter *that brilliant orb, so propitious and helpful to the human race,* and Mars *the ruddy one, dreaded on earth,* the words *brilliant* and *ruddy* are appropriate, for Jupiter glistens and Mars has a ruddy glow; the other words are taken from the treatises of those who believe that good and evil come to mortals from the planets, the evil coming generally from Mars and the good from Jupiter. [20] If anyone should care to inquire how maliciousness came to be associated with the divine so that a planet is called baneful, as is thought to be true of Mars and Saturn, or why Jupiter and Venus are considered clearly beneficial by those who cast horoscopes—this despite the fact that there is only one

---

[16] See below, 1.xxi.5–7. Cf. Chalcidius cxv.

[17] Virgil *Georgicon* 1.137.

[18] Cf. Cicero *De natura deorum* 11.52–53, and note in Mayor edition. See Taylor, pp. 194–95.

nature in things divine—I shall mention a reason found in only one author to my knowledge.

Ptolemy, in the three books he wrote *On Harmony,* offered a reason which I shall briefly explain. [21] There are certain numerical ratios, he says, which are able to afford harmonious relationships among all things that may properly be associated with each other; it is impossible for this association to occur except through these ratios. They are 4:3; 3:2; 9:8; 2:1; 3:1; 4:1.[19] [22] For the present it will be well to keep these numerical ratios in mind, but their nature and power will be explained more appropriately later when we come to the discussion of the harmony of the spheres;[20] let it suffice now merely to accept the fact that without these numbers there can be no coordination or harmony.

[23] The sun and moon, it is true, are the principal guardians of our lives. Of the two faculties identified with terrestrial bodies, sense-perception and growth, the first comes to us from the sun, the second from the moon.[21] Thus we are dependent upon these two planets for the life we enjoy. [24] In our associations and in the outcome of our activities we rely as much upon these two as upon the other five planets; but the numerical relations mentioned above readily coordinate two of the planets with the sun and moon and do not permit any coordination for two others. [25] Venus and Jupiter are favorably aspected to the sun and moon because of these numbers, Jupiter coordinating with the sun in all ratios, with the moon in most of them, Venus with the moon in all ratios and with the sun in most of them.[22] Hence, though each is considered a beneficent planet, Jupiter is more closely related to the sun and Venus to the moon, and both are favorable to human life, being in numerical harmony with the two heavenly bodies upon which we depend for life. [26] On the other hand, Saturn and Mars have no such relationship with them, though it is true that Saturn does aspect the sun and Mars the moon in a very slight degree.[23] They are therefore thought to be unfavorable to human life, having no close numerical connection with the authors of life. The reason

[19] *Harmonica* 1.7.
[20] ii.i.
[21] Cf. above, i.xii.14, xiv.7.
[22] *Harmonica* iii.16.
[23] *Ibid.*

they are also believed sometimes to bring wealth and fame to men belongs properly to another treatise; it is enough that we have shown why one is considered baneful and another beneficial.

[27] Indeed, Plotinus declares in a treatise *Are the Stars Effective?* [24] that the power and influence of stars have no direct bearing upon the individual, but that his allotted fate is revealed to him by stations and direct and retrograde motions of the seven planets, just as birds in flight or at rest unwittingly indicate future events by their direction or cries.[25] And so we have good reason to call this planet beneficial and that one baneful since we obtain premonitions of good or evil through them.

CHAPTER XX

[1] IN REFERRING to the sun by so many names, Cicero was not indulging in mere verbiage, nor was he enumerating these designations for his own amusement; every word has a true meaning. He calls it the *leader, chief, and regulator of the other lights, mind and moderator of the universe.*

[2] Plato, when speaking in the *Timaeus* of the eight spheres, remarks: "In order that there might be an exact measurement of the relative speeds, quick and slow, in the eight spheres, God kindled in the second sphere above the earth a light which we now call the sun."[1] [3] You see that this explanation would place the light of all the spheres in the sun; but Cicero, knowing that the other planets also have their own light—that is, with the exception of the moon, which, as we have repeatedly noted, is devoid of light —clarified the vagueness of this statement and at the same time demonstrated that the greatest light, and not the only light, was in the sun when he called it *leader, chief, and regulator of the other lights.* Indeed, he knew that the other planets are lights but that the sun, which Heraclitus calls the "fount of celestial light," [2] is the

---

[24] Plotinus II.iii.

[25] Cf. Plotinus II.iii.3, 7; Chalcidius cxxv. See Duhem, II, 309–18. On the influence of Plotinus' attitude in the Middle Ages, see Thorndike, I, 302, 306–7. On the possible use of Macrobius' text (I.xix.20–27) by Joannes Lydus, see Paul Henry, "Une Traduction grecque d' un texte de Macrobe dans le Περὶ μηνῶν de Lydus," *Revue des études latines,* XI (1933), 164–71.

[1] 39B.

[2] Cf. Stobaeus 1.526.

leader and chief. [4] It is the leader because it excels the others in the splendor of its light, and is the chief because it is so preeminent that it derives its name *sol* from the word *solus*,[3] since it appears to be "alone" of its kind. It is called the regulator of the others because it controls the departing and returning of each planet through a fixed allotment of space. [5] Each planet has a definite limit which it reaches in its course away from the sun and then, as if forbidden to transgress, it is seen to turn back, and again, when it reaches a certain point, it is recalled to its former direction.[4] In this way the sun's power and influence direct the movements of the other planets over their appointed paths.

[6] Cicero's reference to the sun as the *mind of the universe*,[5] like the philosophers' appellation "heart of the sky,"[6] doubtless arises in the fact that all things that we see recurring in the sky under fixed law—the variations of the days and nights, now long, now short, now equal, falling at definite intervals, the gentle warmth of spring, the scorching heat of Cancer and Leo,[7] the mildness of the autumn breeze, and the biting cold of winter, midway between autumn and spring—all follow the course and plan of the sun.[8] It is proper to call it the heart of the sky, for we see that all things in the divine plan are accomplished through it. [7] There is another reason for calling it the heart of the sky: the nature of fire is always involved in motion and perpetual agitation; the sun, moreover, as we have stated, has been regarded as the source of ethereal fire; therefore, the sun's function in the ether is the same as the heart's function in the animal.[9] The heart is so constituted as not to cease moving; a brief cessation of beating for any reason would quickly kill the animal.

[8] This much will suffice about the sun as the mind of the universe. The reason why it is called the *moderator of the universe* is quite clear: it is known for a certainty that not only the earth but

---

[3] Cf. Varro v.68; Isidore of Seville III.70; Byrhtferth 17.

[4] Cf. Pliny II.12; Cleomedes 1.18–19; Theo Smyrnaeus 187.

[5] Cf. Macrobius *Saturnalia* I.xviii.15; Pliny II.13.

[6] Cf. Theo Smyrnaeus 138, 187; Chalcidius c. On the Copernican character of this passage, see K. Reinhardt, *Kosmos und Sympathie* (Munich, 1926), pp. 332–37; Duhem, I, 442–45.

[7] That is, when the sun is passing through those constellations.

[8] Cf. Pliny II.13.

[9] Cf. Theo Smyrnaeus 187–88; Plutarch *De facie in orbe lunae* xv.928B–C; Chalcidius c.

the sky itself, which he has good reason to designate here as the universe, are warmed by the sun in such a way that the extremities which are farthest removed from the sun's path are deprived of heat and are ever stiff with cold. The explanation of this will come later.[10]

There still remains for brief consideration the important matter of the size of the sun, which Cicero expressed so well. [9] Astronomers, in every discussion of the magnitude of the sun, have been particularly interested in determining how much larger it was than the earth.[11] Eratosthenes, in his book *On Dimensions*,[12] says: "The size of the sun is twenty-seven times greater than that of the earth," while Posidonius' estimate is many, many times greater.[13] Each bases his opinion on the lunar eclipses. [10] Now when they wish to prove that the sun is greater than the earth they use the proof of the moon's eclipse, and when they attempt to account for the moon's eclipse they use as evidence the magnitude of the sun; as a consequence, since either argument is based upon the other, neither is proven successfully, the common evidence inclining now this way, now that.[14] How can proof rest upon a supposition not yet proven?

[11] The statements of the Egyptians, however, left nothing to conjecture but were based upon an independent proof which did not require the assistance of lunar eclipses. They wished to prove how many times greater the sun is than the earth, so that they might demonstrate by its size just why the moon is eclipsed. [12] It was quite clear to them that the solution could not be reached unless a measurement of the earth and sun were obtained in order to establish a comparison. Indeed, it was easy for them to determine the dimensions of the earth with the aid of their eyes, but the meas-

---

[10] II.vii.

[11] The remainder of this chapter is quoted in a gloss on Bede *De temporum ratione* xxvii (Migne, *Pat. Lat.*, XC, 417–20). Cf. also Vincent of Beauvais *Speculum naturale* xv.ii. For further influence of material in this chapter on the Middle Ages, see Manitius, II, 744, 787, III, 116.

[12] Lost.

[13] F. Hultsch (*Poseidonios über die Grösse und Entfernung der Sonne*, pp. 5–6) points out that Eratosthenes' estimate, as reported by Macrobius, must refer to the ratio of their volumes and not diameters inasmuch as Posidonius' estimate is that the sun's diameter is 39¼ times greater than the earth's diameter, and 39¼ is not "many, many times greater" than 27.

[14] Cf. Cleomedes II.79–81. Macrobius is soon to be found guilty of the circular reasoning which he condemns here. See below, I.xxii.2.

urements of the sun, they soon found, could be obtained only by measuring the sky through which it coursed. So they decided to measure that portion of the sky which was the sun's path in order to learn the size of the sun. [13] But, I pray, if anyone is ever so unoccupied or so disengaged from serious matters as to attempt his own investigation of these problems, let him not be shocked or scornful of such presumption on the part of the ancients as an almost insane undertaking; for in this question, the solution of which seemed utterly impossible, human ingenuity opened the way and discovered, through using the earth, what the measurement of the sky is.

That the method used may be clearly understood, it would be well to offer a few introductory words of explanation; then we shall be better prepared to take up what follows. [14] In every orbit or sphere the middle is called the center, which is nothing more than a point that accurately fixes the middle of the orbit or sphere. Now a straight line drawn from any point on the circumference to any other point on that circumference must divide the circle into two parts. [15] But the circle is not necessarily halved by the chord which divides it, for that chord alone divides a circle into two equal parts which is drawn from one point on a circumference to another point on the circumference and which passes through the center. The line which divides a circle equally is called the diameter. [16] Furthermore, the diameter of every circle, when tripled with the addition of a seventh part, gives the measurement of the circumference in which it is inclosed;[15] for example, if a diameter is seven inches long and you desire to know the length of the circumference, you triple seven, making twenty-one, and add a seventh part or one, and the circumference of a circle whose diameter is seven inches is twenty-two inches. [17] We could prove these statements by obvious geometrical processes were it not that we believe everyone assents and that we are anxious to keep this commentary reasonably brief.

[18] We must recognize this fact, too, that the earth's shadow, which the sun after setting and passing into the lower hemisphere sends upwards, creating on earth the darkness called night, is sixty times the diameter of the earth; its full extent reaches the circle of

[15] Cf. Archimedes *Dimensio circuli* Prop. iii; Theo Smyrnaeus 124.

the sun's path[16] and, by cutting off the light, causes darkness to fall
back upon the earth. [19] Now we must reveal the length of the
earth's diameter in order to determine the distance that would be
sixty times as long, and thus fulfill our promise.

[20] By most obvious and accurate methods of measurement we
know that the earth's circumference, including the habitable and
uninhabitable areas, is 252,000 stades.[17] This being the circumference,
the diameter will of course be 80,000 stades, or slightly more, according to the method explained above of tripling the diameter with
the addition of a seventh part to get the circumference. [21] Now,
since it is the diameter of the earth and not the circumference which
is multiplied sixty times to obtain the measurement of the earth's
shadow—inasmuch as this is the dimension that casts the shadow—
sixty times 80,000 stades (the earth's diameter) gives the distance
of 4,800,000 stades from the earth to the sun's path,[18] the point we
said that the earth's shadow reaches.[19] [22] The earth, moreover, is
at the midpoint of the orbit in which the sun revolves, and so the
length of the earth's shadow is equal to half the diameter of the
sun's orbit; and if an equal distance is measured in the opposite
direction from the earth to the sun's orbit, we have the diameter
of the circle in which the sun moves. [23] Double 4,800,000 stades
and you get 9,600,000 stades, or the diameter of the sun's orbit, after
which it is an easy matter to find the circumference. [24] You must

[16] Macrobius offers no proof or authority for these startling statements. His estimate of the
distance of the sun's orbit as sixty earth-diameters happens to be approximately twice as great
as Ptolemy's estimate for the distance of the moon, and we know that Macrobius followed
the Platonists who believed that the sun's distance was twice as great as the moon's (see
below, II.iii.14). These calculations are obviously not original with Macrobius. His authority, whoever he was, may have arrived at his estimate of the sun's distance in the
above manner.

One wonders why it did not occur to Macrobius (or his authority) that, if the earth's
shadow extended as far as the sun's orbit and the sun in its revolutions described a perfect circle about the earth, the sun's diameter would then be twice as great as the earth's.
Cleomedes II.78 uses this simple geometrical demonstration. Instead, Macrobius carries his
tedious calculations through the remainder of this chapter and gets a result that is far
from accurate when compared with the result he should have obtained by geometry.

[17] For a description of the method used by Eratosthenes for measuring the earth's circumference, see Appendix B.

[18] This figure is suspiciously close to the estimate of 4,080,000 stades attributed to
Eratosthenes, as given by Stobaeus 1.566; Aetius *Placita* II.xxxi.3 (Diels, pp. 362–63);
Joannes Lydus III.xii. Tannery and Heath reject this figure for Eratosthenes. See Heath,
Aristarchus, p. 340.

[19] Cf. Vincent of Beauvais *Speculum naturale* VI.xiii.

multiply the length of the diameter by 3⅐, as we have often stated, and thus you will find that the circumference of the circle in which the sun moves is roughly 30,170,000 stades.

[25] At this point we have obtained the measurements of the earth's diameter and circumference, and of the sun's orbit and the diameter of that orbit; now let us reveal the diameter of the sun and how the skillful Egyptians ascertained it. As it was possible to learn the measurement of the orbit in which the sun moves from the earth's shadow, so the dimensions of the sun have been found by means of that orbit in the following ingenious manner. [26] On the day of the equinox before sunrise place in an exactly level position a stone vessel that has been hollowed until its cavity forms a perfect hemisphere.[20] On the bottom there must be lines representing the twelve hours of the day which the shadow cast by a stylus will mark off as the sun passes along in the sky. [27] Moreover, we know that with a vessel of this kind, in the exact amount of time that it takes for the shadow to go from one lip of the vessel to the other, the sun will traverse half the sky, from rising to setting, the distance of one hemisphere. A complete circuit of the sky requires a day and a night, and so we may be sure that the shadow in the vessel advances in proportion to the space traversed by the sun. [28] Shortly before sunrise let the observer closely fix his eyes upon this bowl—be sure that it is in a perfectly level position—and then when the first ray of the sun, as its top just steals over the horizon, has cast a shadow of the top of the stylus upon the edge of the bowl, let him carefully mark the place where the shadow first fell. Then he must watch until the moment when the full orb comes into view so that the bottom seems to be just resting on the horizon. [29] Again he must mark the point which the shadow has reached in the bowl. The measurement between the two shadow marks, corresponding to the full orb or diameter of the sun, will be found to be a ninth part of the space in the bowl between the line marking sunrise and the line marking the first hour.

[30] Thus it becomes clear that nine times the sun's diameter is equal to the distance that the sun progresses in one hour at the time of the equinox. Twelve hours complete the sun's course through one hemisphere, and 12 times 9 is 108; so the sun's diameter must

[20] In Greek, *skaphe* or *polos*.

be equal to ⅟₁₀₈ of the equinoctial hemisphere, or ⅟₂₁₆ of the whole equinoctial orbit.[21] [31] We have proved that the sun's orbit is 30,-170,000 stades long, and therefore the sun's diameter will be ⅟₂₁₆ of this.[22] This will be found to be a little less than 140,000 stades; and this, you see, is almost twice the diameter of the earth.[23]

[32] Now geometry teaches us that when the diameter of one sphere is twice as great as the diameter of another sphere, the sphere with the larger diameter is really eight times as great as the other;[24] so we must agree that the sun is eight times greater than the earth.[25] This discussion of the sun's size is only a brief summary of the many things written on the subject.

CHAPTER XXI

[1] INASMUCH AS WE have pointed out that the seven spheres lie beneath the celestial sphere, with each outer sphere encircling the one beneath it, and since all of them are far removed from the celestial sphere and from one another, we must now inquire how it happens, although there is only one zodiac and it is set with its fixed stars in the celestial sphere, that the planets of the lower spheres are said to "pass through" the signs of the zodiac.[1]

The reason is not difficult to find, for it lies on the very threshold of our investigation. [2] The truth is that neither the sun nor moon nor any of the planets passes through the signs of the zodiac in such a way as to mingle with these constellations, but rather each

---

[21] The one responsible for this figure has made a surprisingly poor observation. For a comparison of Macrobius' figure with the estimates of Cleomedes, Aristarchus, Ptolemy, and Capella, see Appendix C.

[22] Cf. Honorius of Autun *De solis affectibus* xxxviii (Migne, *Pat. Lat.*, CLXXII, 112).

[23] Cleomedes II.82 describes a method quite similar to this for determining the sun's diameter, but his figures and result are much different.

[24] According to Euclid's theorem that two spheres are in the same proportion as the cubes of their diameters. See *Elementa* XII.xviii.

[25] Cf. Achilles *Isagoge in Arati Phaenomena* xx. After fairly careful calculations Macrobius concludes that 140,000 is almost double 80,000 and then takes the cube of 2 and gets 8. If he had taken the cube of 1¾ (140,000 : 80,000), he would have gotten 5.36 instead of 8. Nevertheless Macrobius' estimate of the sun's volume as 8 times as great as the earth's was widely adopted in the Middle Ages. See Helpericus of Auxerre *De computo* xx (Migne, *Pat. Lat.*, CXXXVII, 35); Honorius of Autun *De philosophia mundi* II.xxxii; *De solis affectibus* iii (Migne, *Pat. Lat.*, CLXXII, 74, 103).

[1] Sections 1–22 of this chapter are quoted in a gloss on Bede *De temporum ratione* xvi (Migne, *Pat. Lat.*, XC, 365–68).

of them is said to be in that sign which it has over its head, progressing into that region of its course which is directly beneath the
sign;[2] for just as in the case of the zodiac, each of the seven spheres
has been divided into twelve parts, and a planet which has reached
that region in its own sphere which is beneath the region allocated
to Aries is spoken of as having come into Aries itself, the same
being true for planets passing into any of the twelve sectors.

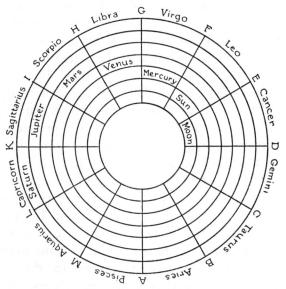

[3] Since our eyes often open the way to the understanding of
a problem, it would be well to draw a diagram. Let a circle marked
A represent the zodiac; within it draw seven concentric circles.
Divide the outer circle into twelve parts, assigning in sequence the
letters A to M to the divisions. Allot the space between A and B to
Aries, between B and C to Taurus, between C and D to Gemini,
the next to Cancer, and so on around the circle. [4] Next, draw
lines from each division on the outer circle towards the center,
passing through the circles and extending to the innermost one;
of course these intersecting lines will divide each circle into twelve
parts.

When the sun or moon or any planet has advanced in its sphere

[2] Cf. Chalcidius lxxiv; Helpericus of Auxerre *De computo* iii (Migne, *Pat. Lat.*, CXXXVII,
26); Vincent of Beauvais *Speculum naturale* III.xix.

to an area that is bounded by the lines originating in the marks at A and B, it will be said to be "in" Aries because in that position it will have directly over it the space marked out on the zodiac as belonging to Aries, as we explained above. Likewise, into whatever sector the planet passes it will be said to be in the sign that is above it.

[5] In addition, this diagram will show us with equal facility why some planets course through the same zodiac and the same constellations in a longer period of time and others in a shorter period. Whenever many concentric circles are placed one within another, the outermost one is the greatest and the innermost the smallest, and likewise the one nearest the outermost circle is greater than those beneath it, and the one next to the innermost circle is smaller than those above it. [6] The time required for each planet's revolution is determined, therefore, by its position among these seven spheres. The planets that course through the greater spaces complete their circuits in longer periods of time, those in the shorter spaces in less time. It is a fact that no planet moves more swiftly or more slowly than the others; since they all move at the same rate of speed, the difference in the distance traversed is alone responsible for the difference in time consumed.[3] [7] For example, omitting the intermediate planets to avoid repetition, Saturn in thirty years passes through the same signs that the moon traverses in twenty-eight days. The only explanation for this difference is the difference in distances covered by their spheres, one being the greatest and the other the smallest; thus the time consumed in each planet's revolution is in proportion to the amount of space traversed.

[8] At this point the diligent inquirer will find something that needs explaining. After noting the marks on the zodiac that were used to assist in the demonstration, he will say: "Who ever discovered or established twelve divisions of the sky when there are no demarcations for any of them apparent to our eyes?" To this reasonable question let history provide the answer, recalling the

[3] Cf. Vitruvius ix.15; Chalcidius cxv; Martianus Capella viii.861. Taylor (p. 173) asks how this statement is to be reconciled with a previous one (i.xix.4) that the sun, Mercury, and Venus all have the same period although the radii of their orbits are different. In the sentence that follows, above, Macrobius gives as his reason for omitting the intermediate planets the desire "to avoid repetition." It is more likely that he is trying to dodge just that contradiction.

occasion when the ancients attempted and accomplished a task so difficult.

[9] The early Egyptians,[4] acknowledged to be the first men who dared to search and measure the sky, being favored by continually clear skies and an unobstructed view of the heavens, discovered that all the stars and constellations were fixed in the sky and that only five planets and the sun and moon roamed. [10] They noticed that these did not wander freely into all regions of the heavens and without laws controlling their courses; that they never strayed to the north polar region, nor plunged into the depths of the south polar region, but kept all their motions within the limits of a path running diagonally;[5] that they did not go forth and return at the same time but that different ones reached a certain region at different times; and again that some of them were drawing near and others were turning away, and that sometimes they seemed to come to a halt. [11] After they saw these things taking place among the planets, they determined to lay off definite divisions on that diagonal path and to note the demarcations carefully in order to give names to the regions and thus be able to declare to each other in which region the planets were, which they had left, and which they were about to enter, and be able to hand down their knowledge to posterity.[6] [12] So they constructed two copper vessels, one of which had a pierced bottom like that of a clepsydra. This, filled with water, but with the hole closed, they placed above the other empty vessel, and then waited for a brilliant and conspicuous fixed star to rise. [13] At the moment that it began to rise above the horizon they removed the obstruction and allowed the water to flow from the upper to the lower vessel. It continued to flow through the night and the following day and the next night until that same star returned again to the horizon. [14] As soon as it reappeared the water in the lower vessel was taken away.

[4] This time Macrobius is not alone in attributing a discovery to the Egyptians. Cleomedes II.75 also gives them credit for devising the apparatus here described.

[5] The zodiac is an imaginary belt on the celestial sphere, about 18 degrees in width, through the middle of which runs the ecliptic, the sun's apparent annual path. The inclination of the ecliptic to the celestial equator is 23½ degress. The ancients believed that the sun, moon, and planets all kept their courses within the zodiac. Actually Venus, Pluto, and some of the asteroids are occasionally found outside.

[6] Cf. Helpericus of Auxerre De computo ii (Migne, Pat. Lat., CXXXVII, 23).

Now since the coming and return of a star under observation indicate a complete revolution of the sky, they determined the measurement of the sky by the amount of water poured into the vessel. [15] Next, they divided the water into twelve exactly equal parts and procured two more vessels, each with a capacity that would contain one of the twelve parts of water. Then all the water was poured back into its original container, with the hole closed, and one of the two smaller vessels was placed beneath and the other kept near by, ready for use. [16] After these preparations on another night, they looked into that portion of the sky which years of observation had taught them was the path of the sun, moon, and the five planets, and which they later named the zodiac, and they observed a constellation ascending, which they later called Aries. [17] When it first began to rise they let the water flow from the upper into the lower vessel. When the latter became full, they removed and emptied it, putting the other vessel like it in its place, and at the same moment they made accurate notation of certain configurations among the fixed stars in the area that was just appearing on the horizon. They knew that in the interval in which a twelfth part of all the water had flowed through, a twelfth part of the sky had risen. [18] From the point on the horizon that was marked when water commenced to pour into the first vessel to the point that was marked when that same vessel was filled, a twelfth part of the sky had been measured off, which they spoke of as one sign. [19] Similarly, the second vessel was filled and withdrawn and the first one, previously emptied, was put in its place; and again careful notation was made of the point on the horizon at the moment that the second vessel became full. The area between the end of the first sign and the point on the horizon when the second vessel became full was marked off as the second sign. [20] Thus, by changing the vessels and by recording the demarcations of the areas of the sky as they ascended with each part of water, they found that when all twelve parts of the water ran through they were back at the beginning of the first sign, and that with the aid of this apparatus they clearly had the twelve regions of the sky divided and identified by demarcations.[7]

[7] Cf. Martianus Capella viii. 860; Honorius of Autun De philosophia mundi ii.xi (Migne, Pat. Lat., CLXXII, 60); Vincent of Beauvais Speculum naturale iii.xix.

[21] This performance required not one night but two, since a complete revolution of the sky occurs not in a night, but half of it in the day and the other half at night. Moreover, the division of the zodiac was not completed by observations on successive nights, but by measuring the sky on nights that were six months apart they were able to mark off both hemispheres according to the equal parts of water. [22] They preferred to call these twelve divisions signs, and to distinguish them one from another, they gave each a name; and because the Greek word for the signs is *zodia*, they called the belt of the signs the zodiac, the sign-bearer, as it were.[8]

[23] Furthermore, they divulged the following reason for wishing Aries to be called the first, although there is nothing first or last in a sphere. According to them, at the beginning of that day which was the first of all days—that is, the time when the sky and the universe took on their brilliant sheen, the day which is rightly called the birthday of the universe—Aries was in the middle of the sky; and because the middle of the sky is the summit of the universe, Aries was considered the first of the signs, since at the first dawn of light it appeared to be the head of the world.[9]

[24] They also offer the reason that these twelve signs are assigned to the influence of different divinities. They say that when the world was being born, at the very hour of birth, Aries, as mentioned above, occupied the middle of the sky and the moon was in Cancer. The sun then rose in Leo, Mercury in Virgo, Venus in Libra, Mars in Scorpio, Jupiter in Sagittarius, and Saturn in Capricorn.[10] [25] Thus it came about that each of the planets was considered lord of the sign in which it was believed to have been when the world was born. The ancients assigned only one sign to the sun and one to the moon, those in which they were at the beginning, Cancer to the moon and Leo to the sun; but to the other five planets five more signs were allotted in addition to those in which they were stationed at the beginning, the second apportionment being resumed where the first left off. [26] The last planet mentioned above was Saturn in Capricorn. In the second apportionment the

[8] Cf. gloss on Bede *De natura rerum* xvi (Migne, *Pat. Lat.*, XC, 231).

[9] Cf. Firmicus Maternus *Matheseos libri* iii.i.17–18; Proclus (Diehl) 30A; Vincent of Beauvais *Speculum naturale* ii.xxx. See Taylor, pp. 219–20.

[10] Cf. Porphyry *De antro nympharum* xxii; pseudo-Bede *Mundi constitutio* (Migne, *Pat. Lat.*, XC, 892–93).

order was reversed and thus Aquarius, following Capricorn, was allotted to Saturn, Pisces to Jupiter, Aries to Mars, Taurus to Venus, and Gemini to Mercury.[11] Attention must here be drawn to the fact that Providence itself or the cleverness of the ancients assigned to the planets the same order at the birth of the world that Plato assigned to their spheres: the moon first, the sun second, Mercury next, Venus fourth, then Mars, Jupiter, and Saturn. But the Platonic order was well supported by a reason already stated,[12] without reliance upon this last one.

[28] Of the questions which arose from the recently quoted words of Cicero, and which we proposed to investigate, I believe we have already answered, as briefly as was possible, all those which were concerned with the outermost sphere or *aplanes* and the region as far as the moon, the lowest limit of the divine. [29] We have shown that the celestial sphere revolves and why it does so; we have plainly demonstrated that the seven spheres undoubtedly move in the opposite direction; and we have discussed the differences of opinion about the order of the spheres, what caused them, and which opinion is the more reliable. [30] We explained why the moon was the only one of the planets dependent upon another for light; and how the distances involved compelled those who placed the sun in the fourth position to say that it was not exactly in the middle but almost so. [31] That the names applied to the sun had significance and were not merely meant to glorify it, was also made clear. We revealed the dimensions of the sun, of its orbit, and of the earth, and how they were determined. [32] We explained why the planets of the lower spheres were said to pass through the zodiac, which is above all of them, and why some planets take longer than others to complete their circuits. How the zodiac was divided into twelve parts, why Aries is considered the first, and how the influence of different divinities is ascribed to the planets, was also explained.

[33] Now all things that lie between the topmost border and the moon are holy, imperishable, and divine because they always have in them the same ether and are never subject to the vacillations of change. Below the moon, air and the realm of change begin together,

[11] Cf. Porphyry *De antro nympharum* xxii.
[12] I.xix.7–9.

and the moon, being the boundary of ether and air, is also the demarcation between the divine and the mortal.[13] [34] When Cicero said, *Below the moon nothing is divine, with the exception of the souls bestowed upon the human race by the benevolence of the gods,* he did not mean that because souls were here they were born here, but rather that, just as we say that the sun is on earth, whose rays descend to us and leave us, so is the origin of souls heavenly;[14] they are merely exiled to earth, sojourning here for a time. The region below possesses nothing divine but only receives it; for it receives it and sends it back, whereas it would only be said to possess it if it had been permitted to keep it always. [35] Is it at all surprising if the soul does not come from this region which is unable by itself to create a living body? Below the moon are earth, water, and air; but a body capable of living cannot be made from these alone; it requires the aid of heavenly fire to enable the terrestrial limbs to sustain life and breath, and to instill and keep vital heat. [36] These remarks will suffice in regard to air; we must yet discuss the necessary questions about the earth, the ninth and last sphere of the universe.

CHAPTER XXII

[1] *NOW IN THE CENTER, the ninth of the spheres, is the earth,* he says, *never moving and at the bottom. Towards it all bodies gravitate by their own inclination.* [2] Those reasons are truly incontrovertible which are mutually confirmed, the one substantiating the other and each arising from the other, never abandoning each other's support. With such bonds nature has held the earth fast: all things tend towards it since, being the middle, it does not move; again, it does not move because it is at the bottom; finally, it must be at the bottom since all things tend towards it.

Let us take up these statements, each inextricably and inevitably bound up with the other. [3] He says that the earth does not move. Indeed, it is the center and, as we have pointed out, the center is the only stationary portion of a sphere, since there must be something immovable around which the sphere rotates.[1] [4] He adds that

[13] Cf. above, I.xi.6, and note; Plotinus II.i.2.
[14] Cf. Plotinus IV.viii.4.
[15] Cf. Theo Smyrnaeus 149, 188; Chalcidius lxxvi.

it is at the bottom. This is also correct, for that which is the center is in the middle, and in a sphere only that which is in the middle can be at the bottom.[2] Now if the earth is at the bottom, it follows that all things must gravitate towards it. Nature always draws weights towards the bottom; obviously this was done that there might be an earth in the universe.[3]

[5] Of all the matter that went into the creation of the universe, that which was purest and clearest took the highest position and was called ether; the part that was less pure and had some slight weight became air and held second place; next came that part which was indeed still clear but which the sense of touch demonstrates to be corporeal, that which formed the bodies of water; [6] lastly, as a result of the downward rush of matter, there was that vast, impenetrable solid, the dregs and off-scourings of the purified elements, which had settled to the bottom, plunged in continual and oppressing chill, relegated to the last position in the universe, far from the sun.[4] Because this became so hardened it received the name *terra*.[5] [7] Compact air, closer to the chill of the earth than to the heat of the sun, supports the earth on all sides and keeps it in its place by its very density. The power of this belt of atmosphere, supporting on every side with equal force, or perhaps the spherical nature of the sky itself, keeps the earth from moving in one direction or another.[6] If it should deviate from the midpoint it would move nearer to the surface and leave the bottom since only the midpoint is equidistant from any point on the surface of a sphere. [8] To this point which is the bottom and middle, so to speak, and is stationary because it is the center, all weights must be drawn since the earth itself, like a weight, has fallen to this place.

We might cite countless arguments as proof, but particularly convincing is that of the rains that fall upon the earth from every region of the atmosphere.[7] Not only do they fall upon this portion of the earth that we inhabit, but on the slopes that give the earth

[2] Cf. Theo Smyrnaeus 120, 128; Martianus Capella VI.599–600.

[3] Cf. Adelard *Quaestiones naturales* xlviii.

[4] Cf. Theo Smyrnaeus 149–50.

[5] Varro V.21 derives *terra*, "earth," from *terere*, "to tread upon." Cf. pseudo-Bede *Mundi constitutio* (Migne, *Pat. Lat.*, XC, 888); Isidore of Seville XIV.i.1.

[6] Cf. Parmenides and Democritus, cited by Aetius *Placita* III.xv.7 (Diels, p. 380); Plato *Phaedo* 108E–109A; Aristotle *De caelo* II.xiii.295B; Martianus Capella VI.599.

[7] Cf. Martianus Capella VI.600.

its sphericity; and, what is more, there is the same sort of rainfall in the region that we consider the underside. [9] If air is condensed by the chill of the earth and forms a cloud which sends down a shower,[8] and if, moreover, air surrounds the whole of the earth, then, assuredly, rain falls from all regions of the air except in those places parched by constant heat.[9] From all quarters it drops upon the earth, which is the only resting place for objects possessing weight. [10] Anyone who rejects this theory will be forced to admit that any precipitation of snow, rain, or hail falling outside the

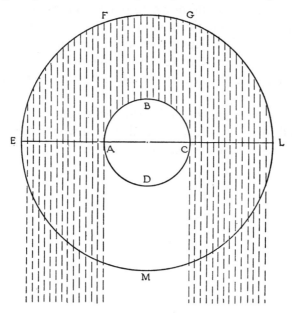

region inhabited by us would continue on down from the air into the celestial sphere. The sky is of course equidistant from the earth in every direction and is as far beyond the sloping regions and that portion which we regard the underside as it is beyond us. If all weights were not drawn to the earth, therefore, the rain that falls beyond the sides of the earth would not fall upon the earth but upon the celestial sphere, an assumption too ridiculous to consider.

[11] Let a circle represent the earth; upon it inscribe the letters

[8] Cf. Lucretius *De rerum natura* VI.495–526; Plutarch *Stromateis* xi; *De placitis philosophorum* iii.4; Stobaeus I.664.

[9] Cf. below, II.vii.19.

ABCD. About this draw another circle with the letters EFGLM inscribed, representing the belt of the atmosphere. Divide both circles by drawing a line from E to L. The upper section will be the one we inhabit, the lower the one beneath us. [12] If it were not true that all weights are drawn towards the earth, then the earth would receive a very small portion of the rainfall, that which falls from A to C. The atmosphere between F and E and G and L would send its moisture into the air and sky. Furthermore, the rain from the lower half of the celestial sphere would have to continue on into the outer regions, unknown to our world, as we see from the diagram. [13] To refute this notion would not befit a sober treatise; it is so absurd that it collapses without discussion.

In conclusion, we may therefore say that we have clearly proved that all weights are drawn to the earth by their own inclination. The statements made in substantiation of this will aid us when we discuss the passage in which Cicero speaks of the antipodes.[10] It will be well to stop at this point and reserve what is left for discussion in the second book of our commentary.

[10] II.v.

Book Two

CHAPTER I

[1] IN THE FIRST BOOK of our commentary, Eustachius, my son dearer to me than life itself, our discussion progressed as far as the motions of the starry sphere and the seven underlying spheres. At this point let us take up their musical harmonies.

[2] *"What is this great and pleasing sound that fills my ears?" I asked. "That," replied my grandfather, "is a concord of tones separated by unequal but nevertheless carefully proportioned intervals, caused by the rapid motion of the spheres themselves. The high and low tones blended together produce different harmonies. Of course such swift motions could not be accomplished in silence, and, as nature requires, the spheres at one extreme produce the low tones and at the other extreme the high tones. [3] Consequently the outermost sphere, the star-bearer, with its swifter motion gives forth a higher-pitched tone, whereas the lunar sphere, the lowest, has the deepest tone. Of course the earth, the ninth and stationary sphere, always keeps the same position in the middle of the universe. The other eight spheres, two of which move at the same speed, produce seven different tones, this number being, one might almost say, the key to the universe. Gifted men, imitating this harmony on stringed instruments and in singing, have gained for themselves a return to this region."*

[4] Since we have explained the order of the spheres and have pointed out how the seven underlying spheres rotate in the opposite direction to the celestial sphere's motion, it is fitting for us next to investigate the sounds produced by the onrush of such vast bodies. [5] From the very rotation of the spheres sound must come forth because air, when lashed, at the very instant of the blow sends forth from itself the force of the contact, as is natural; thus a violent crashing of two bodies ends in a noise.[1] But a sound produced by

[1] Cf. Aristotle *De anima* ii.viii.419B; pseudo-Plutarch *De musica* ii.1131D.

any lashing of air comes to the ears as something either sweet and melodious or dissonant and harsh. [6] An agreeable concord results when the percussion is in keeping with certain numerical relations, but a grating discord results from a random blow, lacking proportionate intervals.[2] [7] Now it is well known that in the heavens nothing happens by chance or at random, and that all things above proceed in orderly fashion according to divine law. Therefore it is unquestionably right to assume that harmonious sounds come forth from the rotation of the heavenly spheres, for sound has to come from motion, and Reason, which is present in the divine, is responsible for the sounds being melodious.[3]

[8] Pythagoras was the first of all Greeks to lay hold of this truth.[4] He realized that the sounds coming forth from the spheres were regulated by divine Reason, which is always present in the sky, but he had difficulty in determining the underlying cause and in finding ways by which he might discover it. When he was weary of his long investigation of a problem so fundamental and yet so recondite, a chance occurrence presented him with what his deep thinking had overlooked.

[9] He happened to pass the open shop of some blacksmiths who were beating a hot iron with hammers. The sound of the hammers striking in alternate and regular succession fell upon his ears with the higher note so attuned to the lower that each time the same musical interval returned, and always striking a concord. [10] Here Pythagoras, seeing that his opportunity had been presented to him, ascertained with his eyes and hands what he had been searching for in his mind. He approached the smiths and stood over their work, carefully heeding the sounds that came forth from the blows of each. Thinking that the difference might be ascribed to the strength of the smiths he requested them to change hammers. Hereupon the difference in tones did not stay with the men but followed the hammers.[5] [11] Then he turned his whole attention

[2] Cf. pseudo-Euclid *Sectio canonis* Introd.; Theo Smyrnaeus 50.

[3] Cf. Plato *Timaeus* 36D; Aristotle *De caelo* ii.ix.290B; pseudo-Plutarch *De musica* xliv.1147.

[4] Cf. Pliny ii.84; Chalcidius lxxiii; Simplicius *In Aristotelis De caelo commentaria*, ed. by Heiberg, p. 463; Favonius 18; Censorinus xiii.3–5; Johannes Scottus xi.8.

[5] This quaint expression is also used in Boethius *De institutione musica* i.10: Sed sonorum proprietas non in hominum lacertis haerebat, sed mutatos malleos comitabatur.

to the study of their weights, and when he had recorded the difference in the weight of each, he had other hammers heavier or lighter than these made. Blows from these produced sounds that were not at all like those of the original hammers, and besides they did not harmonize. [12] He then concluded that harmony of tones was produced according to a proportion of the weights, and made a record of all the numerical relations of the various weights producing harmony.

Next he directed his investigation from hammers to stringed instruments, and stretched intestines of sheep or sinews of oxen by attaching to them weights of the same proportions as those determined by the hammers. Again the concord came forth which had been assured by his earlier well-conceived experiment, but with a sweeter tone, as we might expect from the nature of the instruments.[6] [13] After discovering this great secret, Pythagoras chose the numbers from which consonant chords might be produced so that when stringed instruments had been adjusted with regard to these numbers, certain ones might be pitched to the tonics and others to other consonant notes, numerically harmonious; then when one was struck with a plectrum another, though set off at a distance,

---

[6] Modern scholars also credit Pythagoras with the discovery of the numerical ratios of the fundamental musical concords. See J. Burnet, *Greek Philosophy* (London, 1914), Pt. I, p. 45; Heath, *Gr. Math.*, I, 85; D'Ooge, p. 18. Heath calls it "probably Pythagoras' greatest discovery" in *The Legacy of Greece*, ed. by R. W. Livingstone (Oxford, 1921), p. 109.

Nevertheless the ancient account of the way he chanced upon his discovery, reported by a dozen or more classical authors, has to be rejected because it is physically impossible. Nicomachus *Manuale harmonicum* vi (*Musici scriptores graeci*, ed. by C. von Jan, pp. 245–48) tells essentially the same story with a little greater detail and gives the ratios of the weights used in stretching the strings. According to Nicomachus' report, weights of twelve and six units produced the octave, of twelve and eight or nine and six units gave the fifth, of twelve and nine or eight and six the fourth, and weights of nine and eight units gave the tone. But the vibrations of the strings are not proportional to the number of units of weight but to the square root of these units. Assuming that the linear density of two similar strings of equal length remains constant, one weight (or the tension) would have to be four times as great as the other to produce the octave.

That the account is fabricated, and that it is not simply a matter of discrepancy arising from incorrect numerical values for the weights, is shown by a repetition of the experiment. If one beats a piece of iron upon an anvil with hammers of different weights, there is little if any difference in the pitch of the sounds. When a one-pound hammer and a two-pound hammer were used, it was not possible, if one turned his back, to tell which hammer was striking the metal. For other ancient accounts, see Iamblichus *De vita Pythagorica* xxvi.115–21; *In Nicomachi Arithmeticam introductionem liber*, ed. by Pistelli, pp. 121–22; Gaudentius *Harmonica introductio* xi; Boethius *De institutione musica* i.10. Cf. Theo Smyrnaeus 56; Censorinus x; Chalcidius xlv; Adelard 27.

yet numerically attuned, might sound forth at the same time. [14]
Of the infinite store of numerical combinations those that would
unite to produce harmony were found to be few and simple. They
are six: sesquitertian, sesquialter, double, triple, quadruple, and
superoctave.[7]

[15] The sesquitertian is the combination formed by an integer
and a number one third greater than it, as four is to three. This
numerical relation produces the musical interval known as the
fourth, or *dia tessaron*. [16] The sesquialter is the combination
formed by an integer and a number one half greater than it, as three
is to two, a numerical relation resulting in the interval known as
the fifth, or *dia pente*. [17] The double proportion is formed by an
integer and a number twice as great, as four is to two, resulting in
the interval known as the octave, or *dia pason*. [18] The triple
proportion is formed by an integer and a number thrice as great,
as three is to one, and produces the interval known as the octave
and fifth, or *dia pason ḳai dia pente*. [19] The quadruple proportion
is formed by an integer and a number four times as great, as four
is to one, and produces the interval known as the double octave, or
dis dia pason. [20] The superoctave proportion is formed by an
integer and a number one eighth greater than it, as nine is to eight.
This last proportion produces the interval known to musicians as
the tone, or *tonos*.[8]

[21] The ancients chose to call the interval smaller than a tone
a semitone, but this must not be taken to mean half a tone any more
than we would call an intermediate vowel sound a semivowel. [22]
The tone by its very nature cannot be divided equally: inasmuch as
it originates in the number nine, which cannot be equally divided,
the tone refuses to be divided into two halves;[9] they have merely
called an interval smaller than a full tone a semitone, but it has

---

[7] Cf. Nicomachus ii.xxvi; Theo Smyrnaeus 56–58.

[8] On the numerical ratios of the concords, cf. Aristoxenus *Elementa harmonica* ii.45–46;
Nicomachus *Manuale harmonicum* vi; pseudo-Plutarch *De musica* xxiii.1139C–F; Ptolemy
Harmonica i.v; Chalcidius xlv; Proclus (Diehl) 191D; Boethius *De institutione musica*
i.7; Cassiodorus *De artibus ac disciplinis liberalium litterarum* v (Migne, *Pat. Lat.*, LXX,
1209–10). See J. F. Mountford, "The Harmonics of Ptolemy," *Transact. of the Amer.
Philol. Assoc.*, LVII (1926), 71–72; P. R. Coleman-Norton, "Cicero and the Music of
the Spheres," *Classical Journal*, XLV (1950), 237–41.

[9] Because the ratio 9:8 has no rational square root, there cannot be a mathematically
exact semitone. Cf. pseudo-Euclid *Sectio canonis* xvi; Theo Smyrnaeus 70; Chalcidius l.

been discovered that there is as little difference between it and a full tone as the difference between the numbers 256 and 243.[10] [23] The early Pythagoreans called this semitone *diesis*,[11] but those who came later decided to use the word *diesis* for the interval smaller than the semitone.[12] Plato called the semitone *leimma*.[13]

[24] And so the consonant chords are five in number, the fourth, the fifth, the octave, the octave and fifth, and the double octave. This number of consonant chords has to do only with the music that the human breath can produce or the human ear can catch; beyond this there is still the range of celestial harmony, which reaches even four times the octave and fifth.[14]

Now there is more to be said about the five we have named. [25] The interval of the fourth consists of two tones and a half-tone if, to avoid confusion, we omit to mention a slight addition, and comes from the sesquitertian; the fifth consists of three tones and a half-tone, and comes from the sesquialter; the octave consists of six tones, and comes from the double; the octave and fifth consists of nine tones and a half-tone, and comes from the triple; and the double octave contains twelve tones, and comes from the quadruple.[15]

CHAPTER II

[1] NOW WHEN PLATO, guided by Pythagoras' revelation and drawing upon the godlike power of his own extraordinary genius, had recognized that no union could be lasting except one based on those numbers, he constructed his World-Soul by interweaving them,

---

[10] Cf. Theo Smyrnaeus 67; Gaudentius *Harmonica introductio* xiii; Chalcidius i; Proclus (Diehl) 195B.

[11] Cf. Theo Smyrnaeus 55; Chalcidius xlv; Proclus (Diehl) 191E.

[12] Cf. Aristoxenus *Elementa harmonica* ii.46.

[13] Cf. Theo Smyrnaeus 67.

[14] Because twenty-seven was the largest number in the construction of the World-Soul (see above, i.vi.46, and note), and because, according to his statement in the next paragraph, there would be four octaves and a fifth in twenty-seven and a half tones. See Proclus (Diehl) 192C, 203D.

[15] Aristoxenus regarded musical intervals spatially, as linear measurements, and supposed that a tone was exactly divisible into half and quarter tones. For him the octave consisted of six tones, the fifth three tones and a half, and the fourth two tones and a half. But the mathematicians who came later realized that the octave was less than the sum of six whole tones and that a tone could not be divided equally. See R. P. Winnington-Ingram, "Aristoxenus and the Intervals of Greek Music," *The Classical Quarterly*, XXVI (1932), 195.

imitating the ineffable wisdom of the divine Creator. If we digress here in order to explain how the World-Soul was constructed, it will be a great help in understanding Cicero's words, which seem so obscure, on the subject of music. [2] But in order that what is offered in explanation of something else may not itself be considered puzzling, a few statements must be made to simplify the understanding of both at the same time.

[3] All solids have three dimensions, length, breadth, and thickness; there can be no fourth in any body, but these three confine every solid body.[1] [4] Geometricians propose other bodies for their own use which they call mathematical bodies, in the realm of thought and not of the senses.[2] They say that a point is an indivisible body, which lacks length, breadth, and thickness since it cannot be divided. [5] The extension of it produces a line, which is a body of one dimension: it is long without being broad or thick, and is bounded by two points at either extremity, which confine only length. [6] If a second line is drawn, another mathematical body will result, thought of as two-dimensional, having length and breadth but lacking thickness; this they call a surface. It is bounded by four points, two for each line. [7] If these two lines are duplicated and two others put directly over them, thickness is added, and hence a solid body is formed, which of course is bounded by eight points, as we see in the case of the die, which the Greeks call *kubos*.[3]

[8] To these geometrical steps numbers are applied. The monad represents the point because, like the point, which is not a body but which produces bodies from itself, the monad is said to be not a number but the source of numbers.[4] [9] The first number, therefore, is two, which is like the line protracted from the point by giving it two termini. The number two doubled gives four, representing the mathematical body which is limited by four points, having length and breadth. [10] Four doubled gives eight, the number representing a solid body, to repeat what was previously stated, that two lines placed above two others and limited by eight points produced the solid body; this explains why geometricians

---

[1] Cf. above, i.v.9.
[2] Cf. above, i.v.7.
[3] Cf. above, i.v.11.
[4] Cf. above, i.vi.7.

speak of two times two times two as a solid body. [11] Thus with even numbers progression up to eight represents a solid body, and on this account Cicero attributed fullness to this number in particular.[5]

We must now examine the uneven numbers to see how the same thing is accomplished with them. [12] Since the monad is the source of even and uneven numbers alike, the number three should be considered the first line. This tripled gives nine, which from its two lines, as it were, produces a body with length and breadth, as was the case with the number four, the second of the even numbers. In the same way the number nine tripled supplies the third dimension. Thus with the uneven numbers a solid body is formed in twenty-seven, three times three times three, just as with even numbers eight or two times two times two made a solid body. [13] In either case the monad is necessary to produce a solid body, in addition to the other six numbers, three even and three uneven, two, four, and eight being the even numbers and three, nine, and twenty-seven the uneven.[6]

[14] Plato's Timaeus, in disclosing the divine plan in the creation of the World-Soul, said that the Soul was interwoven with those numbers, odd or even, which produce the cube or solid,[7] not meaning by this that the Soul was at all corporeal; rather, in order to be able to penetrate the whole world with its animating power and fill the solid body of the universe,[8] the Soul was constructed from the numbers denoting solidity.

[15] At this point we may well examine Plato's words. When speaking of God's construction of the World-Soul he said: "First he took one portion from the whole mixture, then a second portion double the first, then a third portion one and one-half times as great as the second and three times as great as the first, then a fourth portion double the second, then a fifth three times as great as the third, then a sixth eight times as great as the first, and a seventh twenty-seven times as great as the first. After that he filled up the intervals between the numbers of both series by inserting further

---

[5] Cf. above, i.v.18.
[6] Cf. above, i.vi.3, and note.
[7] Cf. *Timaeus* 32B.
[8] That is, having length, breadth, and thickness.

portions so that there might be two means in each interval. From these means came the sesquialter, the sesquitertian, and the super-octave." [9]

[16] Plato's words have been so interpreted by some that they regard the first portion as the monad, the second portion, which I said was twice as great as the first, as the number two, the third portion as the number three, which is one and one-half times greater than the second and three times as great as the first, the fourth as the number four, which is twice as great as the second, that is two, the fifth portion as nine, which is three times as great as the third, that is three, the sixth as eight, which is eight times as great as the first, and the seventh portion as twenty-seven, which is, as I have explained, the third increase among uneven numbers. [17] The fabrication of the World-Soul, as we may easily see, proceeded alternately: after the monad, which is both even and uneven, an even number was introduced, namely, two; then followed the first uneven number, three; fourth in order came the second even number, four; in the fifth place came the second uneven number, nine; in the sixth place the third even number, eight; and in the seventh place the third uneven number, twenty-seven. [10]

Since the uneven numbers are considered masculine and the even feminine, God willed that the Soul which was to give birth to the universe should be born from the even and uneven, that is from the male and female; [11] and that, since the Soul was destined to penetrate the solid universe, it should attain to those numbers representing solidity in either series. [12]

[18] And then the Soul had to be a combination of those numbers that alone possess mutual attraction since the Soul itself was to instill harmonious agreement in the whole world. Now two is double one and, as we have already explained, the octave arises from the double; three is one and one-half times greater than two, and this combination produces the fifth; four is one and one-third times greater than three, and this combination produces the fourth; four is also four times as great as one, and from the quadruple ratio the double

[9] *Timaeus* 35B–36A.
[10] See above, I.vi.46, and note.
[11] Cf. above, I.vi.1–2.
[12] Cf. Theo Smyrnaeus 65; Chalcidius xxxiii; Proclus (Diehl) 192B.

octave arises. [19] Thus the World-Soul, which stirred the body of the universe to the motion that we now witness, must have been interwoven with those numbers which produce musical harmony in order to make harmonious the sounds which it instilled by its quickening impulse. It discovered the source of these sounds in the fabric of its own composition.[13]

[20] Plato reports, as we have previously stated, that the divine Creator of the Soul, after weaving it from unequal numbers, filled the intervals between them with sesquialters, sesquitertians, superoctaves, and semitones. [21] In the following passage Cicero shows very skillfully the profundity of Plato's doctrine: *"What is this great and pleasing sound that fills my ears?" "That is a concord of tones separated by unequal but nevertheless carefully proportioned intervals, caused by the rapid motion of the spheres themselves."* [22] You see here how he makes mention of the intervals and states that they are unequal and affirms that they are separated proportionately; for in Plato's *Timaeus*[14] the intervals of the unequal numbers are interspersed with numbers proportional to them, that is, sesquialters, sesquitertians, superoctaves, and half-tones, in which all harmony is embraced.

[23] Hence we clearly see that these words of Cicero's would never have been comprehensible if we had not included a discussion of the sesquialters, sesquitertians, and superoctaves inserted in the intervals, and of the numbers with which Plato constructed the World-Soul, together with the reason why the Soul was interwoven with numbers producing harmony. [24] In so doing we have not only explained the revolutions in the heavens, for which the Soul alone is responsible; we have also shown that the sounds which arose from these had to be harmonious, for they were innate in the Soul which impelled the universe to motion.

CHAPTER III

[1] IN A DISCUSSION in the *Republic* about the whirling motion of the heavenly spheres, Plato[1] says that a Siren sits upon each of

---

[13] Cf. Porphyry, cited by Proclus (Diehl) 205E.
[14] 36A–B.
[15] x.617B.

the spheres, thus indicating that by the motions of the spheres divinities were provided with song; for a singing Siren is equivalent to a
god in the Greek acceptance of the word.[2] Moreover, cosmogonists
have chosen to consider the nine Muses as the tuneful song of the
eight spheres and the one predominant harmony that comes from
all of them.[3] [2] In the *Theogony*,[4] Hesiod calls the eighth Muse
Urania because the eighth sphere, the star-bearer, situated above the
seven errant spheres, is correctly referred to as the sky;[5] and to show
that the ninth was the greatest, resulting from the harmony of all
sounds together, he added: "Calliope, too, who is preeminent among
all."[6] The very name shows that the ninth Muse was noted for the
sweetness of her voice, for Calliope means "best voice."[7] In order to
indicate more plainly that her song was the one coming from all the
others, he applied to her a word suggesting totality in calling her
"preeminent among all." [3] Then, too, they call Apollo, god of the
sun, the "leader of the Muses," as if to say that he is the leader and
chief of the other spheres,[8] just as Cicero, in referring to the sun,
called it *leader, chief, and regulator of the other planets, mind and
moderator of the universe*. [4] The Etruscans also recognize that the
Muses are the song of the universe, for their name for them is
Camenae, a form of *Canenae,* derived from the verb *canere*.[9]

That the priests acknowledged that the heavens sing is indicated
by their use of music at sacrificial ceremonies, some nations pre-
ferring the lyre or cithara, and some pipes or other musical instruments. [5] In the hymns to the gods, too, the verses of the strophe
and antistrophe used to be set to music, so that the strophe might
represent the forward motion of the celestial sphere and the antistrophe the reverse motion of the planetary spheres; these two motions produced nature's first hymn in honor of the Supreme God.[10]

---

[2] Cf. Proclus (Kroll), II, 236–39. See Mras, pp. 266–67.
[3] Cf. Theo Smyrnaeus 146–47; Plutarch *De procreatione animi in Timaeo* xxxii.1029C;
Porphyry *Vita Pythagorae* xxxi; Proclus (Diehl), 203E; Proclus (Kroll), II, 237–38.
[4] Line 78.
[5] The Greek *ourania* means "heavenly one."
[6] Line 79.
[7] From *kalos,* "beautiful," and *ops,* "voice." On the interpretation "best voice," cf. Plato
Phaedrus 259D.
[8] Cf. Proclus (Diehl) 203E; Macrobius *Saturnalia* i.xix.7.
[9] *Canere* in Latin meaning "to sing." This derivation is also found in Varro vii.27; Festus
De significatu verborum xliii.
[10] Cf. Censorinus xii.2.

[6] In funeral processions, too, the practices of diverse peoples have ordained that it was proper to have musical accompaniment, owing to the belief that souls after death return to the source of sweet music, that is, to the sky.[11]

[7] Every soul in this world is allured by musical sounds so that not only those who are more refined in their habits, but all the barbarous peoples as well, have adopted songs by which they are inflamed with courage or wooed to pleasure; for the soul carries with it into the body a memory of the music which it knew in the sky,[12] and is so captivated by its charm that there is no breast so cruel or savage as not to be gripped by the spell of such an appeal. [8] This, I believe, was the origin of the stories of Orpheus and Amphion, one of whom was said to have enticed the dumb beasts by his song, the other the rocks. They were perchance the first to attract in their song men lacking any refinement and stolid as rocks, and to instill in them a feeling of joy.[13] [9] Thus every disposition of the soul is controlled by song. For instance, the signal for marching into battle and for leaving off battle is in one case a tune that arouses the martial spirit and in the other one that quiets it.[14]

It gives or takes away sleep,[15]

it releases or recalls cares, it excites wrath and counsels mercy, it even heals the ills of the body, whence the statement that gifted men "sing out remedies" for the ailing.[16] [10] Is it at all strange if music has such power over men when birds like the nightingale and swan and others of that species practice song as if it were an art with them, when creatures of land, sea, and air willingly fall into nets under the spell of music, and when shepherd's pipes bring rest to the flocks in pasture?[17]

[11] We have just explained that the causes of harmony are traced to the World-Soul, having been interwoven in it; the World-Soul,

[11] Cf. Martianus Capella IX.925.
[12] Cf. Censorinus xii.3; Adelard 25. See above, I.xii.10, and note.
[13] Cf. Quintilian *Institutio oratoriae* I.x.9. See Lobeck, p. 235.
[14] Cf. Gellius I.xi.1–7; Athenaeus *Deipnosophistae* XIV.627D; Censorinus xii.3; Martianus Capella IX.925; Boethius *De institutione musica* I.1; Isidore of Seville III.xvi.2.
[15] Virgil *Aeneid* IV.244.
[16] Cf. Tibullus *Elegiae* I.v.12; Apuleius *Apologia* xl; Censorinus xii.4–5; Martianus Capella IX.926; Boethius *De institutione musica* I.1; Isidore of Seville III.xvi.3.
[17] Cf. Martianus Capella IX.927; Adelard 26.

moreover, provides all creatures with life: "Thence the race of man and beast, the life of winged things, and the strange shapes ocean bears beneath his glassy floor."[18] Consequently it is natural for everything that breathes to be captivated by music since the heavenly Soul that animates the universe sprang from music. [12] In quickening the spheres to motion it produces tones *separated by unequal but nevertheless carefully proportioned intervals,* in accordance with its primeval fabric.

Now we must ask ourselves whether these intervals, which in the incorporeal Soul are apprehended only in the mind and not by the senses, govern the distances between the planets poised in the corporeal universe. [13] Archimedes, indeed, believed that he had calculated in stades the distances between the earth's surface and the moon, between the moon and Mercury, Mercury and Venus, Venus and the sun, the sun and Mars, Mars and Jupiter, Jupiter and Saturn, and that he had also estimated the distance from Saturn's orbit to the celestial sphere.[19] [14] But Archimedes' figures were rejected by the Platonists for not keeping the intervals in the progressions of the numbers two and three. They decided that there could be but one opinion, that the distance from the earth to the sun was twice as great as from the earth to the moon, that the distance from the earth to Venus was thrice as great as from the earth to the sun, that the distance from the earth to Mercury was four times as great as from the earth to Venus, that the distance from the earth to Mars was nine times as great as the distance from the earth to Mercury, that the distance from the earth to Jupiter was eight times as great as from the earth to Mars, and that the distance from the earth to Saturn was twenty-seven times as great as from the earth to Jupiter.[20] [15] Porphyry includes this conviction of the Platonists in his books which

[18] Virgil *Aeneid* vi.728–29. Cf. above, i.xiv.14.

[19] See Duhem, II, 43.

[20] Cf. Plato *Timaeus* 36D; Chalcidius xcvi. On the two different interpretations of the *Timaeus* passage offered by Macrobius and Chalcidius, see Taylor, pp. 162–63; Heath, *Aristarchus*, p. 164. How is the above statement to be reconciled with an earlier one (i.xix.4) that Venus, Mercury, and the sun are so close together that their periods are approximately the same, and another (i.xxi.6) that all planets course at the same rate of speed and the difference in their orbits is alone responsible for the difference in their periods? A moment later (ii.iv.2) Macrobius states that the outer spheres revolve at high speeds but the lunar sphere at low speed. Obviously he is too busily engaged in commenting upon each Ciceronian passage as it comes up to be concerned with his gross inconsistencies.

pour light upon the obscurities of the *Timaeus;*[21] he says they believed that the intervals in the corporeal universe, which were filled with sesquitertians, sesquialters, superoctaves, half-tones, and a *leimma,* followed the pattern of the Soul's fabric, and that harmony was thus forthcoming, the proportional intervals of which were interwoven into the fabric of the Soul and were also injected into the corporeal universe which is quickened by the Soul.[22] [16] Hence Cicero's statement, that the heavenly harmony is a *concord of tones separated by unequal but nevertheless carefully proportioned intervals,* is in all respects wise and true.

CHAPTER IV

[1] AT THIS POINT we are reminded that we must discuss the differences between high and low notes of which Cicero speaks. *Nature requires that the spheres at one extreme produce the low tones and at the other extreme the high tones. Consequently the outermost sphere, the star-bearer, with its swifter motion gives forth a higher-pitched tone whereas the lunar sphere, the lowest, has the deepest tone.*

[2] We have stated that sound is produced only by the percussion of air. The blow regulates the pitch of the sound: a stout blow swiftly dealt produces a high note, a weak one lightly dealt produces a low note. [3] For example, if one lashes the air with a staff, a swift movement produces a high note, a slower movement a lower tone.[1] We see the same phenomenon in the case of the lyre: strings stretched tight give high-pitched notes, but when loosened produce deep notes.[2] [4] Accordingly the outer spheres, revolving at high speeds on account of their great size and constrained by a breath that is more powerful because it is near its source, as Cicero puts it, *with their swifter motion give forth a higher-pitched tone, whereas the lunar sphere, the lowest, has the deepest tone;* the latter is motivated

---

[21] This is Macrobius' only reference to this lost work which many modern commentators feel was the chief source of his *Commentary.*

[22] See Porphyry, cited by Proclus (Diehl), 205E. Cf. Theo Smyrnaeus 140–41; pseudo-Iamblichus 75; Chalcidius lxxii; Honorius of Autun *De imagine mundi* i.lxxxi (Migne, *Pat. Lat.,* CLXXII, 140). For the literature on the musical intervals of the spheres, see Boyancé, pp. 104–15.

[1] Cf. Aristotle *De anima* ii.viii.420A.

[2] Cf. Theo Smyrnaeus 65.

by a breath which at that great distance is weak, and revolves at a slow speed because of the small space in which it, the sphere last but one, is confined. [5] We have further proof in pipes, which emit shrill notes from the holes near the mouthpiece but deep notes from those near the other end, and high notes through the wide holes but low notes through the narrow holes.[3] A single explanation underlies both circumstances: the breath at the start is vigorous but weakens as it is spent, and it rushes with greater force through broad openings; but when the openings are narrow and far removed from the source the opposite is true. [6] Therefore the outermost sphere, being of immense proportions and constrained by a breath that is more vigorous as it is near its source, emits in its motion high-pitched sounds, whereas the lowest sphere, because of its narrow confines and remoteness, has a feeble sound.[4]

[7] Here we also have a clear demonstration that the breath, as it draws downwards away from its source, becomes slower and slower; consequently it gathers about the earth, the last of the spheres, in such a dense and sluggish mass that it is responsible for the earth's remaining in one place and never moving.[5] That the lowest portion in a sphere is the center has been proven in a preceding passage. [8] Now there are nine spheres in the whole body of the universe. The first is the star-bearer, properly called the celestial sphere, and *aplanes* by the Greeks, *confining and containing all the others.* It always revolves from east to west, whereas the seven lower spheres, the so-called errant spheres, revolve from west to east, and the earth, the ninth, is without motion. [9] Thus there are eight moving spheres but only seven tones producing harmony from the motion of the spheres, since Mercury and Venus accompany the sun at the same rate of speed and follow its course like satellites;[6] they are thought by some students of astronomy to possess the same force, whence Cicero's statement: *The other eight spheres, two of which*

---

[3] Cf. *ibid.* 60–61, 66.

[4] Another group, followed by Milton's "bass of Heaven's deep organ" ("The Hymn on the Nativity," stanza xiii), assigned the lowest note to the celestial sphere and the highest to the moon. Nicomachus (*Musici scriptores graeci,* ed. by C. von Jan, pp. 271–72) reports both views. See Taylor, pp. 166–67; Heath, *Aristarchus,* pp. 108, 110.

[5] Cf. above, I.xxii.5–7.

[6] A crude attempt to obtain the seven notes of the heptachord from the eight circles. On the errors involved, see Taylor, p. 173.

move at the same speed, produce seven different tones, this number being, one might almost say, the key to the universe. [10] That seven is the key to the universe we clearly showed in an earlier discussion about numbers.[7]

I believe that this discussion, extremely condensed, will suffice to clarify the obscurity in Cicero's words on music. [11] To refer even cursorily to the *nete* and *hypate* and the other strings[8] and to discuss the subtle points about tones and semitones and to tell what corresponds in music to the letter, the syllable, and the whole word[9] is the part of one showing off his knowledge rather than of one teaching. [12] The fact that Cicero made mention of music in this passage is no excuse for going through all the treatises on the subject, a mass of literature that, it seems to me, is without end; but we should follow up those points which can clarify the words we have undertaken to explain, for in a matter that is naturally obscure the man who in his explanation adds more than is necessary does not remove the difficulty but aggravates it.

[13] Accordingly, we shall conclude this chapter in our treatise with one addition which seems worthy of cognizance: although there are three types of musical harmony, the enharmonic, the diatonic, and the chromatic,[10] the first is no longer used because of its extreme difficulty, and the third is frowned upon because it induces voluptuousness;[11] hence the second, the diatonic, is the one assigned to celestial harmony in Plato's discourse.[12]

[14] Then, too, we must not overlook the fact that we do not catch the sound of the music arising in the constant swirl of the spheres because it is too full to be taken into the narrow range of our ears.[13] Indeed, if the Great Cataract of the Nile withholds the ominous

[7] I.vi.34.

[8] See Nicomachus *Manuale harmonicum* xii; Theo Smyrnaeus 206; Cleonides *Introductio harmonica* iv; Gaudentius *Harmonica introductio* vi; Martianus Capella IX.931; Boethius *De institutione musica* I.20.

[9] Cf. Theo Smyrnaeus 49; Chalcidius xliv.

[10] This classification of harmony into three genera was originated by Archytas, according to Porphyry *In Harmonica Ptolemaei commentarius* xii (Düring ed., p. 136).

[11] Cf. pseudo-Plutarch *De musica* xvii.1136E. Gaudentius in the fourth century reports that both the enharmonic and chromatic had become obsolete. See J. F. Mountford, "Greek Music and its Relation to Modern Times," *The Journal of Hellenic Studies*, XL (1920), 38.

[12] Cf. Theo Smyrnaeus 56; Proclus (Diehl), 191E.

[13] Cf. Aristotle *De caelo* II.ix.290B; Censorinus xiii.1.

thunder of its falls from the ears of the inhabitants,[14] why is it surprising that the sound coming from the vastness of the universe sur-
passes our hearing? [15] No idle words were these: *What is this
great and pleasing sound that fills my ears?* Cicero would have us
understand that if the ears of a man who deserved to participate in
the heavenly secrets were filled with the vastness of the sound, surely
the hearing of other mortals would not catch the sound of celestial harmony.

CHAPTER V

[1] LET US NOW turn our attention to what follows. *You see,
Scipio, that the inhabited portions on earth are widely separated and
narrow, and that vast wastes lie between these inhabited spots, as
we might call them; the earth's inhabitants are so cut off that there
can be no communication among different groups; moreover, some
nations stand obliquely, some transversely to you, and some even
stand diametrically opposite you; from these of course you can expect
no fame. [2] You can also make out certain belts, so to speak, which
encircle the earth; you observe that the two which are farthest apart
and lie under the poles of the heavens are stiff with cold, whereas the
belt in the middle, the greatest one, is scorched with the heat of the
sun. [3] The two remaining belts are habitable: one, the southern,
is inhabited by men who plant their feet in the opposite direction to
yours and have nothing to do with your people; the other, the northern, is inhabited by you Romans. But look closely, see how small is
the portion allotted to you! The whole of the portion that you inhabit is narrow at the top and broad at the sides and is in truth a
small island encircled by that sea which you call the Atlantic, the
Great Sea, or Ocean. But you can see how small it is despite its name!*

[4] After Cicero had treated of the celestial sphere, which incloses
the universe, the order and movements of the underlying spheres,
the celestial harmony coming forth from those movements, and the
atmosphere situated beneath the moon, he was obliged to deal with
the earth, a subject closely related to the work at hand; his description

[14] Cf. Cicero *Scipio's Dream* v.3; Shakespeare, *The Merchant of Venice*, V, i, 63-65:
Such harmony is in immortal souls;
But, whilst this muddy vesture of decay
Doth grossly close us in, we cannot hear it.

of it, though brief, abounds in information. [5] In speaking of the inhabited areas as *spots* and of the earth's inhabitants as *cut off*, some obliquely, some transversely, and some in a diametrically opposite region, he presented a vivid picture of the spherical nature of the earth. [6] The completeness of his knowledge is also demonstrated in his not permitting us to fall into the common error of those who believe that Ocean encircles the whole earth. Now if he had said, "The whole earth is a small island encircled by that sea," he would have given us to understand that one ocean surrounded the earth; but by qualifying his words, *The whole portion that you inhabit,* he revealed to the attentive reader the actual divisions of the earth, a matter which we shall discuss a little later.

[7] As regards the five belts, I beg you not to think that the two founders of Roman eloquence, Virgil and Cicero, disagree in their views because the latter says that the belts *encircle the earth* and the former that the belts, which he calls by their Greek name zones, "hold the sky";[1] a later discussion will prove that they are both correct and still not contradictory.[2] [8] But in order to clarify all the difficulties we have undertaken to explain at this time, we must first discuss these belts, for when we have the location of each set before our eyes we shall more easily understand the rest.

We must first explain how they girdle the earth and then how they hold the sky. [9] The earth is the ninth and lowest sphere. The horizon—that is, the circular boundary to which we have previously referred—divides this equally: one half, a part of which we inhabit, lies beneath that portion of the sky which is above the horizon, and the other half lies beneath that portion of the sky which in its revolutions has descended to the regions that seem to be below us. The earth, fixed in the middle of the universe, looks out upon the sky from every direction.[3] [10] Insignificant as it is in comparison with the sky—it is only a point in comparison,[4] though a vast sphere to us —it is divided into regions of excessive cold or heat, with two temperate zones between the hot and cold regions.[5] [11] The northern and southern extremities are frozen with perpetual cold, two belts,

---

[1] *Georgicon* 1.233.
[2] II.vii.
[3] Cf. Cleomedes I.10.
[4] Cf. above, I.xvi.10, and note.
[5] Cf. Pythagoras, cited in Aetius *Placita* III.xiv.1 (Diels, pp. 378–79).

so to speak, that go around the earth but are small since they encircle the extremities. Neither zone affords habitation, for their icy torpor withholds life from animals and vegetation; animal life thrives upon the same climate that sustains plant life. [12] The belt in the middle and consequently the greatest, scorched by an incessant blast of heat, occupies an area more extensive in breadth and circumference, and is uninhabited because of the raging heat.[6] Between the extremities and the middle zone lie two belts which are greater than those at the poles and smaller than the one in the middle, tempered by the extremes of the adjoining belts; in these alone has nature permitted the human race to exist.[7]

[13] Here again a diagram will be easier to understand than a discussion.[8] Let us draw a circle to represent the earth with the letters ABCD inscribed. On either side of A inscribe the letters N and L; beside B inscribe M and K; beside C, G and I; and beside D, E and F. Draw straight lines connecting the letters just mentioned, that is, from G to I, from M to N, from K to L, and from E to F. [14] The two spaces at the extremities, one extending from C to the line GI and the other from D to the line EF are to

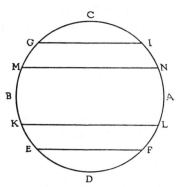

represent the regions perpetually stiff with cold, the upper one being the northern and the lower the southern extremity. The middle belt from N to L is to be the torrid zone. As a result, the belt from I to N is tempered by the heat beneath and the cold above it, and the zone from L to F is tempered by the heat above and the cold beneath it.[9] [15] The lines drawn for our diagram must not be thought of as straight lines, for they are the circles mentioned earlier,[10] the arctic and antarctic circles and the two tropics. The equator has no place

---

[6] Cf. Cleomedes 1.12; Theo Smyrnaeus 133; Geminus xv.1–3; Chalcidius lxvii.
[7] Cf. Martianus Capella vi.602.
[8] Sections 13–17 are quoted in a gloss on Bede *De temporum ratione* xxxii (Migne, *Pat. Lat.*, XC, 443–44).
[9] Cf. Cleomedes 1.12.
[10] I.xv.13.

in this discussion of the earth; it will be treated later in a more appropriate place.

[16] Although the two so-called temperate zones "by the grace of the gods have been vouchsafed to feeble mortals," [11] the men of our race have not fallen heir to both zones: only the upper one, between I and N, is inhabited by the races we are privileged to know, whether Romans, Greeks, or barbarians.[12] [17] That the zone from L to F is also inhabited is inferred solely from reason, for it has the same climate as our zone, but by whom it is occupied we have never been permitted to learn and never shall be, since the torrid zone lying between denies the people of either zone the opportunity of communicating with each other.[13]

[18] Of the four cardinal points in our region, the east, west, and north are referred to by their proper names because we know about them from their beginnings; the northern extremity, though uninhabited, is still not far removed from us. [19] But the fourth cardinal point received another name, not being known as *australis*, "southern," but rather as *meridies*, "midday," for two reasons: first, because only that region is properly called southern which originates in the other extremity, lying opposite the north pole; second, the region where the south wind is first felt by the inhabitants of our quarter is the *mid*-part of the earth on which the light of *day* falls; hence the name *medidies*, and then by the substitution of a letter *meridies*.[14] [20] You must realize that Auster, the wind that reaches us from that direction, is at its starting point cold, as is our north wind, which pleases us with its refreshing chill, but that as it passes through the burning torrid zone, it gathers heat and reaches us as a warm wind though it was originally cold.[15] [21] Indeed, it would be contrary to reason and nature for winds originating at the two poles that are subjected to the same degree of cold to differ much in temperature.[16] It is also obvious for the same reason that our north

---

[11] Virgil *Georgicon* 1.237–38.

[12] Cf. Cleomedes 1.12.

[13] Cf. *ibid.* 15; Geminus xvi.19–20; Isidore of Seville xiv.v.17. For the restrictive effect that Macrobius' doctrine had upon the development of geographical knowledge, see Wright, p. 18.

[14] Cf. Varro vi.4; Isidore of Seville iii.xli.3; Honorius of Autun *De imagine mundi* i.xxvi (Migne, *Pat. Lat.*, CLXXII, 150).

[15] Cf. Honorius of Autun *De philosophia mundi* iii.xv.

[16] Cf. Aristotle *Meteorologica* ii.v.362B–63A.

wind reaches the inhabitants of the south temperate zone as a hot wind, and that the south wind agreeably affects their bodies with its innate chill.[17] [22] It is then impossible to doubt that over that portion of the earth's surface which we think of as the underside the continuation and complete circuit of the zones that above are temperate are there also to be considered temperate,[18] and accordingly, that the same two zones lie as far apart there as here, and are likewise inhabited. [23] If anyone refuses to believe in this let him state his objections.

If life is possible for us in this quarter of the earth that we inhabit because we tread on the ground and look up at the sky overhead, and thrive upon the abundant air that we inhale,[19] and because the sun rises and sets for us, why should we not assume that there are men living there as well where similar conditions always obtain?[20] [24] We must agree that the men who are supposed to be dwelling there breathe the same air as we because both zones have the same moderate temperature over their entire circuit; the same sun will of course be setting for them when it is rising for us and will be rising for them when setting for us;[21] they will tread the ground as well as we and above their heads will always see the sky. [25] Have no fear that they will fall off the earth into the sky, for nothing can ever fall upwards. If for us *down* is the earth and *up* is the sky—to affirm it is to be jesting—then for those people as well *up* will be what they see above them, and there is no danger of their falling upwards. [26] I can assure you that the uninformed among them think the same thing about us and believe that it is impossible for us to be where we are; they, too, feel that anyone who tried to stand in the region beneath them would fall.[22] But just as there has never been anyone

[17] Cf. Cleomedes 1.33.
[18] Cf. Geminus XVI.13–14; Cleomedes 1.34.
[19] Cf. Cleomedes 1.46.
[20] Cf. *ibid.* 15.
[21] Cf. Eudoxus, cited in Aetius *Placita* IV.i.7 (Diels, p. 386); Cleomedes 1.14; Martianus Capella VI.606.
[22] Lucretius *De rerum natura* 1.1052–82 and Plutarch *De facie in orbe lunae* VII.924A–C scoff at the idea of antipodes. Some Christian fathers also refused to accept the doctrines of the philosophers. Probably the best known attitudes are those of Lactantius *Divinae institutiones* III.xxiv and Augustine *De civitate Dei* XVI.ix. For instances of the belief in the earth's sphericity and in antipodes being regarded as heretical in the early Middle Ages, see M. L. W. Laistner, *Thought and Letters in Western Europe* (New York, 1931), pp. 145–46; Wright, pp. 160–61; J. O. Thomson, *History of Ancient Geography*, p. 386.

among us who was afraid he might fall into the sky, so no one in their quarter is going to fall upwards since we saw from a previous discussion that all weights are borne by their own inclination towards the earth.[23]

[27] Finally, who does not admit that upon the spherical earth those regions that are called lower are opposite those that are called upper as the east is to the west? Diameters drawn in any part are considered equal. Now since we know that the east and west are inhabited in much the same way,[24] what is to prevent us from believing in a habitation that is diametrically opposite these?

[28] No inattentive reader will get all the meaning out of Cicero's concise statement. When he says that the earth is encircled by belts, he implies that all over the earth the temperate belts have the same mild climate; when he speaks of habitations appearing as *spots,* he is not referring to the inhabited places in our quarter of the globe that are interspersed with desolate areas. [29] If he were speaking of these deserted areas among which definite places of habitation were regarded as spots, he would not expressly say, *Vast wastes lie between these inhabited spots;* but inasmuch as his *spots* refer to the four inhabited quarters, of which, as our argument has proven, there are two in each hemisphere, he was wise in saying that *vast wastes lie between.* [30] Indeed, just as the quarter inhabited by us is interrupted by many a region of waste land, so we may be assured that the other three inhabited quarters have a similar distribution of waste and cultivated land.

[31] But Cicero defined the four inhabited regions by location and by the position in which the inhabitants stood. First he says that others besides us inhabit the earth, so cut off from each other that they have no opportunity of communicating with each other; his very words show that he is not speaking about one race of men on our side of the earth, cut off from us by the barrier of the desolate

---

[23] I.xxii.4.

[24] Cf. Geminus xv.4; Strabo ii.v.6. Ptolemy greatly overestimated the dimensions of the known portion of the earth. He placed the Fortunate Isles (the Canaries) on the prime meridian and the city of Sera in China on the 180th meridian. The distance is in reality about 130 degrees. His overestimate of the extent of land in the eastern hemisphere became a doctrinal tradition in the late Middle Ages and had an encouraging influence upon Columbus. See G. E. Nunn, *The Geographical Conceptions of Columbus* (New York, 1924), pp. 29–30. Macrobius and Martianus Capella were largely responsible for the belief in a spherical earth and in the antipodes in the Middle Ages. See Wright, pp. 160, 258, 386.

torrid zone. Were this so he would rather say, "They are so cut off that they can have no communication with you," but by saying that they are *so cut off that there can be no communication among the different groups,* he shows how those other inhabited quarters are also segregated. [32] Then referring to our quarter, indeed, and speaking about those who are separated from us and from each other, he says, *Some nations stand obliquely, some transversely, and some even stand diametrically opposite us;* hence not only the barrier that separates us from another people but also the barriers that separate all of them from each other are intended. They must be divided as follows: [33] those who are separated from us by the torrid zone, whom the Greeks named *antoikoi,* the Antoeci; next, those who live on the underside of the southern hemisphere, the Antipodes, separated from the Antoeci by the south frigid zone; next, those who are separated from their Antoeci, that is, the inhabitants of the underside of our zone, by their torrid zone; they are in turn separated from us by the north frigid zone.[25]

[34] Since there is no continuous succession of peoples but waste lands are interposed, preventing communication because of heat or cold, he called the quarters of the earth, which are inhabited by the four populations, the *spots* of habitations. [35] He clearly indicated how the other people are believed to plant their feet with respect to us, and emphatically declared that the people of the southern hemisphere stand in the opposite direction to us when he said, *One, the southern, is inhabited by men who plant their feet in the opposite direction to yours;* their posture is the opposite of ours because they dwell in that part of the sphere that is opposite ours. [36] We still have to consider what he meant by people standing transversely and obliquely to us, but here again there can be no doubt: by those standing transversely he means the inhabitants of our zone in the lower hemisphere, and by those standing obliquely he means the inhabitants of the south temperate zone in our hemisphere.

CHAPTER VI

[1] THERE STILL remains the question of the areas of the earth: we must reveal how much is allotted to habitations and how much

[25] Cf. Geminus XVI.1–2; Cleomedes 1.12–13; Martianus Capella VI.604–5.

is desolate, that is to say, what the dimensions of each zone are. To understand this clearly we shall have to return to the diagram of the earth which we used a little while ago; our measurements will be better understood by referring to the letters of that diagram.

[2] The whole sphere of the earth or the circle ABCD, which represents the circumference, has been divided into sixty intervals by those who have calculated its measurements.[1] [3] The whole circumference measures 252,000 stades, and so each interval measures 4,200 stades; thus half of the circumference, for example, from D eastward to C through A, has thirty intervals and measures 126,000 stades; a quarter part, from A to C, beginning at the middle of the torrid zone, has fifteen intervals and measures 63,000 stades.

By giving the measurements for this quarter we can determine the corresponding measurements for the whole sphere.[2] [4] The distance from A to N, beginning at the middle of the torrid zone, comprises four intervals or 16,800 stades; the whole torrid zone, therefore, comprises eight intervals or 33,600 stades. [5] The breadth of our temperate zone, that is from N to I, is five intervals or 21,000 stades, while the measurement of the frigid zone, that is from I to C, is six intervals or 25,200 stades.[3] [6] From this fourth part of the earth's surface, the dimensions of which have been clearly set forth, you will obtain the measurements of another fourth part from A to D by applying the same distances. When you have learned the dimensions of our side of the sphere's surface, comprising half of the whole, it will be a simple matter similarly to measure off the lower half, that is from D to C through B.

[7] Now since we have represented the circumference of the earth on a plane and, moreover, since it is impossible for a plane to show the protuberance of a sphere about the middle, we have assumed the swelling from our orientation of a circle which really seems to be a

---

[1] This was Eratosthenes' method. Hipparchus is believed to have introduced the division by 360 degrees.

[2] On Hipparchus' method of treating of the whole globe by considering the dimensions of the known quarter, see Strabo ii.v.7.

[3] The degrees and dimensions of the breadth of the zones coincide with those given by Geminus v.45–46, xvi.7–8, and the degrees with those of Theo Smyrnaeus 202–3. Hipparchus placed the Tropic of Cancer at 16,800 stades north of the equator (Strabo ii.v.7), as did Macrobius, but he set the northern habitable limit roughly at 22,200 stades beyond the tropic (Strabo ii.i.13, v.7), whereas Macrobius' limit would be at 21,000 stades. Cf. pseudo-Bede *Mundi constitutio* (Migne, *Pat. Lat.*, XC, 883).

horizon rather than a meridian: I should like to have you regard the diagram above as if from D to C through A were the upper face of the earth, the one inhabited by us, and from D to C through B were the lower half of the earth.

CHAPTER VII

[1] HAVING CONCLUDED this particular discussion, let us now furnish proof, as we promised, for the assertion that both Virgil and Cicero were correct, the former assigning the zones to the sky and the latter to the earth, and that their words were not contradictory but rather in agreement.

[2] The physical nature of the sky is responsible for the differences between the temperate and extremely warm and cold zones upon earth: the same sort of heat or cold that grips any sector of the upper air at any time is conducted to that portion of the earth which lies directly below.[1] [3] Since the diverse regions of the sky with their definite demarcations have been referred to as zones, we must assume the same zones here on earth, just as the image of a large object in a small mirror reproduces its exact features and lineaments on a reduced scale in their correct proportions.

Once again we shall lessen the difficulty of proving our point by using a diagram. [4] Let the circle ABCD represent the celestial sphere, and include within it the circle SXTV representing the earth. Draw upon the celestial sphere the line IO to represent the arctic circle, GP to represent the summer tropic, BA to represent the equator, FQ to represent the winter tropic, and ER to represent the antarctic circle. Then draw the zodiac line from F to P. Next draw upon the earth the same demarcations for the zones mentioned above, lines terminating at N, M, L, and K.[2]

[5] With this diagram you will have no difficulty in seeing that each zone on the earth gets a climate that is temperate or extreme from the portion of the sky directly above it. The upper tract from D to R looks down upon the area on earth from S to K; the celestial sphere from R to Q affects the earth from K to L; the heavens from Q to P have a similar effect upon the earth from L to M; the zone

[1] Cf. Cleomedes 1.19–20.
[2] Cf. gloss on Bede De natura rerum xlvii (Migne, Pat. Lat., XC, 267–68).

from P to O influences the earth from M to N, and the same is true for OC and NT. [6] Both extremes of temperature are found in the upper air; the regions from D to R and from C to O are ever stiff with cold, and consequently the same holds true for the earth from S to K and from T to N. Again, the heavens from Q to P seethe with excessive heat, and the same is true upon earth from L to M. The temperate zones in the sky are from O to P and from Q to R and, correspondingly, the temperate zones on earth are from N to M and from L to K. The equatorial circle drawn from A to B divides the torrid zone at the middle.

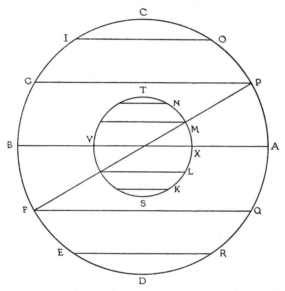

[7] That Cicero himself was aware of the connection between the earth's zones and those of the heavens is shown by his words, *You observe that the two which are farthest apart and lie under the poles of the heavens are stiff with cold.* It is clear that he implies that the ultimate source of cold is the sky. [8] He also says concerning the torrid middle zone, *The belt in the middle, the greatest one, is scorched with the heat of the sun.* His obvious inference that cold comes to the earth's zones from the poles of the sky and that heat comes from the sun shows that he first assumed corresponding zones in the sky.

[9] Now that it is agreed that the earth and sky do have corre-

sponding zones or belts (the two words have the same meaning), we must tell what is responsible for this difference in temperature in the upper air. [10] The torrid zone is hemmed in by the two tropics, the summer tropic GP and the winter tropic FQ. In our diagram, FP represents the zodiac line, P being taken as the tropical sign Cancer and F the tropical sign Capricorn. Now we know that the sun never travels north beyond Cancer nor south beyond Capricorn, but when it reaches the limits of the tropics it turns back; for this reason they are called the solstices.[3] [11] Inasmuch as the summer tropic is also the boundary of our temperate zone, the sun, when it reaches that boundary, subjects us to summer heat, burning the regions directly beneath it with greater fervor. At that time, too, there can be no doubt that winter has come to the people of the southern hemisphere, for the sun is then farthest removed from them. Likewise, when it has reached F, that is the sign of Capricorn, it produces winter for us and restores the heat of summer to those in its proximity.[4]

[12] Attention must here be drawn to the fact that sunlight can enter any building from only three directions and never from the fourth. Windows facing the east and west will receive sunlight in the morning or afternoon, and windows to the south as well, since the whole path of the sun is to the south of us, as our diagram showed; never will a north window admit sunlight, because the sun never invades the area from P to O, always turning back at P and never approaching the borders of the north-polar region, and consequently never pouring its light in from this direction.

[13] The shadow of any object will furnish further proof of this truth. At sunrise the shadow falls to the west and at sunset to the east; at midday, the sun being in the south, the shadow is cast to the north. But in our quarter of the earth it is impossible for a shadow to fall to the south since the shadow is always cast in the direction opposite the sun, and since for us the sun can never be opposite the south because it never approaches the arctic boundaries.

[14] Now inasmuch as the portion of the torrid zone that borders upon the temperate zone does permit habitation, it is obvious that in a location which is just across the tropic shadows will be cast to the south at the season of the year when the sun is at Cancer. As

[3] From *sol*, "sun," and sistere, "to cause to stand still."
[4] Cf. Geminus v.41.

long as the sun is at the tropic it will be north to the people there because it will have gone beyond them. [15] Syene, in the nome of Thebais, the first city beyond the desolate mountainous regions, is set directly beneath the summer tropic. At noon of the day when the sun reaches Cancer, as it is directly over that city, there can be no shadow cast upon the earth by any object, not even by the stylus or gnomon of a sundial, which marks the passage of the hours on the dial.[5] [16] This is what the poet Lucan meant to express though his actual statement is inadequate; for the words "Syene never casting shadows"[6] allude to the phenomenon but confound the truth. To say that it never casts shadows is incorrect; the only time it does not has been reported and explained above.

[17] From these remarks it is clear that the sun never crosses the limits of the torrid zone, for the zodiac slants from tropic to tropic.[7] It is easy to see why this zone is always oppressed by heat; indeed, the sun, source and dispenser of all heavenly heat, never withdraws from it. [18] Hence the two remote regions, arctic and antarctic, which are never approached by the sun, have to endure perpetual cold; but there are, as we have noted, two zones that are tempered by cold from one direction and heat from another.

[19] Finally, in this zone which we inhabit, all of which is spoken of as temperate, there are portions near the torrid zone which are hotter than the rest—Ethiopia, Arabia, Egypt, and Libya, for example. In these lands the atmosphere has become so rarefied because of the heat that it is seldom or never condensed into clouds.[8] Consequently there is almost no rainfall there. [20] Then there are the regions that closely press the frigid zone: the Palus Maeotis [Sea of Azov],[9] and the lands about the Don and Danube rivers, and the

---

[5] The knowledge that Syene lay beneath the Tropic of Cancer served as the basis for Eratosthenes' procedure and calculations to determine the measurement of the earth's circumference. See above, i.xx.20, and note.

[6] *De bello civili* ii.587. Macrobius' observation is pointless because it is based upon a faulty reading *numquam* "never" for *nusquam* "nowhere." See A. E. Houseman's note on this line in his edition, Oxford, 1926.

[7] The remainder of this chapter is quoted in a gloss on Bede *De temporum ratione* xxxii (Migne, *Pat. Lat.*, XC, 444).

[8] Cf. Honorius of Autun *De philosophia mundi* iv.iii.

[9] The notion that the Sea of Azov extended deep into Russia and that it and its environs bordered upon the frigid zone was an old and persistent one. Strabo (ii.i.12) places the mouth of the Dnieper in the latitude of the northern coast of France. Pliny (iv.78) nearly doubles the true length of the Sea of Azov. Ptolemy (*Geographia* ii.viii) places the mouth

territory north of Scythia, the inhabitants of which were called Hyperboreans in antiquity, as if they had passed beyond the source of Boreas; those regions are so oppressed with almost constant cold that it is not easy to determine how much harm they suffer from such extreme temperatures. [21] The countries lying between have mild climates since they are far removed from either extreme; they enjoy conditions that are really temperate and healthy.

CHAPTER VIII

[1] SINCE IT IS impossible to refute our assertions that the two tropics mark the limits of the zodiac, that the sun can never pass over either tropic in its journeys back and forth, and that beyond the belt of the zodiac—that is to say, beyond the torrid zone, which is hemmed in by the two tropics—the temperate zones commence on either side, it behooves us at this time to inquire into the meaning of certain words of Virgil, a poet who has never been caught in error on any subject: "Two zones by the grace of the gods have been vouchsafed to feeble mortals; and a path is cut across the two, wherein the slanting array of the Signs may turn." [1] [2] He seems to say here that the zodiac is drawn "across" the temperate zones and that the sun's course lies over them; but this of course cannot be since the sun does not cross either tropic.

Is he here alluding to something we noted a short while ago, that there are people living across the tropic in that part of the torrid zone which borders upon the temperate? [3] Syene is directly under the tropic and Meroë is over in the torrid zone, 3,800 stades south of Syene, and the Cinnamon-producing Country is another 800 stades farther south;[2] over all this span of the torrid zone habitations,

---

of the Rhine at the fifty-third parallel and (*ibid.* v.viii) the upper reaches of the Sea of Azov above it at the fifty-fourth. Martianus Capella (VIII.876) has his seventh latitude cut through Britain, Germany, and the mouth of the Dnieper, and places the Sea of Azov above that.

[1] *Georgicon* I.237–39.

[2] Eratosthenes placed Meroë at 10,000 stades south of Alexandria and the limit of human habitation at 3,400 stades south of Meroë (Strabo I.iv.2). We saw above that Eratosthenes estimated the distance between Alexandria and Syene (directly beneath the tropic) to be 5,000 stades, so that he would place Meroë at 5,000 stades south of the tropic. Hipparchus also placed Meroë at 5,000 stades south of Syene (Strabo II.v.7), but placed the Cinnamon-producing Country 3,000 stades south of Meroë (Strabo II.i.13).

though sparse, are maintained; but beyond this point none can go because of the great heat. [4] This much of the torrid zone supports life, and there is no doubt that in the vicinity of the southern temperate zone a corresponding amount of space in the torrid zone with its similar climate supports the Antoeci[3]—for on either side all conditions are the same. Is it for these reasons that we are to believe that in using the grand epic style, which exalts everything above reality, Virgil said that the sun's path was cut across the temperate zones, and that he had in his mind that the torrid regions on either border are similar to the temperate zones in that they permit habitations?

[5] Or perhaps with poetic license he substituted one particle for another like it, and preferred to say *per ambas,* "across both," though meaning *sub ambas,* "under both." In fact, the zodiac does come up under both temperate zones, for at its junction with the tropics it embraces them on both sides; but it does not go across them. Moreover, we know that Homer himself often substituted such particles, and Virgil was his imitator in all respects.[4]

[6] Or, which seems still more reasonable, by *per ambas* he may have meant *inter ambas,* "between both." The zodiac goes between both temperate zones and not across both; besides, it is not unusual for him to substitute *per* for *inter,* as we may see from another passage:

River-like, about and between the two Bears.[5]

[7] The constellation of the Dragon does not cut across the Bears; it embraces them and goes between them but not through them. Thus if we should assume that by *per ambas* the poet meant *inter ambas,* as is his wont, it would be possible for us to support our interpretation.

[8] We have nothing else to suggest in addition to the foregoing explanations. Now that we have clearly set forth the limits which the sun never transgresses and have pointed out, moreover, what Virgil said, a man admittedly above error, each one is free to exercise his own ingenuity to suggest a better solution of this question.

---

[3] This hypothesis is ascribed to Crates by Geminus (xvi.26–27).
[4] Cf. Macrobius *Saturnalia* v.xiv.1, xvi.5.
[5] *Georgicon* 1.245. Cf. this comment with that of Servius, III, 188.

CHAPTER IX

[1] AFTER GIVING these matters an examination that is by no means useless, as it seems to me, let us now confirm the statement we made about Ocean, that the whole earth is girt about not by a single but by a twofold body of water whose true and original course man in his ignorance has not yet determined.

That Ocean which is generally supposed to be the only one is really a secondary body, a great circle which was obliged to branch off from the original body. [2] The main course actually flows around the earth's torrid zone, girdling our hemisphere and the underside, and follows the circumference of the equator. In the east it divides, one stream flowing off to the northern extremity, the other to the southern; likewise, in the west, streams flow to the north and south, where they meet the streams from the east at the poles.[1] [3] As they rush together with great violence and impetus and buffet each other, the impact produces the remarkable ebb and flow of Ocean;[2] and wherever our sea[3] extends, whether in narrow straits or open coast, it shares in the tidal movement of Ocean's streams. These we now speak of as Ocean proper because of the fact that our sea is filled from Ocean's streams. [4] But the truer bed of Ocean, if I may call it that, keeps to the torrid zone;[4] it follows the circuit of the equator as the streams originating in it follow the circuit of the horizon in their course, thus dividing the whole earth into four parts and making each inhabited quarter, as we previously stated, an island.

[5] Separating us from the people of the southern hemisphere, Ocean flows along the whole extent of the equator; again, as its streams branch out at the extremities of both regions, it forms two

---

[1] This theory of an equatorial and a meridional Ocean dividing the earth into four parts and making each quarter an island is believed to have been originated by Crates of Mallus (2d cent. B.C.). See Pauly, XI (1922), col. 1637; *Enc. Brit.*, 11th ed., XVII, 635; Wright, pp. 18–19.

[2] This explanation of the cause of tides is also attributed to Crates by Aetius (*Placita* III.xvii.7 [Diels, p. 383]). Cf. Perscrutator *Septima conclusio* (Thorndike, III, Appendix 7). On the influence of Macrobius' doctrines upon tidal theories in the Middle Ages, see Wright, pp. 192–94.

[3] The Mediterranean.

[4] Cf. Cleomedes 1.33; Porphyry *De antro nympharum* xi; Stobaeus 1.526.

Mappamundi in the 1485 Edition of the *Commentary*

islands on the upper face of the earth and two on the underside. [6] Cicero, wishing to imply this, did not say, "The whole earth is a small island," but rather, *The whole of the portion that you inhabit is a small island,* since each of the four inhabited quarters becomes an island, with Ocean flowing about them all in two great circles, as we have explained.

[7] The accompanying diagram will lay everything before our eyes; the origin of our sea, one part of the whole, and the sources of the Red Sea and the Indian Ocean will be evident; here, too, you will see where the Caspian Sea rises, although I am aware that there are some who deny that it has any connection with Ocean.[5] It is certain, too, that in the temperate zone of the southern hemisphere there is a sea comparable to ours flowing in from Ocean, but we do not have the evidence for marking this off since its location continues to be unknown.[6]

[8] From our diagram we shall also understand Cicero's statement that our quarter is *narrow at the top and broad at the sides.* As the tropical circle is greater than the arctic circle, so our zone is narrower at the top than at the sides, for the top is pressed together by the smallness of the northern circle, whereas the sides extend in either direction over the broad expanse of the tropics. Indeed, the ancients remarked that the whole of our inhabited quarter was like an outspread chlamys.[7]

[9] Furthermore, since the whole earth, including Ocean, is but a point in comparison with any circle in the celestial sphere, Cicero was obliged to add, when speaking about Ocean, *But you can see*

[5] Hecataeus believed that the Caspian Sea emptied into the eastern Ocean. Herodotus and Aristotle made it a closed body, and Alexander the Great, according to Arrian (*Anabasis Alexandri* vii.xvi.1–2), had in mind sending a fleet along its shores to settle the question. Strabo revived the Hecatean view. Pliny (vi.58) records the remarkable voyage of Seleucus and Antiochus around India into the Caspian. Ptolemy again closed the Caspian but it was frequently reopened thereafter. See M. Cary and E. H. Warmington, *The Ancient Explorers,* p. 189; H. F. Tozer, *A History of Ancient Geography,* p. 367. The ignorance of Macrobius and others regarding the Caspian Sea is not so appalling. Ptolemy represented its long axis as running east and west, and this error persisted in maps at least into the seventeenth century.

[6] It appears that the basis for this assumption is the desire to achieve a symmetrical scheme, as seems to have been the case with Crates. The Mediterranean (including the Euxine) bisects the western part of the known quarter. Possibly the Caspian was regarded as the counterpart on the east.

[7] Popularly known as "Strabo's cloak," although Strabo was not the first to draw the comparison. See Strabo ii.v.6, 14, xi.xi.7.

how small it is despite its name! Although we call it the Atlantic Sea
and the Great Sea, it cannot seem great to those who behold it from
the sky, since in comparison with the sky the earth is a mark that
cannot be divided.[8] [10] His reason for emphasizing the earth's
minuteness was that worthy men might realize that the quest for
fame should be considered unimportant since it could not be great
in so small a sphere.

CHAPTER X

[1] THIS PURPOSE of his counsel will be no less evident in the
words that follow. *Not even if the children of future generations
should wish to hand down to their posterity the exploits of each one
of us as they heard them from their fathers, would it be possible for
us to achieve fame for a long time, not to mention permanent fame,
owing to the floods and conflagrations that inevitably overwhelm the
earth at definite intervals.*

[2] The wise man places the reward of virtuous deeds in his own
consciousness of them while the less enlightened man places it in
reputation; accordingly, Scipio the Elder, trying to make his grandson truly enlightened, acts as his counsellor and urges him to find sat-
isfaction in his own knowledge of his services and not to look for
glory.

[3] In the quest for glory there are two things which may be
sought above all others: that the fame reach as far as possible, and
that it last as long as possible. Hence, he removes the first hope, that
of an extensive reputation, by revealing in the preceding passage
about the narrow limits of our habitation that the men of our race
occupy only a minute portion of the whole earth, which in comparison with the sky is but a point, and by showing that no man's
reputation can extend over the whole of even that small part if, as
we see, the great name of Rome herself has not been able to pass the
Ganges or to cross the Caucasus. Now he desires to remove the hope
of a lasting reputation as well, so that he, the possessor of glory but
not its advocate, may instill a contempt for it in his grandson's mind.

[4] He says that the fame of a wise and brave man cannot endure
for long even within the small area over which it can spread, for its

[8] Cf. above, i.xvi.10 and note.

endurance is cut short by the destruction that results from a general conflagration or a flood.

Let us look into this matter further. [5] In this chapter of our treatise we shall unobtrusively answer a question that vexes the thoughts of many—the puzzle of the earth's age. [6] For who would readily agree that the earth has always existed when historians assure us that the development and improvement and even the discovery of many things are of recent date, and when in the memories and tales of the ancients we find crude men, unkempt rustics, not far removed from wild beasts in their savagery, who did not use the food that we enjoy, but subsisting at first on nuts and berries, only recently began to look for nourishment from the plowed furrow;[1] and when we have such faith in the beginning of the world and of the human race itself that we believe that the Golden Age was the first and that subsequent ages degenerated through the baser metals to the last Age of Iron?[2]

[7] And, lest we seem to rely entirely upon the authority of legends, who would not conclude that the earth began at a definite time not so very far in the past when even Greek history does not record salient events more than two thousand years ago? Before Ninus, believed by some to be the father of Semiramis, there is no reliable record.[3] [8] If the world was in the beginning or, as philosophers would have it, before the beginning, why, in the passage of countless ages, was the culture that we now enjoy not discovered? And the knowledge of writing, the sole means of preserving the past? Why, finally, did so many types of experience come so late to some nations, witness the Gauls learning about the vine and the raising of olives at the time when our nation was already fully developed,[4] and other peoples still ignorant of many things that have proved boons to us? [9] All of which seems to argue against the eternity of nature, and forces us to conclude that each innovation proceeded gradually after a definite beginning of the universe.[5] Yet

---

[1] Cf. Lucretius *De rerum natura* v.925–1027.

[2] Cf. Hesiod *Opera et dies* 109–201.

[3] Cf. Diodorus Siculus *Bibliotheca historica* ii.i.4. According to legends preserved in Greek and Latin authors, Ninus was the eponymous founder of Nineveh, first king of Assyria, and husband of Semiramis.

[4] Cf. Diodorus Siculus *op. cit.* v.xxvi.2; Varro *De re rustica* i.vii.8.

[5] Cf. Augustine *De civitate Dei* xii.x.

from the teachings of philosophy arises the belief that the world existed always and that God made it, but not after time; indeed, time could not have been before the world because the sun's course and nothing else creates time.[6]

While the world goes on, our civilizations often perish almost completely, and they rise again when floods or conflagrations in their turn subside. [10] The cause of this alternation is as follows. Natural philosophers have taught us that ethereal fire feeds upon moisture, declaring that directly under the torrid zone of the celestial sphere, which is occupied by the sun's course or zodiac, nature placed Ocean, as is shown by our diagram, in order that the whole broad belt over which the sun, moon, and the five errant planets travel might have the nourishment of moisture from beneath.[7] [11] They claim that Homer, the originator of all conceits about the gods, hid this subtle truth beneath the cloak of poetic imagery when he said that Zeus, invited to feast with the Ethiopians, went off to Ocean with the other gods,[8] that is with the planets. They say that by this allegory Homer meant that the planets drew their nourishment from the water[9] and that he called the Ethiopians "kings of the celestial tables" because only Ethiopians inhabit the bank of Ocean, a race whose skin has been burned black because of the sun's nearness.[10]

[12] Since heat is nourished by moisture, there is an alternation set up so that now heat, now moisture predominates. The result is that fire, amply fed, reaches huge proportions, and the moisture is drained up. The atmosphere in this changed state lends itself readily to conflagration, and the earth far and wide is ablaze with raging flames; presently their progress is checked and the waters gradually recover their strength since a great part of the fire, allayed by the conflagration, now consumes less moisture. [13] Then, after a great interval of time, the moisture thus increasing prevails far and wide so that a flood covers the lands, and again fire gradually resumes its place; as a result the universe remains, but in the alternation of ex-

[6] Cf. Plato Timaeus 37E; Cicero De natura deorum 1.21.

[7] Cf. Cleomedes 1.33; Porphyry De antro nympharum xi; Stobaeus 1.526; Isidore of Seville III.xxxviii; pseudo-Bede Mundi constitutio (Migne, Pat. Lat., XC, 884).

[8] Iliad 1.423–25.

[9] Cf. Macrobius Saturnalia I.xxiii.1–5. See R. M. Jones, "Posidonius and Solar Eschatology," Classical Philology, XXVII (1932), 132–34.

[10] Ethiopian means "burnt face," from aithein, "to burn," and ops, "face." Cf. Geminus XVI.28.

cessive fire and flood civilizations frequently perish and are born again when temperate conditions return.[11]

[14] Never does a flood or conflagration sweep all lands and the whole race of men, however. Egypt, it is true, as Plato states in the *Timaeus*,[12] never suffers from excesses of heat or moisture, and hence it alone records countless millennia in its monuments and books.[13]

[15] Certain portions of the earth, escaping utter destruction, become the seedbeds for replenishing the human race, and so it happens that on a world that is not young there are young populations having no culture, whose traditions were swept away in a debacle;[14] they wander over the earth and gradually put aside the roughness of a nomadic existence and by natural inclination submit to communities and associations; their mode of living is at first simple, knowing no guile and strange to cunning, called in its early stage the Golden Age. [16] The more these populations progress in civilization and employment of the arts, the more easily does the spirit of rivalry creep in, at first commendable but imperceptibly changing to envy; this, then, is responsible for all the tribulations that the race suffers in subsequent ages.[15] So much for the vicissitudes that civilizations experience, of perishing and arising again, as the world goes on unchanged.

CHAPTER XI

[1] *INDEED, among those who can possibly hear of the name of Rome, there is not one who is able to gain a reputation that will endure a single year. [2] Men commonly reckon a year solely by the return of the sun, which is just one star; but in truth when all the stars have returned to the same places from which they started out and have restored the same configurations over the great distances of the whole sky, then alone can the returning cycle truly be called a*

---

[11] Cf. Plato *Timaeus* 22C–23C; Proclus (Diehl), 37E–F; Seneca *Quaestiones naturales* III.xxix; Censorinus xviii.11.

[12] 22D.

[13] Taylor (p. 54), suggests that the assumption that Egypt was exempt from the excesses of flood or conflagration probably arose from the fact that the Nile reaches its greatest height in the summer.

[14] Cf. Plato *Leges* III.677.

[15] Cf. Lucretius *De rerum natura* v.1105–42; Tibullus *Elegiae* I.iii.35–50, x.1–10, and notes in K. F. Smith edition.

*year; how many generations of men are contained in a great year I
scarcely dare say.* [3] *As, long ago, the sun seemed to be failing and
going out when Romulus' soul reached these very regions, so at the
time when it will be eclipsed again in the very same quarter, and at
the same season, and when all constellations and planets have been returned to those former positions, then you may consider the year
complete; indeed, you may be sure that not a twentieth part of that
year has yet elapsed.*

[4] The grandfather steadfastly continues the same argument, in-
sisting that glory is not to be sought after. He showed above that its
area is circumscribed and that in addition it is not eternal; now he
informs Scipio that it is so far from being eternal that it cannot even
be prolonged to the span of a single year. The meaning of this assertion we shall now discuss.

[5] That period of time which is now universally accepted as the
year is not the only year, but when each planet has traversed the
whole of the sky, leaving a definite place and returning to it, it has
completed its own year. [6] Thus the moon's year is the month required to make its circuit of the heavens. The name of the period,
mensis, is derived from the moon, for in Greek the word for the
moon is *mene.* Virgil, wishing to refer to the year that is measured
by the sun's course as distinguished from the brief year of the moon,
said, "Meanwhile the sun completes its great year."[1] He called it
"great" in comparison with the moon's year. [7] Now the revolutions of Venus and Mercury are nearly equal to that of the sun,[2]
whereas Mars' year is almost two solar years; it requires that amount
of time to complete its circuit. Jupiter, moreover, consumes twelve
years and Saturn thirty in their revolutions. [8] These facts regarding the planets, often stated, are now familiar. But the so-called
world-year, which is the true year's round, since it is measured by a
revolution of the whole universe, is accomplished in very long ages,
the explanation for which is here presented.

[9] All stars and constellations which seem fixed in the sky and
whose peculiar motions no human eye can ever discern nevertheless
do move, and in addition to the rotation of the celestial sphere by
which they are pulled along they proceed at a pace of their own

[1] *Aeneid* III.284. Cf. Macrobius *Saturnalia* I.xiv.5.
[2] See above, I.xix.4 and note.

which is so slow that no mortal's life span is sufficiently long to detect by continuous observation any movement away from the position in which he first saw them. [10] A world-year will therefore be completed when all stars and constellations in the celestial sphere have gone from a definite place and returned to it, so that not a single star is out of the position it previously held at the beginning of the world-year, and when the sun and moon and the five other planets are in the same positions and quarters that they held at the start of the world-year.[3] [11] This, philosophers tell us, occurs every 15,000 years. Thus the lunar year is a month, the solar year twelve months, and the years of the other planets are as mentioned above; similarly, the world-year is estimated to be 15,000 of the years we reckon by at the present. [12] That must truly be called the revolving year which we measure not by the return of a single star, the sun, but by the return of all stars in every quarter of the sky to their original positions, with the same configurations over all the sky; hence it is called the world-year, for it is proper to refer to the sky as the world.

[13] Then, just as we assume a solar year to be not only the period from the calends of January to the calends of January but from the second day of January to the second day of January or from any day of any month to the same day in the following year, so the world-year begins when anyone chooses to have it begin, as Cicero did when he marked the beginning of his world-year by the sun's eclipse at the hour of Romulus' death. [14] Although solar eclipses have frequently occurred since then, it is not assumed that a world-year has been completed each time; but the span will be fulfilled when the sun is again eclipsed in the same position, and finds all the stars and constellations of the sky in the same positions that they held when it was eclipsed at Romulus' death. [15] Accordingly, 15,000 years after

[3] Also known as a "great" or "perfect year." Cf. Plato *Timaeus* 39D; Cicero *De finibus* II.102; *De natura deorum* II.51, and note in Mayor edition; Chalcidius cxviii; Honorius of Autun *De imagine mundi* II.lxx (Migne, *Pat. Lat.*, CLXXII, 155). Although there is no statement of the duration of a great year in Plato, it is frequently assumed, on the basis of a passage in his *Republic* VIII.546, that his estimate was 36,000 years. This tradition seems to have been strengthened by the fact that Hipparchus, discoverer of the precession of the equinoxes (Ptolemy VII.i–ii), estimated a precessional period to be 36,000 years. But it is quite clear that there is no connection between Plato's great year and Hipparchus' precessional period. See Heath, *Aristarchus*, pp. 171–73; Taylor, pp. 217–19; P. R. Coleman-Norton, "Cicero's Doctrine of the Great Year," *Laval théologique et philosophique*, III (1947), 293–302. For survivals of the doctrine of the great year in the Middle Ages, see Thorndike, Indexes: "magnus annus."

his death, as the philosophers reckon, the sun will again enter an eclipse in the same position in the sky and all the other stars and constellations will have returned to the same positions they held at his death.

[16] At the time that Scipio was campaigning in Africa, 573 years had elapsed since Romulus' death. Scipio celebrated his triumph over Carthage in the 607th year of the founding of the city,[4] and by subtracting thirty-two years for Romulus' reign and two more for the interval between the dream and the end of the war, 573 years remain for the interval between the dream and Romulus' death. [17] So Cicero's observation was quite correct that a twentieth part of a world-year had not yet elapsed since then. One has only to count on his fingers to find how many years remain in a twentieth part after subtracting the 573 years from Romulus' death to Scipio's campaign.

CHAPTER XII

[1] *DO YOU then make that effort, and regard not yourself but only this body as mortal; the outward form does not reveal the man but rather the mind of each individual is his true self, not the figure that one designates by pointing a finger.*[1] *Know, therefore, that you are a god if, indeed, a god is that which quickens, feels, remembers, foresees, and in the same manner rules, restrains, and impels the body of which it has charge as the supreme God rules the universe; and as the eternal God moves a universe that is mortal in part, so an everlasting mind moves your frail body.* [2] As he approaches the end of his instruction, the elder Scipio completes the offices of a good teacher, addressing these wise and appropriate remarks to his grandson.

To review hastily what is contained in the dream, he first foretold the year of his grandson's death and the treachery awaiting him at the hands of relatives, his purpose being to impress upon him that life was transient so that he might no longer put all his hope in it; then, that he might not be crushed by the thought of his impending death, the elder Scipio revealed to him that wise and virtuous citizens were destined to pass into immortality; but when that glorious ex-

---

[4] 146 B.C.
[1] Quoted in John of Salisbury *Metalogicus* III.vii (Migne, *Pat. Lat.*, CXCIX, 906).

pectation led Scipio to yearn for death, his father Paulus stepped in with a timely admonition and turned him from his rash impulse to destroy himself. [3] Thus, after the dreaming Scipio had been firmly convinced by both father and grandfather of the wisdom of hoping and waiting, the elder Scipio then bent himself to the task of inflaming his grandson's mind, not permitting him to get a glimpse of the earth until he had learned about the nature, movements, and regulation of the sky and stars, and understood that all these were to be the rewards of virtue. [4] Then, when his mind had been filled with rapture at the assurance of what was to come, he was bidden to despise glory, a thing which to the uninstructed is the crowning reward of virtue, but which, as he was shown, is restricted by an earth narrow in its confines and exposed to calamities. [5] At this point Scipio had almost put behind him his mortal nature and purged his mind; and now, finally prepared to assume his true nature, he is here clearly told to realize that he is a god.

This is also the consummation of the present treatise: to make it clear that the soul is not only immortal but is a god.[2] [6] If one who has already been received into heaven at death intends to impress on a man still bound to an earthly existence the need to realize that he is a god, he does not entrust such a secret to a mortal before the mortal has comprehended his true nature, lest the mortal be led to suppose that even what is frail and perishable in us is also divine. [7] Cicero has a habit of concealing his deep knowledge of things beneath a concise form of expression, and hence he again introduces with amazing brevity a profound truth which Plotinus, who is terser than anyone, discussed in a whole treatise, entitled *Which Is Creature and Which Is Man?*

[8] In this work Plotinus asks where our pleasures, sorrows, fears, yearnings, ardor, anguish, and finally our thoughts and understanding originate, whether in pure soul or in soul functioning with body;[3] and after discussing a multiplicity of subjects which we must omit here for fear of boring our readers, he concludes with this pronouncement, that the creature is a body quickened with a soul. [9] He does not overlook or leave unexamined, moreover, the question of the soul's service, and the way in which the soul and body

---

[2] Cf. Plato *Leges* x.899D; *Republic* x.611E; *Phaedo* 80A; Plotinus iv.viii.5.
[3] Plotinus i.i.1.

are joined together.[4] All of the aforementioned experiences he assigns to the creature, but the true man he declares to be soul itself. Therefore, that which is seen is not the true man, but the true man is he by whom that which is seen is ruled.[5] Consequently, when at the death of the creature its quickening force has departed, the body is prostrated, deprived of its lord, and this is the part that is mortal in man; but the soul, which is the true man, is completely free of mortality;[6] so, you see, it rules the body in the same manner that God rules the universe, being self-moved. [11] That is the reason why philosophers called the universe a huge man and man a miniature universe;[7] and by way of alluding to the other prerogatives in which the soul seemed to copy God, the early philosophers and Cicero spoke of the soul as a god.

[12] In the words *a universe that is mortal in part* he inclines a little to the popular belief that some things seem to perish within the universe, as in the case of a creature deprived of a soul, or a fire extinguished, or a body of water dried up, for all these are thought to have perished. [13] But it is unquestionably true, on the basis of sound arguments, of which Cicero was aware and which Virgil had in mind when he said, "No place is there for death" [8] —it is unquestionably true, I say, that within the living universe nothing perishes; but of those things that seem to perish only the appearance is changed,[9] and that which has ceased to be as it formerly was returns to its original state and to its component parts. [14] Again, when Plotinus in another passage discussed the destruction of bodies and said that whatever passes away can be dissolved, he asked himself this question: "Why are the elements whose dis-

---

[4] *Ibid.* 1.i.4.

[5] *Ibid.* 1.i.7. Henry (pp. 150–53) offers a detailed comparison of the texts of Macrobius and Plotinus, but his conclusion that Macrobius derived his doctrines directly from Plotinus is open to question. See the section on Sources in the Introduction.

[6] Quoted by Thomas Aquinas *De unitate intellectus* v.

[7] Cf. Democritus *Frag.* xxxiv; Plato *Philebus* xxix; Aristotle *Physica* viii.ii.252B; Philo Judaeus *Quis rerum divinarum heres* xxxi.155; Porphyry, quoted by Stobaeus *Florilegium* xxi.27; Chalcidius ccii; Proclus (Diehl), 62D. See F. M. Cornford, "Mysticism and Science in the Pythagorean Tradition," *The Classical Quarterly*, XVI (1922), 142. For the many survivals in the Middle Ages of the doctrine that man is a miniature universe, see Thorndike, Indexes: "Microcosm"; Schedler, p. 158; Wright, pp. 147–50.

[8] *Georgicon* iv.226. Cf. note on this passage in Servius III, 337–38.

[9] Cf. Adelard *Quaestiones naturales* iv; Hugh of Saint Victor *Eruditio didascalica* i.vii (edition by Buttimer [Washington, D. C., 1939]).

solution is evident not themselves ultimately destroyed in a like manner?" Then succinctly and firmly he answers his question: "The elements, though they pass out of union, are never themselves dissolved, since they do not pass off anywhere." [10] [15] That which flows off bodies withdraws from them, but the flow of elements never withdraws from the elements themselves; and so in this universe no part is mortal according to sound reasoning. [16] When Cicero spoke of a *universe that is mortal in part,* he wanted to incline a little to the popular belief, as we said; but at the conclusion he offered a most convincing argument for the immortality of the soul, the fact that it furnishes the body with motion.

CHAPTER XIII

[1] CICERO'S EXPLANATION of the soul's immortality you will find in his words that follow. *For that which is always self-moved is eternal, but when that which conveys motion to another body and which is itself moved from the outside no longer continues in motion, it must of course cease to be alive. Therefore, only that which is self-moved never ceases to be moved, since it never abandons itself; rather, it is the source and beginning of motion for all other things that move.* [2] *Now a beginning has no origin: all things originate in a beginning, but a beginning itself cannot be born from something else, since it would not be a beginning if it originated elsewhere.* [3] *But if it has no beginning, then indeed, it has no ending: for if a beginning were destroyed it could not be reborn from anything else; nor could it create anything else from itself if, indeed, everything has to come from a beginning.* [4] *Thus it happens that the beginning of motion, that which is self-moved, originates in itself; moreover, it cannot experience birth or death; otherwise the whole heavens and all nature would have to collapse and come to a standstill and would find no force to stir them to motion again.* [5] *Therefore, since it is clear that which is self-moved is eternal, is there anyone who would deny that this is the essence possessed by souls? Everything that is set in motion by an outside*

---

[10] Plotinus II.i.1–3. Plato maintained that materially nothing is created or destroyed. On Plotinus' interpretation of Plato's theory of matter, see Whittaker, *Neo-Platonists,* pp. 70–71.

force is inanimate, but that which has soul is moved by its own in-ward motion, for this is the peculiar function and property of soul. If the soul is unique in being self-moved, surely it is without birth and without death.

[6] The whole of this passage is literally translated by Cicero from Plato's *Phaedrus*.[1] It affirms by most convincing arguments the im-mortality of the soul, and this is the conclusion reached: the soul is not subject to death since it is self-moved.

[7] You must know, however, that there are two interpretations of immortality. A thing is immortal either because it is itself in-capable of dying or because it is kept alive by the efforts of another. Of these the first case applies to the immortaliy of the soul, the second to the immortality of the universe.[2] The soul escapes death by its very nature, but the universe enjoys deathlessness through the offices of the soul.[3]

[8] There are also two interpretations of eternal motion. It is predicated of that which derives its motion from that which is eter-nal and also of that which is both eternal and always moving; the second interpretation is that by which we refer to the eternal motion of the soul.[4]

[9] At this point it is fitting to make known the syllogisms with which the diverse followers of Plato accounted for the immortality of the soul. There are some who arrive at a conclusion by using two syllogisms, beginning the second syllogism where the first left off. [10] They begin in this manner: "The soul is self-moved; but that which is self-moved is always moving; therefore the soul is always moving." Their second syllogism originates in the conclusion of the first: "The soul is always moving; but that which is always moving is immortal; therefore the soul is immortal."[5] Thus in two syllo-gisms two truths are demonstrated: in the first, that the soul is al-ways moving, and in the second, that the soul is immortal. [11] Others carry their sorites further, using three syllogisms: "The soul

---

[1] 245C–246A. Cicero must have admired this passage; he repeats this translation in *Tusculanae disputationes* 1.53–54. Chalcidius lvii includes a translation of the same passage. For a comparison of the texts of Plato, Cicero, and Chalcidius, see Mras, pp. 274–75.
[2] Cf. Plotinus II.i.4.
[3] Cf. Vincent of Beauvais *Speculum naturale* XXIII.lxxiv.
[4] Cf. Plato *Leges* x.894B.
[5] Cf. Plato *Phaedrus* 245C.

is self-moved; but that which is self-moved is the beginning of motion; therefore, the soul is the beginning of motion." With this conclusion the second begins: "The soul is the beginning of motion; but that which is the beginning of motion has no birth; therefore the soul has no birth." And the third step is: "The soul has no birth; but that which has no birth is immortal; therefore the soul is immortal."[6] [12] Still others limit their whole argument to one syllogism: "The soul is self-moved; that which is self-moved is the beginning of motion; that which is the beginning of motion has no birth; that which has no birth is immortal; therefore the soul is immortal."[7]

CHAPTER XIV

[1] BUT IN EACH of the above syllogisms the final conclusion regarding the immortality of the soul can be accepted only by those who do not reject the major premise, namely, that the soul is self-moved; if this is not accepted then everything that follows is undermined. [2] The Stoics, indeed, assented to it, but Aristotle did not, and even went so far as to attempt to prove not only that the soul is not self-moved but that it does not move at all.[1] By skillful argumentation he maintains that nothing is self-moved, so that even if he were to grant that something does move itself, he assures us that it would not be soul. [3] "For if the soul is the beginning of motion," he says, "my contention is that the beginning of motion cannot move."

This is the method he dexterously follows: first, to show that there is something immovable in nature, and second, to attempt to demonstrate that this is soul. [4] He reasons thus:[2] "The following must be true: either all things that exist are immovable, or all are in motion, or some are in motion and some are not. Moreover, if we grant both motion and rest, it follows either that some things are

[6] Cf. *ibid.* C–D.
[7] Cf. Vincent of Beauvais *Speculum naturale* xxiii.lxv.
[1] Cf. Plutarch *De placitis philosophorum* iv.6.899B; Stobaeus 1.812; Proclus (Diehl), 226D.
[2] Cf. *Physica* viii.iii.253A–54B. Macrobius' summary of Aristotle's arguments is so different from the original, particularly in the order of the arguments, and presents the master in so vulnerable a position that it is evident that he did not consult Aristotle's works but drew his material from the clichés of Platonists and Neoplatonists. See the section on Sources in the Introduction.

always in motion and some things are never in motion, or that all things are at one time at rest and at another in motion. Let us see which of these is the more probable. [5] Observation tells us that not all things are immovable, for there are things whose movement we see; again, our eyes attest that not all things are in motion, for we see things at rest. But we cannot say that all things are now in motion and now at rest because there are some things which we see are always moving, the celestial bodies for instance, as everyone admits. It therefore follows that as there are some things always in motion, so there is something always immovable."

[6] No one denies or rejects his inference that there is something always immovable, for his premises are correct and are not repugnant to the followers of Plato; but it does not follow that if there is something immovable, it is soul, nor does one who says the soul is self-moved assert that all things are self-moved, but he merely affirms the method by which the soul is moved; if there is something else that is immovable it will have nothing to do with this point that is made about the soul. [7] Aristotle himself recognizes this, and after proving that there is something immovable he wishes to demonstrate that this is soul; he begins by maintaining that nothing can be self-moved but that all things that are in motion are moved by something else. If he had proved this there would be no defense left for the Platonists; for how could one maintain that the soul is self-moved if it were agreed that nothing can be self-moved?

Aristotle arranges the steps of his argumentation in the following way. [8] "Of all things that are in motion, some are moved essentially and some accidentally.[3] Those bodies are accidentally moved which, though they are themselves not in motion, are nevertheless in something that is in motion, as in the case of cargo or a motionless passenger aboard a ship,[4] or, again, when a part is moving but all the rest of a body is quiet, as in the case of a person standing still and moving a foot, a hand, or his head. [9] But a body is essentially moved which is not moved accidentally nor in part, but is all of it moved together, as when flames mount upwards. No one hesitates to admit that those bodies which are moved accidentally are moved by something else; but I will also prove," he says, "that those

[3] Cf. *Physica* VIII.iv.254B–56A.
[4] Cf. *De anima* I.iii.406A.

bodies whose motion is essential are likewise moved by something else. [10] Of all the bodies having essential motion, some contain within themselves the cause of motion, as, for instance, the animals and trees, which are obviously understood to be moved by something else, that is, by a cause that lies hidden in them; for reason distinguishes the cause of motion from that which is moved; there are other bodies which, it is plain to see, are moved from the outside by some force, or by nature. [11] We say that a javelin is moved by force; when it has left the thrower's hand it seems to be borne along by its own motion, but the beginning of its motion is traced to force.[5] Likewise, we sometimes see earth going upwards and fire downwards, undoubtedly because some outside force constrains them.[6] [12] But heavy bodies are moved by nature when they are being borne downwards or light bodies when they are being borne upwards; even these, it must be admitted, are moved by something outside, although it is uncertain what force is operating. [13] Reason affirms that there is something, I know not what, that moves these bodies. If they were moved of their own accord, they would also halt of their own accord; and they would not always be moving in one direction but would move in different directions if they were being driven by their own impetus. But inasmuch as they are unable to do this, and light bodies tend always to go upwards and heavy bodies downwards, it is evident that their motion originates in a definite and fixed law of nature."

[14] By these arguments and others like them Aristotle believed he had proved that everything in motion is moved by something else. But the Platonists, as will be shown a little later, revealed his arguments to be more subtle than true. [15] Now the second demonstration, in which he takes pains to point out that the soul could not be self-moved even if this could be predicated of other things, has to be joined to the first. He derives the major premise for this assertion from the conclusion that he thought he had just established.

[16] This is his reasoning: "Since it has been proved that everything in motion is moved by something else, then without doubt that which first causes motion, since it is not moved by anything else—it would not be considered the first if it were moved by some-

---

[5] Cf. *Physica* VIII.x.266B.
[6] Cf. *ibid.* VIII.iv.254B.

thing else—must of course be admitted to be either stationary or self-moved. [17] For if we should admit that it is moved by something else, then we must admit that that which moves it is also moved by something else, and that in turn by some other force; our search will continue indefinitely, never coming upon the beginning if something always lies beyond that which you regarded as the first. [18] It follows, therefore, that if that which is the first cause of motion is not said to be stationary, then it must be self-moved. Thus there will be in one and the same thing something which moves and something which is moved if, indeed, in all motion three things are necessary: that which moves, that which conveys the motion, and that which is moved. [19] Of these, that which is moved is only moved and does not cause motion, while that which is the instrument of motion is both moved and causes motion, and that which causes motion is not also moved; thus, of the three we understand that one is common or the mean and the other two are contraries. [20] Now just as there is something that is moved and does not cause motion, so there is something that causes motion and is not moved, for the reason already stated that since everything in motion is moved by something else, if that which causes motion is itself in motion, then we shall always be searching for the beginning of that motion and will never find it. [21] Besides, if anything should be said to be self-moved, we would have to assume that the whole is moved by the whole, or a part by a part, or a part by the whole, or the whole by a part; and whether that motion is derived from the whole or a part, it will nevertheless require some originator." [7]

[22] From all these steps Aristotle draws his inference thus: "Everything in motion is moved by something else; that which is the first cause of motion is either stationary or else moved by something else; but if it is moved by something else then it cannot be called the first cause, and the search for the first cause will always continue; it follows that it must be stationary; therefore the original mover is stationary." [23] In contradiction of Plato, who says that the soul is the beginning of motion, he forms a syllogism in this

---

[7] Cf. *ibid.* VIII.v.256A–258B.

fashion: "The soul is the beginning of motion; but the beginning of motion is not moved; therefore the soul is not moved."[8]

This is his first impetuous objection; and he is not content with persuading us that the soul does not move, but continues to annoy us with other arguments no less provoking: [24] "No beginning can be the same as that of which it is the beginning. Geometricians call the beginning of a line a point, not a line, and arithmeticians say that the beginning of numbers is itself not a number. Likewise, the cause of birth is itself not born, and the cause or beginning of motion is not moved. Therefore the soul, which is the beginning of motion, is not moved."[9]

[25] He also adds: "It will never be possible for contraries to be present in one and the same thing at the same time; but since we know that to move is active and to be moved passive, that which moves itself would undergo the contrary experiences of acting and being acted upon, which is impossible; therefore the soul cannot be self-moved."[10]

[26] He further argues: "If motion were the essence of soul, the soul would never cease moving, for there is nothing which admits the opposite of its essence; fire will never be cold and snow will never grow warm of its own accord; but the soul sometimes ceases moving, for our bodies are not always active;[11] therefore the essence of soul is not in motion since it admits its opposite."

[27] Again he says: "If the soul is the cause of motion for other things, it cannot be the cause of its own motion; there is nothing that can be the cause of the same thing for itself as it is for something else. The doctor and trainer, for example, by no means impart to themselves the health which the one bestows upon the sick or the vigor which the other bestows upon the athletic."[12]

[28] Another argument is offered: "Every motion requires an instrument for its exercise,[13] as experience with the arts teaches us; we must therefore consider whether the soul does not need an in-

[8] Cf. *ibid.* VIII.vi.258B–260A.
[9] Cf. *ibid.* VIII.vii.261B; *Metaphysica* XII.iv.1070B, XIV.i.1087A, 1088A.
[10] Cf. *Physica* VIII.vii.261B, v.257B.
[11] Cf. *ibid.* VIII.vi.259B; *Categoriae* X.12B.
[12] Cf. *Physica* VIII.v.256B–257B.
[13] Cf. *ibid.* VIII.v.256A–B.

strument to move itself; for if this is considered impossible, then it will also be impossible for the soul to move itself."

[29] Still again he says: "If the soul is moved, then, assuredly, it is moved with other movements from place to place. If this is so it now enters a body and now leaves it and does this frequently;[14] but we see that this is impossible, and therefore it does not move."

[30] To this he adds: "If the soul is self-moved, it will have to move with some kind of motion; therefore it moves in space, or moves by begetting or consuming itself, or by increasing or diminishing itself, for these are the varieties of motion. [31] Let us examine each of these to see how possible they are. If it moves itself in space it either moves in a straight line or with a rotary motion. [32] But no straight line is infinite, for every line conceived of in nature is of course terminated somewhere; if the soul moves itself over a line that has an end it will not always be moving, for when it reaches the end and turns about towards the other end there will have to be a slight interval of cessation in the act of reversing its direction. [33] But neither can its motion be rotary, for every sphere revolves about some immovable point called the center; if the soul's motion is rotary it has within it something immovable, and thus of course not all of it moves; if this is not within it, the subsequent hypothesis is no less absurd: that the center is outside, which is impossible; therefore the conclusion is that it does not move in space. [34] But if it begets itself, then we are forced to say that the same thing both is and is not; or if it consumes itself, it will not be immortal; or if it increases or diminishes itself, then the same thing will be found to be now greater than itself, now smaller." [35] From these arguments he draws the following syllogism: "If the soul is self-moving, it moves itself with some kind of motion; but no kind of motion by which it could move itself is found; therefore it does not move itself."[15]

CHAPTER XV

[1] AGAINST ARGUMENTATION so subtle, cunning, and apparently sound as this we must gird ourselves, following the ad-

[14] Cf. De anima i.iii.406B.
[15] Cf. Physica viii.viii.261B–ix.266A; De anima i.iii.406A.

herents of Plato, who undermined the very first contention by which Aristotle tried to invalidate so true and so logical a premise of the master. [2] Indeed, I am not so unmindful of my own limitations nor am I so presumptuous as with my small powers to offer resistance to Aristotle or support to Plato; but inasmuch as each of the great men who were proud to be called followers of Plato has by way of attracting attention to his own studies left a single or twofold refutation,[1] I have here collected these into one continuous body of defense, supplementing their arguments with anything that it was right to offer as an opinion or permissible to hazard as a conjecture. [3] And since there were two conclusions that he tried to maintain, saying first that nothing is self-moved, and second that, if there were, it certainly could not be soul, our refutation must be twofold, proving that something can be self-moved, and revealing that this is soul.

[4] We must be particularly careful to avoid the deception of that reasoning in which Aristotle specifies certain things which are self-moving and shows that they, too, are really moved by something else, by a cause lying hidden within, and then thinks that he has proved that all moving things, even though they are called self-moved, are still moved by some other force.[2] [5] Part of the argument is true, but the conclusion is false. It is true that there are some things which, though they seem to be self-moved, are really moved by something else, and we do not deny it; but this does not mean that all things that are self-moved have to be moved by something else. [6] When Plato says that the soul is self-moved and calls it *autokinetos*,[3] he does not wish it to be included among those things that seem to be self-moved but are really moved by a cause hidden within them, as is true of animals moved by some other hidden agency (for it is soul that moves them), or as trees, which, although the agent is not visible, are nevertheless unquestionably moved by some nature concealed within them. Plato, in calling the soul self-moved, does not mean that some other cause impelling it from outside or hidden within it is responsible for the motion. What he does mean we shall explain here.

[1] Cf. Proclus (Diehl) 226D.
[2] Cf. above, II.xiv.10–13.
[3] *Phaedrus* 246A.

[7] We speak of fire as hot and of iron as hot also, of snow as cold and of a stone as cold, of honey as sweet and of mulse as sweet, and yet the meanings of the words vary in the different examples. [8] The word *hot* has one meaning when referring to fire and another when referring to iron, since fire is intrinsically hot and does not become so through something else, whereas iron will only become hot through an outside agency; snow is not cold nor honey sweet as the result of an outside cause, but a stone grows cold or mulse sweet by the action of snow or honey. [9] Similarly the verbs *to halt* and *to be moved* apply as much to those bodies which are still or are moved of their own accord as they do to those which are brought to a halt or are moved by some outside agency; but those which are moved or halted because of something else do not always continue to be moved or halted, whereas those bodies for which being and being in motion are the same thing never cease moving since they cannot exist apart from their essence; thus iron loses its heat, but fire never.[4] [10] Therefore the soul is self-moved. To be sure, animals and trees seem to be self-moved, but they have deep within them a cause, hidden but nevertheless accidental, in the one case a soul, in the other a natural cause, which furnishes the motion; consequently they lose that which they obtained from something else; the soul, on the other hand, is self-moved just as fire is self-heated, with no contributing cause warming the one or moving the other. [11] When we speak of fire as hot we do not imagine two distinct parts, one that heats and the other that is made hot, but we call the whole of it hot in accordance with its nature; and when we call snow cold and honey sweet we are not distinguishing between that which furnishes these qualities and that which receives them. [12] Likewise, in calling the soul self-moved no distinction arises between the moving and the moved, but in the very motion we acknowledge its essence;[5] for just as the word *hot* applies to fire and *cold* to snow and *sweet* to honey, so we must understand the word *autokinetos,* rendered in Latin *per se moveri* [self-moved], as applying to soul.

---

[4] Cf. Plotinus vi.iv.10; Porphyry, quoted by Eusebius *Praeparatio evangelica* xv.xi (Migne, *Pat. Gr.,* XXI, 1336).
[5] Cf. Plotinus vi.ii.15.

[13] Do not be puzzled at the fact that the verb *to be moved* is in the passive voice; nor should you think, because in the verb *to be cut* there are two things involved, that which cuts and that which is cut, and in the verb *to be held* that which holds and that which is held, that there are also two things meant here, that which moves and that which is moved. [14] The verbs *to be cut* and *to be held* denote passivity and therefore include consideration of both the agent and the thing acted upon; the verb *to be moved,* when referring to those things which are moved by something else, also presents two aspects; but when the verb *to be moved* refers to something which is self-moved so that it is *autokinetos,* since it is moved by itself and not by something else, it can have no suggestion of passivity about it. [15] Though the verb *to stand* does not seem active, yet when it refers to something which stands because it was placed there, as "the spears stand fixed in the ground," [6] it signifies passivity; similarly, although *to be moved* sounds passive, it cannot have anything passive in it since there is nothing active present. [16] To make it still clearer that passivity is indicated not by the words used but by what is involved, consider this instance: when fire is borne upwards there is no passivity involved, but when it is borne downwards there undoubtedly is, because fire does not act this way unless compelled by something; although the same verb is used in both cases we shall admit that passivity is present in the one and absent in the other. [17] So the verb *to be moved* is in the same category as *to be hot:* when we say that iron is hot or a stylus is being moved, since both conditions depend upon an outward agency, we must admit they are passive; but when fire is said to be hot or soul to be moved, since the essence of the one is in heat and of the other in motion, there is no possibility of passiveness, but the one will be said to be hot as the other will be said to be moved.

[18] At this point Aristotle contrives a cunning misrepresentation of a quotation, claiming that Plato had two things in mind, that which moves and that which is moved, when he made the statement, "Only that which is self-moved never ceases to be moved since it never abandons itself"; [7] he openly avows that Plato referred

---

[6] Virgil *Aeneid* VI.652.
[7] *Phaedrus* 245C.

to two things in these words: that which moves and that which is moved.[8] A man with Aristotle's mind, it seems to me, could have let nothing escape him, but in his use of such devices he seems to have willfully twisted the argument in his own interest. [19] Who would not understand, when something is said to move itself, that two things are not meant? When one is said to be punishing himself there is not one individual doing the punishing and another being punished, and when one is said to ruin himself, to entangle himself, or to free himself, it does not follow that an agent and a subject are both represented; but this alone is expressed in the meaning of the words, that one who punishes himself or frees himself is not regarded as receiving the action from someone else but as having brought it upon himself; just so, when something that is self-moved is said to move itself, the author has in mind to preclude the suggestion that something outside is doing the moving. [20] Plato, wishing to keep this clear in his reader's mind, introduced the statement above with these words: "For that which is always self-moved is eternal, but when that which conveys motion to another body and which is itself moved from the outside no longer continues in motion, it must of course cease to be alive."[9] [21] What can be more emphatic than these words which clearly testify that that which moves itself is not moved from the outside, for he says that the soul is eternal for the very reason that it moves itself and is not moved from the outside? Therefore, to move itself signifies only this, that it is not moved by something else; it does not signify both moving and being moved, but rather that to be moved without being moved by something else is to be self-moved. [22] Thus it is obviously true that not everything that is moved is moved by something else. That which is self-moved is able to move without any other agent; but, indeed, it is not self-moved in such a way that there is something in it which moves and something which is moved, nor is it moved wholly or in part, as Aristotle claims;[10] this alone is stated, that it moves itself, in order that it should not be thought that it is moved by something else.

[23] And that Aristotelian inference about motion, recorded

[8] Cf. above, II.xiv.18.
[9] *Phaedrus* 245C.
[10] Cf. above, II.xiv.21.

above, that "just as there is something that is moved and does not cause motion, so there is something that causes motion and is not moved," [11] is more subtle than convincing. [24] It is obvious that anything in motion moves other things, as a rudder is said to move a ship[12] or a ship to move the air or water about it. Is there anything, indeed, that cannot move something else as long as it is in motion? If, therefore, it is not true that there are things in motion which do not move other things, it does not follow that you will find something that moves and yet is itself not moved. [25] Rather, Plato's inference regarding motions, found in the tenth book of the *Laws,* is more probable. "Every motion," he says, "is either self-moved and moves other things, or is moved by something else and moves other things." [13] The former refers to soul and the latter to the corporeal world. These two motions are distinguished by a difference and associated by a similarity: they have in common the ability to move other things, and they differ in that one is self-moved and the other is moved from the outside. [26] From these statements, gleaned from the wealth of Plato's thoughts, it is evident that it is false to assume that all things in motion are moved by something else; therefore, the beginning of motion will not be admitted to be stationary in order to avoid the necessity of something else moving it, since it is able, as we said, to move itself without other help. [27] Consequently the syllogism which he derived previously from various involved inferences, stating that "the soul is the beginning of motion; but the beginning of motion is not moved; therefore the soul is not moved," is undermined.

It remains for us to prove, since there can be something which is truly self-moved without any other agency, that soul is that something, a simple matter if we base our arguments on obvious and indisputable facts. [28] It is either soul or body or a mixture of both that furnishes man with motion. Since there are three possibilities open to question, when it has been proved that motion cannot be furnished by body or by a mixture, then it will unquestionably follow that man is moved by soul.

[29] Let us take them up separately, beginning with body. That

[11] Cf. above, ii.xiv.20.
[12] Cf. Aristotle *De anima* ii.iv.416B.
[13] x.894B–C.

no inanimate body is moved by its own motion is too obvious to maintain; moreover, there is nothing stationary that is able to move something else; therefore, body does not move man. [30] Now we must see if a combination of soul and body does not furnish this motion. But since it is agreed that motion is not present in body, then if it is also absent from soul, no motion can be produced by two things lacking motion; bitterness will not come from two sweet things nor sweetness from two bitter things, nor will heat be produced from two cold things nor cold from two hot things; every quality, when doubled, becomes more pronounced, and never does something opposite result from two similars; therefore, motion will not come from two things that are stationary, and the combination will not move man. [31] Hence an incontrovertible syllogism is formed in the light of evident truths: "The creature is moved; but either soul or body or a combination of both furnishes the creature with motion; but neither body nor a combination furnishes motion; therefore the soul furnishes motion." [14] [32] From this it is apparent that the soul is the beginning of motion; but an earlier discussion showed that the beginning of motion is self-moved; therefore it is obvious that the soul is self-moved.

CHAPTER XVI

[1] AGAIN ARISTOTLE OBJECTS, taking issue with Plato regarding beginnings; in our rejoinder we shall discuss his objections in the order in which they were offered above. "Things," he says, "cannot be the same as the beginnings from which they were produced; therefore soul, which is the beginning of motion, is not moved; otherwise the beginning would be the same as that which springs from the beginning, and motion would seem to have come forth from motion." [1]

[2] To this argument our reply is simple and conclusive: while it is true that first beginnings and those things that come from first beginnings do sometimes differ in some respect, they can never be so contrary to each other as to be both stationary and in motion.

[14] Cf. Plotinus iv.vii.2.
[1] Cf. above, ii.xiv.24.

[3] Now if the beginning of white were called black and dryness were the beginning of wetness, then good would come from bad and sweet would come from sour. But this is not so since nature does not allow beginnings and their immediate offspring to differ to the point of opposition; at times, however, such difference is found between them as is fitting between a beginning and the next step, and as is here found between the motion by which the soul is moved and that by which it moves other things. [4] Plato did not simply call the soul motion but motion moving itself. The difference between motion moving itself and motion by which other things are moved is quite plain, for the first has no agent and the second is the agent of motion for other things.[2] And so we conclude that beginnings and things sprung from beginnings cannot differ to the point of being opposites, and yet that there is a reasonable difference present here; therefore the beginning of motion will not be stationary, a thing which he deduced by clever argumentation.

[5] His third objection, as I recall, was as follows: "A single thing cannot suffer opposite experiences at the same time; since to move and to be moved are opposites the soul cannot move itself; otherwise the same thing would move and be moved."[3] But the evidence presented above invalidates this argument if, indeed, it was agreed that in the soul's motion two things are not to be understood, something that moves and something that is moved; for to be self-moved is nothing more than to be moved without other help. No opposition is present when what is happening is uniform; obviously there are not both an agent and a recipient of motion here, for motion is the very essence of soul.

[6] After this he finds a fourth opportunity to argue, as we reported above. "If the essence of soul is motion," he asks, "why is it sometimes quiet, although nothing else admits the opposite of its essential nature? Fire, the essence of which is heat, never ceases being hot, and since cold is the essential nature of snow, it is always cold; consequently the soul for the same reason ought never to cease moving." (I should like him to tell when he supposes that the soul does cease moving.) [7] "If in moving itself," he says, "it also moves the

---

[2] Cf. Plotinus iv.vii.11.
[3] Cf. above, ii.xiv.25.

body, it follows that when we see that the body is not moving we also understand that soul is not moving." [4]

[8] Two replies to this argument immediately come to mind. First, motion of the soul is not detected in the body's activity, for even when no part of a man's body appears to be moving his thinking, or in the case of any animal, hearing, sight, smell, and other similar functions, and when he is asleep, his breathing and dreaming are all movements of the soul. [9] Second, who would say that the body is motionless, even while it does not appear to be moving, when growth of limbs, or if the age of growth has passed, the incessant beating of the heart, the digestion of food carrying nourishment through the veins and organs according to its natural routine, and even the process of excretion testify to continuous activity in the body? Therefore both the soul with its eternal motion and the body, as long as it is animated by the beginning and cause of movement, are always in motion.[5]

[10] At this point he saw fit to introduce a fifth objection. "If the soul is the cause of motion for other things," he says, "it cannot be the cause of its own motion; there is nothing that can be the cause of the same thing for itself as it is for something else." [6] Although I could easily prove that there are many things that can be the cause of the same thing for themselves as they are for something else, nevertheless, in order not to seem eager to refute every assertion of his, I shall grant this point. Even though it be regarded as true, it will not prejudice the conviction of the soul's motion.

[11] Now we call the soul the beginning and cause of motion. We shall speak about the cause in a moment. Meanwhile, it is agreed that every beginning is present in the thing of which it is the beginning; therefore, whatever sets out from its beginning into something else, is also found in the beginning itself. Thus the beginning of heat has to be hot. Who will deny that fire itself, from which heat passes off to other things, is hot? [12] "But fire," he says, "does not heat itself because by nature it is hot throughout." [7] Here I have what I was seeking, for the soul, too, does not move itself in such

---

[4] Cf. above, II.xiv.26.
[5] Cf. Plotinus IV.iii.23.
[6] Cf. above, II.xiv.27.
[7] Cf. *Categoriae* x.12B.

a way that there is a distinction between what is moved and what moves, but it is moved throughout by its own motion in such a way that you would not be able to isolate that which moves.

[13] So much for the beginning. Now in regard to the cause, since we voluntarily closed our eyes and granted that nothing was the cause of the same thing for itself as it was for something else, we freely acquiesce in the statement that the soul, which is the cause of motion for other things, does not seem to be the cause of its own motion. It is the cause of motion for those things which, if it did not furnish them with the impetus, would not be moved, but it does not furnish itself with the impetus to be moved; rather, its essence is to be moved.

[14] As a result, Aristotle's next objection is already disproved. I will grant that instruments are needed for the production of motion[8] only when the cause of motion and the object moved are entirely different. But to look for this in the soul, whose motion is in its essence, is something not even a vile jester will attempt without a feeling of shame. Since fire, though it is moved by a cause hidden within it, ascends aloft without the aid of instruments, much less are these to be sought in the soul, the motion of which is its very essence.

[15] In the statements that follow, a man of his reputation, and on other occasions the most serious of philosphers, appears to be quibbling. "If the soul is moving, then assuredly among its other movements it is moving from place to place. If this is so it now enters a body and now leaves it and does so frequently; but we see that this is not the case, and therefore it does not move."[9] [16] In reply to this there is no one who would not answer without hesitation that not all things that are moved are moved from place to place. It is fitting and proper for us to direct a similar inquiry to him in turn. "You say that trees are moved?" When he has assented, and I think he will, we will attack him with raillery like his own: "If trees are moved, then of course, as you are accustomed to say, among their other movements they are moved from place to place; but we see that trees cannot do this of their own accord; therefore trees are not moved." [17] But to make this syllogism serious, after

[8] Cf. above, ii.xiv.28.
[9] Cf. above, ii.xiv.29.

we have said, "Therefore trees are not moved," we will add: "But
trees are moved; therefore, not everything that is moved is moved
from place to place."

And now we shall bring this argument to a climax with a rational
conclusion: "If we confess that trees are moved, but with a motion
adapted to them, why do we refuse to believe that the soul, too, is
moved with a motion that harmonizes with its essence?" [18] Even
if the soul were unable to be moved with this sort of motion, our
declaration would be well founded, for inasmuch as it quickens the
body by its entrance and leaves the body after a definitely allotted
span, who will deny that it also moves into a place, so to speak?
[19] For its inability to shuttle in and out of the body at any time
a secret and wise provision of nature is responsible, which, for the
purpose of prolonging the life of the creature, has instilled in the
soul such a longing for its body that the affection extends beyond
the required time; and it rarely happens, when the allotted span is
over, that the soul is not mournful and reluctant to depart.

[20] Having repulsed this attack, as I think we have, let us come
to the other objections with which he seems to challenge us. "If
the soul moves itself," he says, "it moves itself with some kind of
motion. Is it not true that the soul moves itself in space? But that
space is either a circle or a line. Or does it move by begetting or
consuming itself? Or does it increase or diminish itself? Otherwise present to us some kind of motion by which we may say it is
moved." [10] [21] But all of this tiresome investigation is based upon
the device of a false premise. Since he once declared that everything
in motion is moved by something else, he now examines the soul
for every kind of motion in which there is something that moves
and something that is moved, despite the fact that none of these
can apply to the soul; for in it there is no distinction between the
moving and the moved.

[22] But someone will ask: "What is the motion of the soul or
how can it be apprehended if it is none of these?" He will know
who cares to make the effort, with Plato or Cicero as his guide:
*Rather it is the source and beginning of motion for all other things
that move.*[11] [23] How profound the meaning of the phrase *source*

[10] Cf. above, II.xiv.30.   [11] *Scipio's Dream* viii.3.

of motion is, when applied to the soul, you will easily discover if you will imagine the movement of something invisible, without author and therefore without beginning and ending, coming forth and moving other things; the nearest thing to it that one will be able to find will be a spring, which is so truly the beginning of water that though it produces rivers and lakes it is not said to be born from anything, for if it were it would not be the beginning.[12] [24] Just as the sources are not easy to discover from which pour forth the Nile, the Po, the Danube, and the Don, and as you, in wonder at the vastness of such streams and curious about their beginnings, run back in your thoughts to their sources and realize that all this flood originates in little bubbling springs, so when you pause to think about the motion of bodies, whether they be divine or earthy, and wish to seek their beginning, let your mind run back to the soul as the source, the motion of which, even without bodily activity, is evidenced by our thoughts, joys, hopes, and fears. [25] Its motion is the discernment of good and evil, love of the virtues, yearning for the vices, from which flow all the streams of action that arise in us; its motion is what makes us angry and makes us lose our tempers in the heat of argument, till its mounting tide ends in the madness of warfare; its motion causes us to be swept away by pleasures and become slaves to passion. If the soul's motions are governed by reason, their effect is salutary, but if reason is lacking, the end is ruin.[13]

[26] You have learned about the soul's motions, which are exercised at times without affecting the body and at times by using the body. If you are curious about the movements of the World-Soul, follow the revolutions of the sky and the swift movements in the underlying spheres, the rising and setting of the sun and the journeys of the planets back and forth, all of which derive their impulse from Soul; but to say that that which moves all these is itself motionless does not become Aristotle, whose greatness in other respects has been proved. But enough of him who turns his back on nature's powers and obvious conclusions.

[12] Cf. Plotinus III.viii.10.
[13] Cf. Plato *Leges* x.897A–B; Plotinus VI.iv.15.

CHAPTER XVII

[1] AFTER HE HAD revealed and verified the soul's motion, the elder Scipio charged his grandson as to the proper use of it in the following words. [2] *Exercise it in the best achievements. The noblest efforts are in behalf of your native country; a soul thus stimulated and engaged will speed hither to its destination and abode without delay; and this flight will be even swifter if the soul, while it is still shut up in the body, will rise above it, and in contemplation of what is beyond, detach itself as much as possible from the body.* [3] *Indeed, the souls of those who have surrendered themselves to bodily pleasures, becoming their slaves, and who in response to sensual passions have flouted the laws of gods and of men, slip out of their bodies at death and hover close to the earth, and return to this region only after long ages of torment.*

[4] In an early part of this work we noted that men of leisure possessed some virtues and men of affairs others, that the former virtues befitted philosophers and the latter the leaders in public welfare, and that the exercise of both made one blessed.[1] These virtues are sometimes separated, but they are occasionally combined if a man by disposition and training is found to have a capacity for both. [5] If a man is looked upon as possessing no learning but is nevertheless prudent, temperate, courageous, and just in public office, though enjoying no leisure he may nevertheless be recognized for his exercise of the virtues of men of action and receive his reward in the sky as well as the others.[2] [6] And if a man, because of a quiet disposition, is unfit for a life of activity but by virtue of rich gifts for introspection is elevated to the realms above and devotes the benefits of his training solely to divine matters, searching for heavenly truths and shunning the material world, he, too, is taken up into the sky in consideration of his virtues of leisure. [7] It often happens, too, that the same individual is distinguished for excellence both in public life and in private reflections, and he also is assured of a place in the sky.[3] [8] Romulus would be placed in the first

[1] i.viii.
[2] Cf. above, i.viii.6–8.
[3] Macrobius was himself a prominent public official according to the distinguished titles appended to his name in the manuscripts.

group, a man who never failed to exercise courage; Pythagoras belongs in the second, a man who had no experience in public office but who was skillful in reasoning and was concerned only with the virtues of learning and deep thinking; in the third, or mixed, group among the Greeks there would be Lycurgus and Solon, and among the Romans Numa, both Catos,[4] and a host of others, who drank deeply of philosophy and laid a firm basis for the state; Greece, it is true, produced many men whose lives were dedicated solely to the philosopher's retirement, but such men are not found among the Romans.

[9] Since our younger Scipio Africanus, who has just been receiving instructions from his grandfather, belongs to that group of men who both mold their lives according to the precepts of philosophy and support their commonwealths with deeds of valor, he is charged with upholding the highest standards of both modes of life. [10] Of course the virtues of a public career were called to his attention first, for he was at that time stationed in a military camp, enduring the hardships of a campaign: *The noblest efforts are in behalf of your native country; a soul thus stimulated and engaged will speed hither to its destination and abode without delay.* [11] Then, being a man of no less learning than courage, he is informed of the philosopher's virtues: *This flight will be even swifter if that soul, while it is still shut up in the body, will rise above it, and in contemplation of what is beyond, detach itself as much as possible from the body.* [12] These are the rules of that discipline which directs philosophers to seek after that sort of death in which, while still living, they despise the body as an extraneous burden to the fullest extent that nature's laws will permit. The grandfather found it easy to persuade him at this opportune time, after he had pointed out the magnificent heavenly rewards for virtuous conduct.

[13] But because a law that has no stated penalty for its infraction is incomplete, the elder Scipio at the close of Cicero's work revealed the punishment awaiting all who disregard these precepts. In Plato's work this task is well cared for by Er, who points to the countless ages that must elapse before the souls of the guilty can quit their round of torment and at last rise from the lower regions to their

---

[4] The elder Marcus Porcius Cato does not deserve to be ranked as a philosopher. Macrobius is probably thinking of the idealized Cato of Cicero's *De senectute*.

natural origin, the sky, after undergoing purification.[5] [14] Of course every soul must return to its original abode; but those that sojourn in mortal bodies as strangers are recalled home soon after leaving their bodies, while those that are allured by their bodies as if they belonged to them return to the heavens as much later as the effort required to separate them from their bodies determines.

[15] Let us now check our discussion and bring an end to this *Commentary* with one additional remark, which will afford a fitting conclusion: there are three branches of the whole field of philosophy —moral, physical, and rational.[6] Moral philosophy is a guide to the highest perfection in moral conduct, physical philosophy is concerned with the physical part of the divine order, and rational philosophy discusses incorporealities, matters apprehended only by the mind. Accordingly, Cicero included all three in *Scipio's Dream*. [16] What is his exhortation to do virtuous deeds, to love one's country, and to despise glory, if not instruction in moral philosophy? When he discusses the spheres, the unknown stars, the magnitude of heavenly bodies, the sun's dominant position, the celestial circles and terrestrial zones, and the location of Ocean, and when he discloses the secret of the harmony of the spheres, he is dealing with matters of physical philosophy. When he argues the motion and immortality of the soul, about which there is of course nothing corporeal and the nature of which is ascertained not by the senses but by the mind alone, he is ascending to the heights of rational philosophy. [17] Consequently we must declare that there is nothing more complete than this work, which embraces the entire body of philosophy.

[5] *Republic* x.615A–B.
[6] A classification erroneously attributed to Plato by Cicero and other ancients. See Cicero *Academica* 1.19, and note in Reid edition.

Appendices

Appendix A

MACROBIUS AND HERACLIDES' THEORY OF PLANETARY REVOLUTIONS

MY INTERPRETATION of Macrobius' meaning in this paragraph is contrary to the view held by the leading modern authorities on the history of classical astronomy—Dreyer, Heath, and Duhem—and also to the interpretation given to the passage by writers on astronomy since the early Middle Ages. In a chapter on the influence of Macrobius, Chalcidius, and Martianus Capella upon the astronomy of the Middle Ages, Duhem (III, 44–162) has cited a number of authors who assumed that Macrobius was here presenting an exposition of Heraclides' theory of planetary revolutions, and the modern authorities all agree that such is the case. To my mind there is no question that this is a mistaken interpretation.

First it would be well to explain what the Heraclidean system was. Heraclides' contributions to the progress of Greek astronomical theory were outstanding, perhaps even more important than those of Aristarchus, who discovered the heliocentric theory and anticipated Copernicus by seventeen centuries. Heraclides accounted for the rotation of the sky by maintaining that its rotation is only apparent and that instead the earth turns on its axis once daily. He abandoned the concept of a stationary earth surrounded by seven concentric planetary spheres and explained the periodic difference in the brightness of Venus by maintaining that Venus and Mercury do not revolve about the earth but rather about the sun. As to whether Heraclides held still more advanced notions, opinions differ. Some authorities think that he put all the planets in motion about the sun and the sun in motion about the earth (Tycho Brahe's system), and Schiaparelli goes so far as to claim that Heraclides anticipated Aristarchus in arriving at the heliocentric hypothesis. For a fuller summary of the development of Greek planetary theories before and after Heraclides, see my article "The Greek Heliocentric Theory and its Abandonment," *Transact. of the Amer. Philol. Assoc.*, LXXVI (1945), 323–25.

Dreyer (pp. 129–30), Heath (*Aristarchus*, pp. 258–59), and Duhem (III, 51–52) assume that when Macrobius speaks of Mercury and Venus as coursing *per superiores circulorum suorum vertices* . . . *per inferiora circulorum* (which I have translated "upper reaches of their spheres . . . lower tracts"), he is here presenting Heraclides' theory of the revolutions of Mercury and Venus about the sun. I must admit that Macrobius is undoubtedly alluding to the Heraclidean theory in this statement, but either he himself does not understand the theory or he is purposely vague in referring to it.

A careful reading of the first ten sections of this chapter—the modern authorities have ignored sections 8–10—will reveal that the purpose of Macrobius' discussion is to determine which is the correct order of the planets, the Ciceronian (Ptolemaic) or the Platonic. Macrobius of course prefers the Platonic order, for Plato and Plotinus are infallible in his eyes. A moment later (1.xxi.24–27) he refers back to this passage and reaffirms his preference for Plato's order. He feels called upon, as a Neoplatonist, to defend Plato against the growing popularity of the Ptolemaic system, which kept the sun's orbit above the epicycles of Mercury and Venus.

Macrobius could not be expounding the Heraclidean theory here because there can be no fixed order of the planets if two of them are coursing about the sun, now above it and now below it, as Heraclides maintained in order to explain the difference in Venus' brilliance. Macrobius clearly states that the moon is the only planet beneath the sun and that accordingly it must borrow its light, whereas the other planets are bathed in the perpetual light of the upper air. We must conclude that although Macrobius is credited (together with Chalcidius and Martianus Capella) with transmitting the Heraclidean system to the Middle Ages, he did not intend to expound the system but was merely alluding to the behavior of Mercury and Venus and primarily defending the Platonic order. For other arguments supporting this interpretation, see Stahl, 236–42.

Appendix B

ERATOSTHENES' METHOD OF MEASURING
THE EARTH'S CIRCUMFERENCE

THE MEASUREMENT of the earth's circumference is regarded as Eratosthenes' greatest achievement. He ascertained that at noon at the summer solstice the sun casts no shadow at Syene (modern Assuan). Using a hollow hemispherical bowl (such as described by Macrobius in the next paragraph) with a vertical stylus or gnomon in the center, he found that the shadow cast at Alexandria at the summer solstice subtended an arc that was a fiftieth part of the circumference of the sphere from which the bowl was cut.

If hemispherical bowls are placed in perfectly level positions anywhere on the earth's surface, their gnomons will always point to the center of the earth. Eratosthenes' geometrical demonstration, as given by Cleomedes 1.52–55, is as follows:

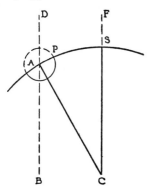

He assumed that Syene and Alexandria were on the same meridian and were 5,000 stades apart, and that the sun was so far away that all its rays falling upon the earth were parallel. The sun's rays falling upon Syene (S), if extended, would pass through the earth's center (C). Let DB represent the sun's rays falling upon Alexandria (A). DB and FC are parallel. AC, the extension of the gnomon at Alexandria, becomes a transversal of parallel lines, and the alternate angles BAC and ACS are therefore equal. In any circle the length of arc subtended by a central angle is proportional to the size of the angle. If the arc subtended by BAC is ⅟₅₀ of the circumference P, then the arc AS is ⅟₅₀ of its circle. The distance between Alexandria and Syene was estimated as 5,000 stades, and by multiplying by 50, he determined the earth's circumference to be 250,000 stades. This figure he later changed to 252,000 stades (Strabo 11.113; Theo Smyrnaeus 124). Good fortune attended his experiment, for aside from the deficiencies of his instruments, the three errors involved seem to have canceled each other instead of accumulating. Syene does not lie directly beneath the Tropic of Cancer, but 37 miles north of it; the figure for the distance between Syene and Alexandria could not be accurately measured by the men who paced it off and was meant to be only a round one; lastly, there was no knowledge of the earth's oblateness and greater diameter at the equator. For further details on his method, see H. F. Tozer, *A History of Ancient Geography,* pp. 170–72. See also A. Diller, "Geographical Latitudes in Eratosthenes, Hipparchus and Posidonius," *Klio* (1934), pp. 258–69.

The problem of determining which stade Eratosthenes used and its equivalent in feet has long puzzled scholars and is not yet settled. The most widely accepted figure of 157.5 meters in a stade, adopted by Tannery, Dreyer, and Heath, would make Eratosthenes' estimate of the earth's circumference 24,662 miles, as compared with the actual mean circumference of 24,857 miles. Recently Lehmann-Haupt's figure of 148.8 meters (Pauly, Second Series, Vol. III, Pt.2 [1929], cols. 1952–60) has found favor with historians of science. Still another figure by A. Thalamas, *La Géographie d' Ératosthène* (Versailles, 1921), pp. 158–59, for the stade is 168 meters. According to Lehmann-Haupt's figure Eratosthenes' estimate of the earth's circumference would be 23,300 miles and according to Thalamas's it would be 26,306 miles.

Appendix C

ANCIENT ESTIMATES OF
THE SUN'S APPARENT SIZE

ARISTARCHUS (according to Archimedes *Arenarius* x) estimates the apparent size of the sun to be ¹⁄₇₂₀ of the complete celestial circle; Cleomedes (II.75, 82) has ¹⁄₇₅₀; Martianus Capella (VIII.860) has ¹⁄₆₀₀. Thus Aristarchus observes that the sun occupies ½ degree, Cleomedes slightly less, but Macrobius 1⅔ degrees. The mean apparent size of the sun actually amounts to slightly more than ½ degree of celestial arc.

Actual mean apparent size:		31′ 59″
Cleomedes' figure	:	28′ 48″
Aristarchus' "	:	30′
Ptolemy's " (mean) :		33′ 20″
Capella's "	:	36′
Macrobius' "	:	1° 40′

We do not know how Aristarchus arrived at his figure. It is possible that he used a hemispherical bowl in the manner described above, since he is credited by Vitruvius (IX.viii.1) with inventing the *skaphe*. The figures of Cleomedes and Martianus Capella were obtained through the use of a water clock which indicated what part of twenty-four hours intervened between the appearance of the sun's first rays and of its full orb on the horizon. There is still another figure given by Aristarchus, but it is so grossly excessive that it is not certain whether he meant to have his estimate (two degrees) taken as a serious value or whether he was assigning a purely arbitrary figure for the purposes of his calculations. Heath is of the opinion that the work in which Aristarchus gives his estimate of two degrees, the *De magnitudinibus et distantiis solis et lunae* (his only extant work), was an early one, written before he had obtained the nearly correct figure given above. But that part of Tannery's explanation in which he conjectures that Aristarchus' figure was not meant to be taken seriously seems quite plausible, since it is hard to imagine how a man of Aristarchus' ability could have arrived at so poor a result from observation. See Heath, *Aristarchus*, p. 312.

Bibliography

Bibliography

THE FOLLOWING LIST is not intended as an exhaustive bibliography of Macrobius. It includes works and studies containing significant contributions to Macrobian scholarship, particularly those which bear upon problems concerning the *Commentary*. Works cited in abbreviated form in the footnotes are listed here under their abbreviations, which are placed between brackets and precede the full bibliographical entry.

[Adelard] Adelardus. De eodem et diverso. Ed. by H. Willner. Münster, 1903.

[Anatolius] Anatolius. De decade. Ed. by J. L. Heiberg. Paris, 1901.

✓Anderson, E. P. "Some Notes on Chaucer's Treatment of the Somnium Scipionis," *Proceedings of the American Philological Association,* XXXIII (1902), xcviii–xcix.

Andrews, M. C. "The Study and Classification of Medieval Mappae Mundi," *Archaeologia,* LXXV (1925), 61–76.

[Artemidorus] Artemidorus. Onirocriticon libri v. Ed. by R. Hercher. Leipzig, 1864.

Beazley, C. R. The Dawn of Modern Geography. Vol. I. London, 1897.

Bede, The Venerable. Bedae opera de temporibus. Ed. by Charles W. Jones. Cambridge, Mass., 1943.

Bitsch, Friedrich. De Platonicorum quaestionibus quibusdam Vergilianis. Berlin, 1911.

Blum, Claes. Studies in the Dream-Book of Artemidorus. Uppsala, 1936.

Boak, A. E. R., and J. E. Dunlap. Two Studies in Later Roman and Byzantine Administration. New York, 1924.

Boissier, Gaston. La Fin du paganisme. Vol. II. Paris, 1913.

Borghorst, Gerhard. De Anatolii fontibus. Berlin, 1905.

[Boyancé] Boyancé, Pierre. Études sur le Songe de Scipion. Limoges, 1936.

[Byrhtferth] Byrhtferth. Manual. Ed. by S. J. Crawford. London, 1929.

[*Cambr. Med. Hist.*] The Cambridge Medieval History. Ed. by H. M. Gwatkin, J. P. Whitney, and others. 8 vols. New York, 1911–1936.

Capelle, P. De luna, stellis, lacteo orbe animarum sedibus. Halle, 1917.

Cary, M., and E. H. Warmington. The Ancient Explorers. London, 1929.

√[Censorinus] Censorinus. De die natali liber. Ed. by F. Hultsch. Leipzig, 1867.

[Chalcidius] Platonis Timaeus interprete Chalcidio, cum eiusdem commentario. Ed. by J. Wrobel. Leipzig, 1876.

Chaucer, Geoffrey. The Complete Works of Geoffrey Chaucer. Ed. by F. N. Robinson. Boston, 1933.

Cicero: see Mai, Angelo.

[Clemens Alexandrinus] Clemens Alexandrinus. Stromateis. Ed. by R. Klotz. Leipzig, 1831.

[Cleomedes] Cleomedes. De motu circulari corporum caelestium libri duo. Ed. by H. Ziegler. Leipzig, 1891.

Collins, S. T. The Interpretation of Vergil with Special Reference to Macrobius. Oxford, 1909.

Comparetti, D. Virgilio nel medio evo. Florence, 1896.

Cook, A. B. Zeus. Vol. II. Cambridge, England, 1925.

[Courcelle] Courcelle, Pierre. Les Lettres grecques en occident de Macrobe à Cassiodore. Paris, 1943. "Bibliothèque des Ecoles françaises d'Athènes et de Rome," Fasc. 159.

[Cumont] Cumont, Franz. "Comment Plotin détourna Porphyre du suicide," Revue des études grecques, XXXII (1919), 113-20.

Curry, Walter Clyde. Chaucer and the Mediaeval Sciences. New York, 1926.

[Diels] Diels, Hermann. Doxographi graeci. Berlin, 1879.

Dill, Samuel. Roman Society in the Last Century of the Western Empire. London, 1896.

√[D'Ooge] Nicomachus Gerasenus. Introduction to Arithmetic. Translated into English by M. L. D'Ooge; with studies in Greek arithmetic by F. E. Robbins and L. C. Karpinski. New York, 1926.

[Dreyer] Dreyer, John Louis Emil. History of the Planetary Systems from Thales to Kepler. Cambridge, England, 1906.

[Duhem] Duhem, Pierre. Le Système du monde; histoire des doctrines cosmologiques de Platon à Copernic. 5 vols. Paris, 1913-1917.

[Eyssenhardt] Macrobius. Ed. by F. Eyssenhardt. Leipzig, 1893.

[Favonius] Favonius Eulogius. Disputatio de Somnio Scipionis. Ed. by A. Holder. Leipzig, 1901.

[Gellius] Aulus Gellius. Noctium atticarum libri xx. Ed by C. Hosius. 2 vols. Leipzig, 1903.

[Geminus] Geminus. Elementa astronomiae. Ed. by K. Manitius. Leipzig, 1898.

Georgii, H. "Zur Bestimmung der Zeit des Servius," Philologus, LXXI (1912), 518-26.

Glover, T. R. Life and Letters in the Fourth Century. Cambridge, England, 1901.

Goetz, Georg. Commentatiuncula Macrobiana. Jena, 1890.

Haskins, Charles Homer. Studies in Mediaeval Science. Cambridge, Mass., 1924.

[Heath, *Aristarchus*] Heath, Thomas L. Aristarchus of Samos, the Ancient Copernicus. Oxford, 1913.

[Heath, *Gr. Math.*] Heath, Thomas L. A History of Greek Mathematics. 2 vols. Oxford, 1921.

[Henry] Henry, Paul. Plotin et l'occident; Firmicus Maternus, Marius Victorinus, Saint Augustin et Macrobe. Louvain, 1934. "Specilegium sacrum Lovaniense, études et documents," Fasc. 15.

Henry, Paul. "Une Traduction grecque d'un texte de Macrobe dans le Περὶ μηνῶν de Lydus," *Revue des études latines*, XI (1933), 164–71.

Highbarger, E. L. The Gates of Dreams; an Archaeological Examination of Aeneid VI, 893–899. Baltimore, 1940. "The Johns Hopkins University Studies in Archaeology," No. 30.

—— "Virgil's Nether World and Elysium; Addenda," *Proceedings of the American Philological Association*, LXXVI (1945), xxxiii.

Hultsch, F. Poseidonios über die Grösse und Entfernung der Sonne. Berlin, 1897.

Iamblichus: see pseudo-Iamblichus.

[Inge] Inge, William Ralph. Philosophy of Plotinus. 2 vols. London, 1923.

[Isidore of Seville] Isidorus Hispalensis. Etymologiarum libri xx. Ed. by F. W. Otto. Leipzig, 1833.

[Jan] Macrobius. Opera quae supersunt. Ed. by L. von Jan. 2 vols. Leipzig and Quedlinburg, 1848–1852.

[Joannes Lydus] Joannes Laurentius Lydus. Liber de mensibus. Ed. by R. Wuensch. Leipzig, 1898.

Joannes Saresberiensis: see John of Salisbury.

[Johannes Scottus] Johannes Scottus. Annotationes in Marcianum. Ed. by C. E. Lutz. Cambridge, Mass., 1939.

[John of Salisbury] Joannes Saresberiensis. Policraticus. Ed. by C. J. Webb. Oxford, 1909.

Kimble, G. H. T. Geography in the Middle Ages. London, 1938.

Lindsay, W. M. "A Bodleian MS. of Macrobius," *The Classical Review*, XIV (1900), 260–61.

Linke, Hugo. "Ueber Macrobius' Kommentar zu Ciceros Somnium Scipionis," in Philologische Abhandlungen, Martin Hertz zum siebzigsten Geburtstage. Berlin, 1888. Pages 240–56.

Lögdberg, G. In Macrobii Saturnalia adnotationes. Uppsala, 1936.

[Lobeck] Lobeck, Christian August. Aglaophamus. 2 vols. Königsberg, 1829.

Lowes, J. L. Geoffrey Chaucer and the Development of his Genius. Boston and New York, 1934.

—— "The Second Nun's Prologue, Alanus and Macrobius," *Modern Philology,* XV (1917), 193–202.

Macrobius: for a list of editions, see pp. 60–63; for translations, see pp. 63–64.

Magnien, Victor. Les Mystères d'Éleusis: leurs origines, le rituel de leurs initiations. Paris, 1938.

Mai, Angelo, ed. M. Tullii Ciceronis de Re publica quae supersunt. Rome, 1822.

[Manitius] Manitius, Max. Geschichte der lateinischen Literatur des Mittelalters. 3 vols. Munich, 1911–1931.

[Martianus Capella] Martianus Capella. Ed. by A. Dick. Leipzig, 1925.

[Migne, *Pat. Lat.*] Migne, Jacques Paul, ed. Patrologiae cursus completus; series latina. 221 vols. Paris, 1844–1864.

[Mras] Mras, Karl. "Macrobius' Kommentar zu Ciceros Somnium," *Sitzungsberichte der preussischen Akademie der Wissenschaften, Philosophisch-historische Klasse,* Jahrg. 1933, pp. 232–86.

Neuburger, Max. "Die Medizin im Macrobius und Theodoretus," *Janus,* XXVIII (1924), 155–72.

[Nicomachus] Nicomachus Gerasenus. Introductionis arithmeticae libri II. Ed. by R. Hoche. Leipzig, 1866. For the English translation, see D'Ooge.

[Pauly] Pauly, August Friedrich. Pauly's Real-Encyclopädie der classischen Altertumswissenschaft. Ed. by G. Wissowa, W. Kroll, and others. Stuttgart, 1894–.

Petersson, Torsten. Cicero; a Biography. Berkeley, 1920. Chap. XIII.

[Petit] Petit, L. De Macrobio Ciceronis interprete philosopho. Paris, 1866.

[Photius] Photius. Bibliotheca. Ed. by I. Bekker. 2 vols. Berlin, 1824–1825.

[Pliny] Plinius. Naturalis historia. Ed. by K. Mayhoff. 6 vols. Leipzig, 1892–1909.

[Plotinus] Plotinus. Enneades. Ed. by R. Volkmann. 2 vols. Leipzig, 1883–1884.

[Proclus (Diehl)] Proclus Diadochus. In Platonis Timaeum commentaria. Ed. by E. Diehl. 3 vols. Leipzig, 1903–1906.

[Proclus (Kroll)] Proclus Diadochus. In Platonis Rem publicam commentarii. Ed. by W. Kroll. 2 vols. Leipzig, 1899–1901.

[pseudo-Iamblichus] Iamblichus. Theologoumena arithmeticae. Ed. by V. de Falco. Leipzig, 1922.

[Ptolemy] Claudius Ptolemaeus. Syntaxis mathematica. Ed. by J. L. Heiberg. 2 vols. Leipzig, 1898.

Robbins, F. E. "The Tradition of Greek Arithmology," *Classical Philology,* XVI (1921), 97–123.

Roscher, W. H. Hebdomadenlehren der griechischen Philosophie und Ärzte. Leipzig, 1906.

―――― Die hippokratische Schrift von der Siebenzahl. Paderborn, 1913.

Sandys, J. E. A History of Classical Scholarship. 3 vols. Cambridge, England, 1906.

Sarton, George. Introduction to the History of Science. Vol. I. Baltimore, 1927. "Carnegie Institution of Washington Publication," No. 376.

Schanz, Martin. Geschichte der römischen Litteratur. 2 vols. Munich, 1914–1920.

[Schedler] Schedler, P. M. Die Philosophie des Macrobius und ihr Einfluss auf die Wissenschaft des christlichen Mittelalters. Münster, 1916. "Beiträge zur Geschichte der Philosophie des Mittelalters . . ." Vol. XIII, No. 1.

[Servius] Servius Grammaticus. In Vergilii carmina commentarii. Ed. by G. Thilo and H. Hagen. 3 vols. Leipzig, 1881–1887.

Smith, William, ed. Dictionary of Greek and Roman Biography and Mythology. Vol. II. Boston, 1849.

[Stahl] Stahl, William Harris. "Astronomy and Geography in Macrobius," *Transactions of the American Philological Association,* LXXIII (1942), 232–58.

[Stobaeus] Joannes Stobaeus. Eclogarum physicarum et ethicarum libri duo. Ed. by A. Meineke. Leipzig, 1860.

[Strabo] Strabo. Geographica. Ed. by A. Meineke. 3 vols. Leipzig, 1915–1925.

[Synesius] Synesius. De somniis. Ed. by J. G. Krabinger. Landshut, 1850.

[Taylor] Taylor, Alfred Edward. A Commentary on Plato's Timaeus. Oxford, 1928.

Teuffel, W. S. Geschichte der römischen Literatur, 6th ed., rev. by W. Kroll and F. Skutsch. Leipzig, 1913.

[Theo Smyrnaeus] Theo Smyrnaeus. Expositio rerum mathematicarum ad legendum Platonem utilium. Ed. by E. Hiller. Leipzig, 1878.

Thomson, J. Oliver. History of Ancient Geography. Cambridge, England, 1948.

[Thorndike] Thorndike, Lynn. A History of Magic and Experimental Science. 6 vols. New York, 1923–1941.

Tozer, H. F. A History of Ancient Geography. Cambridge, England, 1935.

[Varro] Varro. De lingua latina. Ed. by L. Sprengel. Berlin, 1885.

Wessner, Paul. "Macrobius," in Pauly's Real-Encyclopädie der classischen Altertumswissenschaft, XIV (1928), cols. 170–98.

[Whittaker, *Macrobius*] Whittaker, Thomas. Macrobius; or Philosophy, Science and Letters in the Year 400. Cambridge, England, 1923.

[Whittaker, *Neo-Platonists*] Whittaker, Thomas. The Neo-Platonists. 2d ed. Cambridge, England, 1918.

Wissowa, G. De Macrobii Saturnaliorum fontibus capita tria; dissertatio inauguralis philologica. Breslau, 1880.

[Wright] Wright, John Kirtland. The Geographical Lore of the Time of the Crusades. New York, 1925.

Index

Index